IMAGES
of America

PAWTUXET
VALLEY

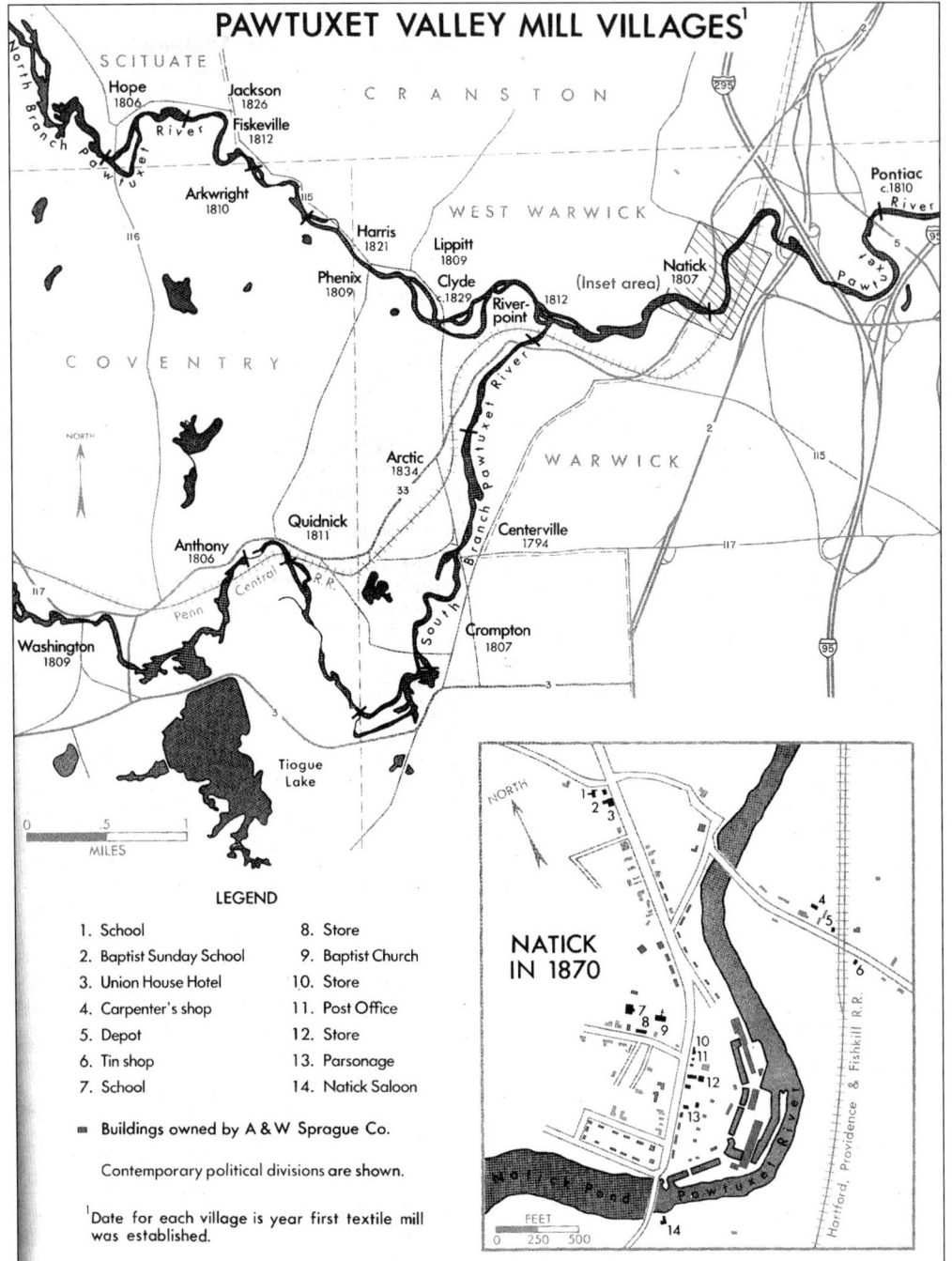

THE TEXTILE MILL VILLAGES OF THE PAWTUXET VALLEY. The mill villages are represented here with relevant dates. (Courtesy *Rhode Island Atlas*, 1982, Marion Wright and Dr. Patrick Conley.)

Contents

Acknowledgments		6
Introduction		7
1.	The Mills and Workers	9
2.	The Rural and Colonial Valley	33
3.	The Immigrants: Starting a New Life	41
4.	Business	67
5.	Sports, Recreation, and Getting Around	81
6.	Familiar Faces, Change, and Continuity	97
7.	Serving the Public	113
8.	Pawtuxet River Rebirth	121

ACKNOWLEDGMENTS

I would like to acknowledge my debt to those who generously provided images for this book, especially Lydia Rapoza, Donald Carpenter, David Perry, Leo and Celia Charbonneau, the Cayouette family, Daniel Burns, Amby Smith and the staff of the Kent County Daily Times, Bob and Anna Tucker, and Al Muschiano. Their patience and willingness to give of their time made this work a pleasure. There are a great many of their photographs and others that were not used here, and perhaps we can explore facets of the Pawtuxet Valley story in greater detail in future books, should there be a demand.

INTRODUCTION

The Pawtuxet Valley was shaped by the flow of the Pawtuxet River both physically and in human experience. An old history of the area—*Patterns on the River*, by Mathias Harpin—captured that reality nicely in its title. The more one looks at the flow of time over this place, the more one feels part of a continuous stream from one space to another. It is also like a great cloth being weaved, the next threads being bound with the previous ones into an inseparable unity. Rather than attempt to systematically pick the cloth apart, I have chosen to try to capture a sense of the flow, the weave of this place, and convey it in the images available to me.

A brief note about the political and social geography of the area may be useful for the reader. The Pawtuxet Valley includes parts of the cities and towns of West Warwick, Warwick, Coventry, Scituate, and Cranston. The traditional identification of residents of the area was with the village in which they lived and worked, then with the Pawtuxet Valley as a whole, and only then with the political entity to which their village belonged. Indeed, some towns (such as West Warwick, created in 1913) are much younger than the villages making them up. From the 1790s on, textile mill villages (miniature company towns) shaped social life in the area, and the effects have been remarkably persistent to the present day. A map on page 2 gives a good overview of the area and should be kept in mind when going through the book.

This is not a comprehensive history of the valley. Such a task would take several more volumes this size and more. It is an introduction to the Pawtuxet Valley, its history, its people, and the spirit of the place. I hope those of you who live there will recognize some of yourselves in it, and I hope that those who do not will learn something about it and its part in the Rhode Island and American experience.

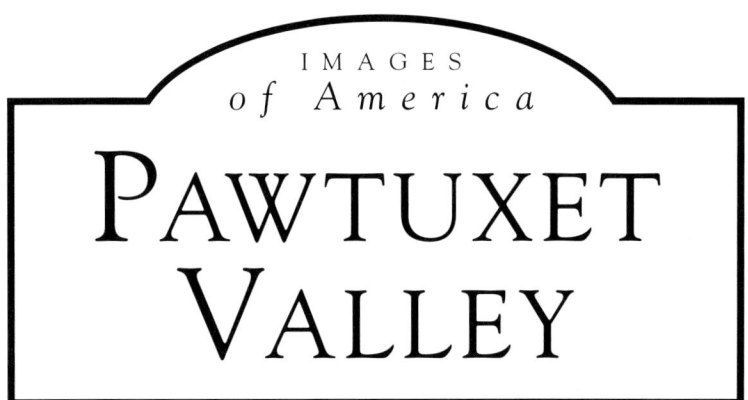

IMAGES of America
PAWTUXET VALLEY

Jeffrey Marc Kos

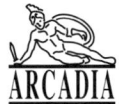

Copyright © 2001 by Jeffrey Marc Kos
ISBN 0-7385-0955-8

First printed in 2001.

Published by Arcadia Publishing,
an imprint of Tempus Publishing, Inc.
2A Cumberland Street
Charleston, SC 29401

Printed in Great Britain.

Library of Congress Catalog Card Number: 2001093037

For all general information contact Arcadia Publishing at:
Telephone 843-853-2070
Fax 843-853-0044
E-Mail sales@arcadiapublishing.com

For customer service and orders:
Toll-Free 1-888-313-2665

Visit us on the internet at http://www.arcadiapublishing.com

I would like to dedicate this book to Jeanette and her generation, who learned how to be Americans the hard way, never forgot who they were, and always had time to tell you the story.

One
THE MILLS AND WORKERS

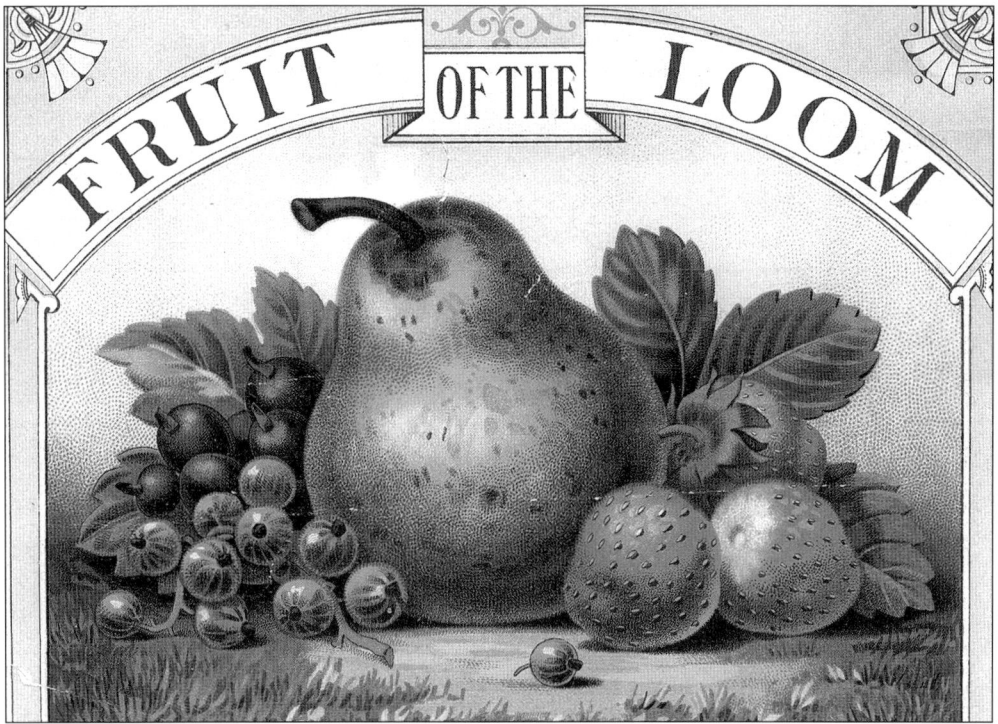

AN ORIGINAL FRUIT OF THE LOOM LABEL. This label would have been attached to the finished products from one of the Knight Company mills in the valley c. 1900. Fruit of the Loom products were produced in the area from the late 1870s to the 1950s at Arctic, Riverpoint, and Pontiac. Note the unusual take on the familiar brand design. (Photograph from the Lydia Rapoza collection.)

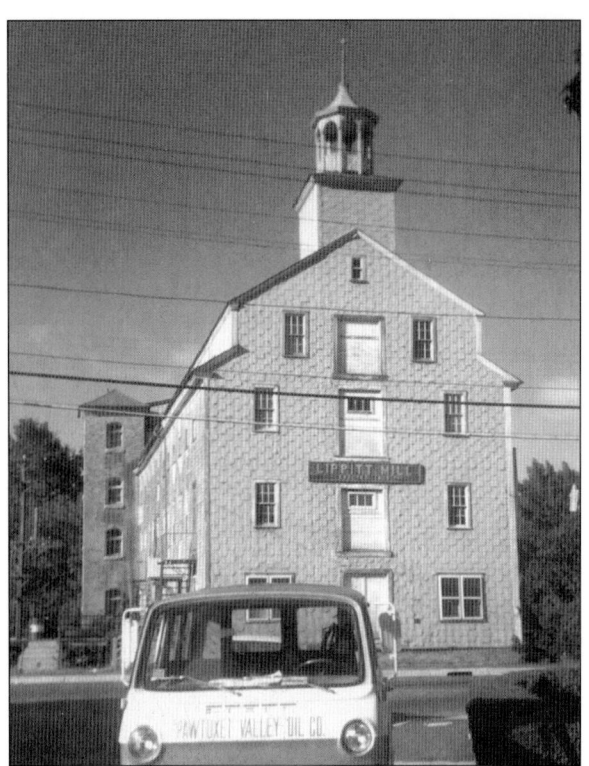

THE 1809 LIPPITT MILL. This mill is an excellent surviving example of early textile architecture. Small entrepreneur mill operators dominated the first decades of the industry, though often with the backing of big-name investors.

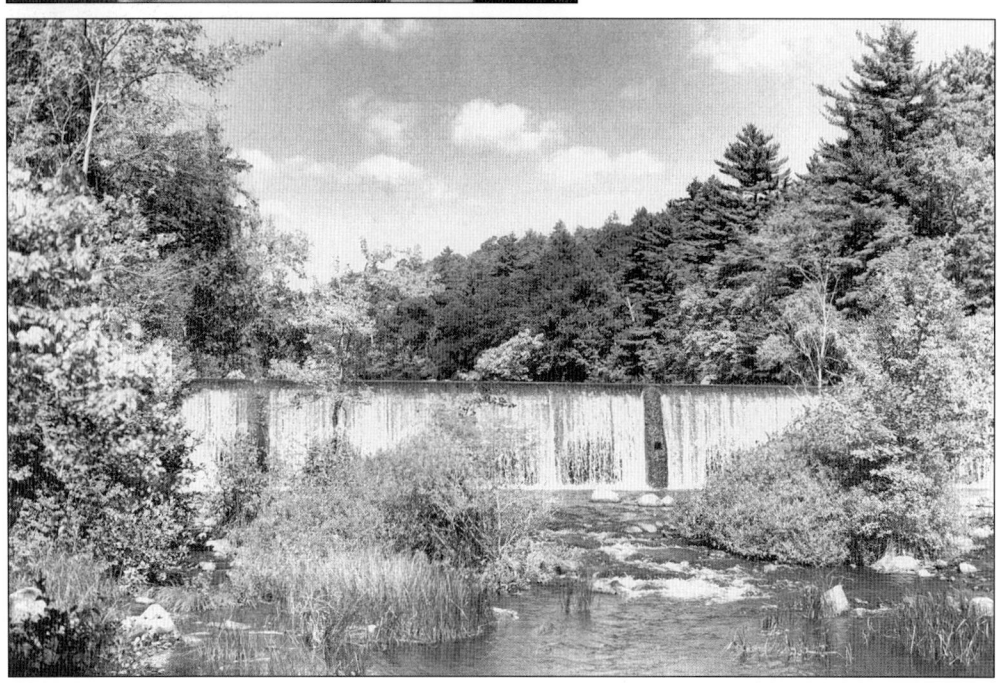

THE HOPE DAM. This photograph of Hope Dam gives an idea of what drew the investment interest to the "river of many falls." In a pre-electric age, waterpower was essential to mill operations, and the North and South Branches of the Pawtuxet River provided many location options in a small space. This dam was built in stages from 1885 to 1925.

THE LIPPITT MILL. The Lippitt Mill also has the distinction of being the oldest working mill in the country. The Riverpoint Company still uses the facility as part of its lace manufacturing.

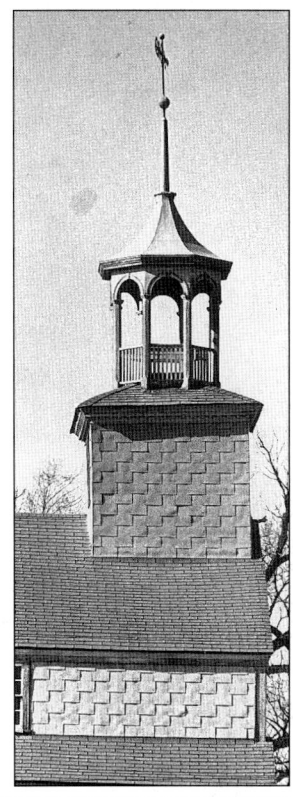

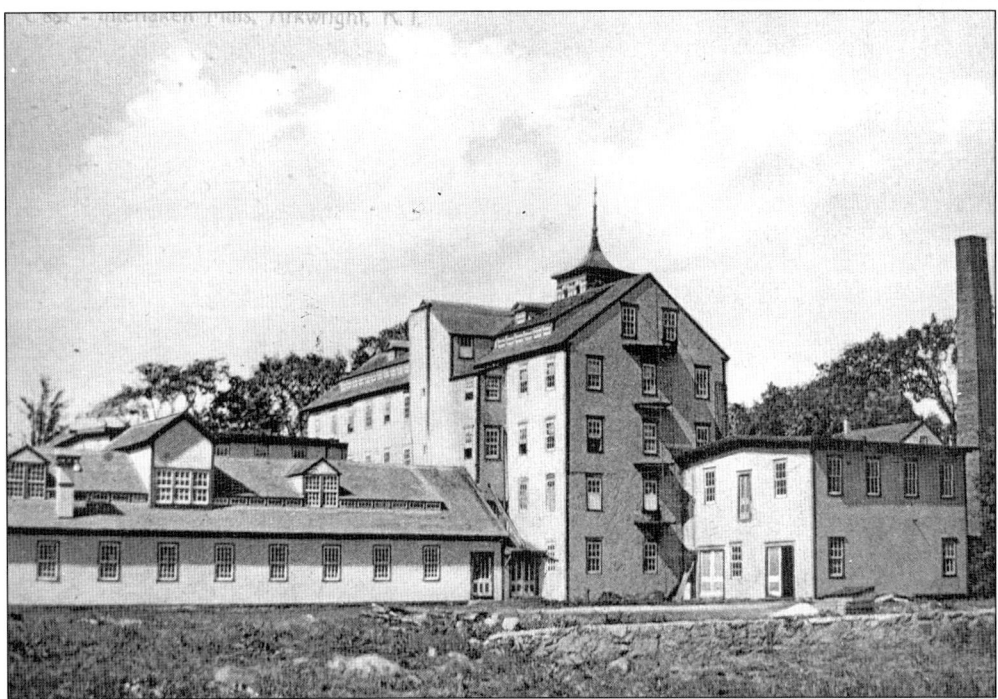

THE 1824 ARKWRIGHT MILL, C. 1900. This company is still in operation in a newer plant on the opposite side of the river.

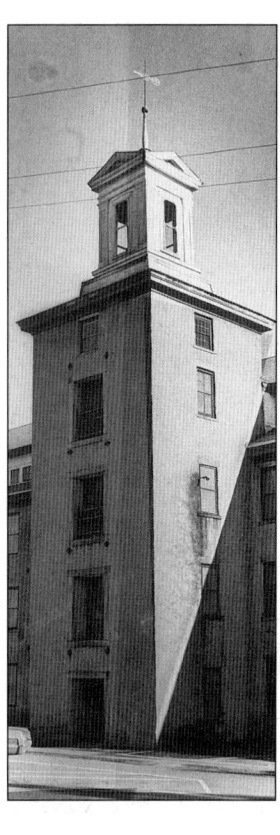

THE HARRIS MILL TOWER.

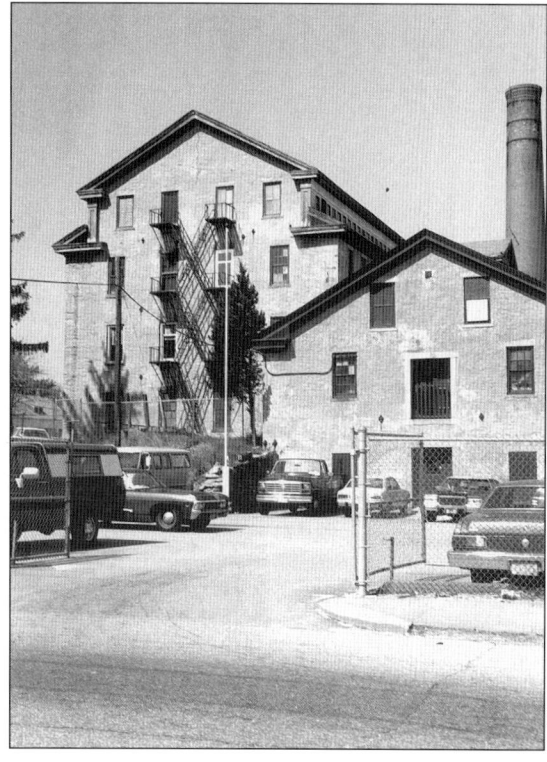

THE REMAINS OF THE HARRIS MILL COMPLEX ON THE NORTH BRANCH OF THE PAWTUXET RIVER IN THE 1970S. This site is now the home of the Pawtuxet Valley Performing Arts Center. It is a good example of how some Industrial Revolution–era buildings are finding new uses in a postindustrial valley.

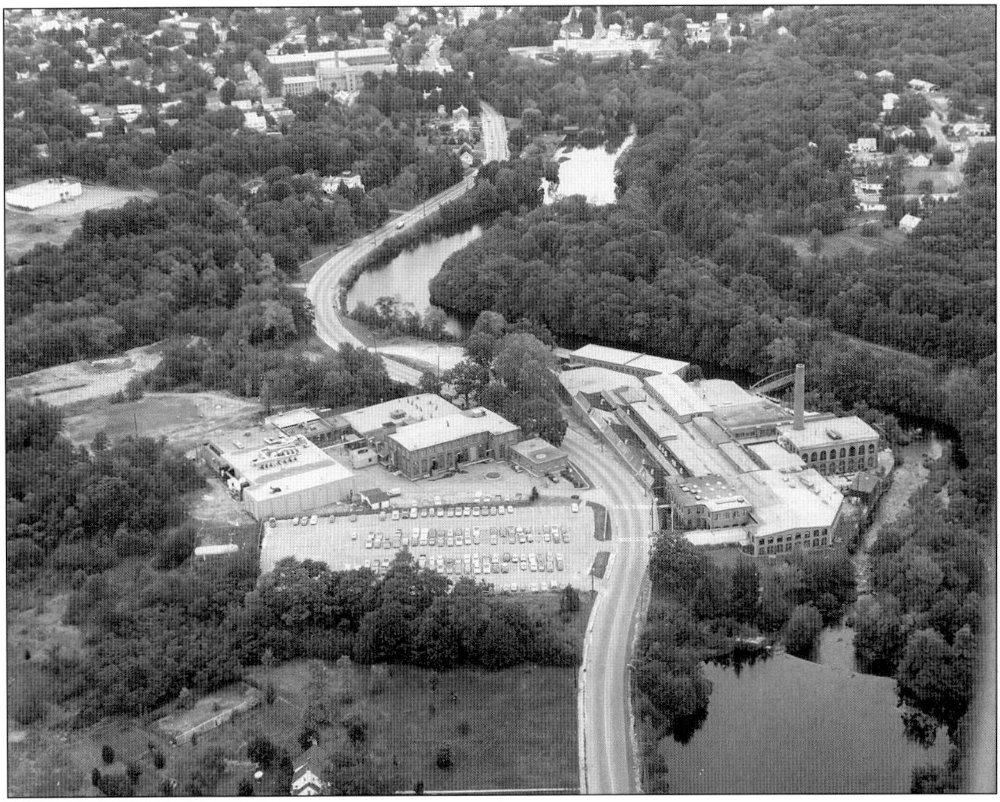

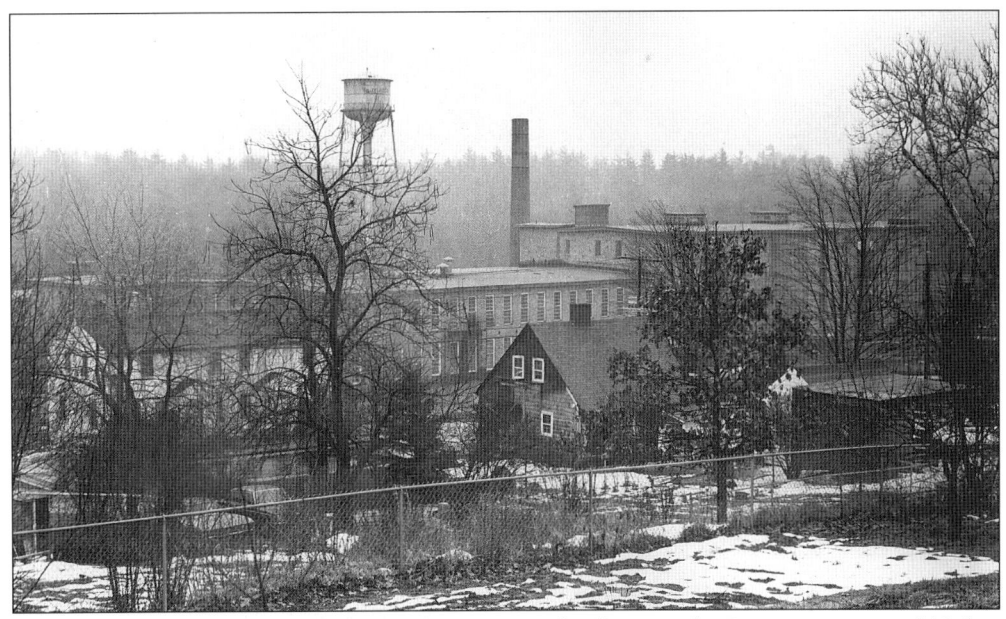

AN AERIAL VIEW OF THE NORTH BRANCH OF THE PAWTUXET RIVER. This view, looking east to Harris and Phenix Villages, shows the present Arkwright complex.

HOPE VILLAGE. Hope Village, the northernmost mill village on the Pawtuxet, is one of 18 that developed along the river.

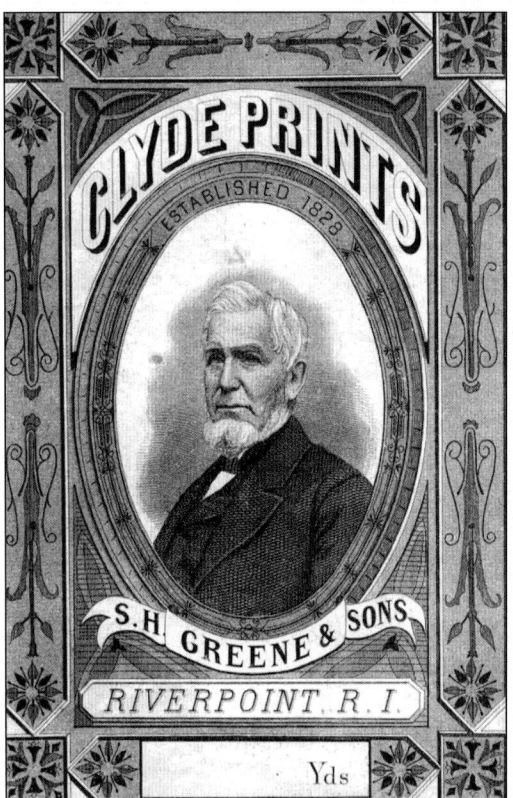

A Clyde Print Works Cloth Label, c. 1880. (Courtesy the Donald Carpenter collection.)

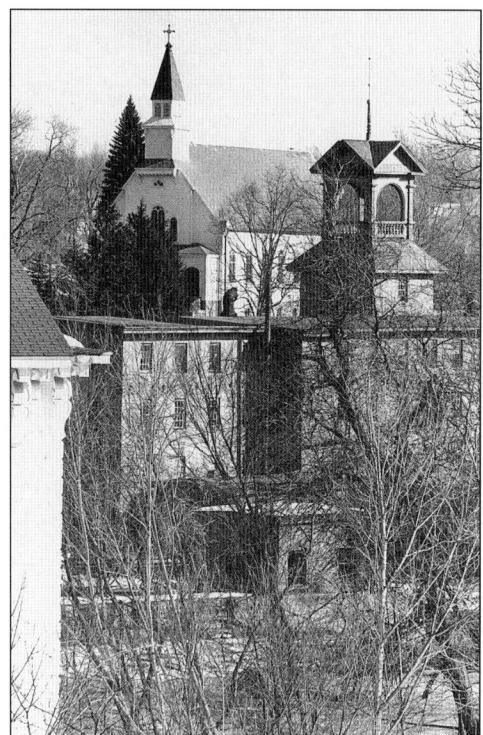

The Phenix Mill Tower, c. 1975. This is the Phenix Mill Tower, built in 1825, with a view of Saints Peter and Paul Church in the background.

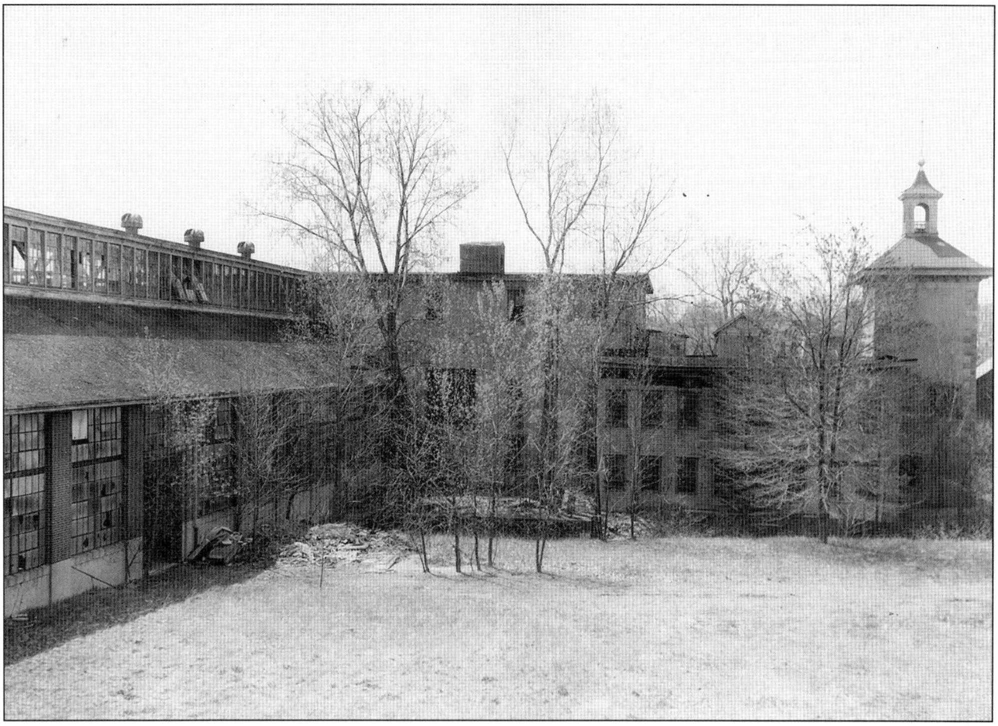

THE CLYDE PRINT WORKS. This is a rare photograph of the Clyde Print Works before demolition in the early 1960s.

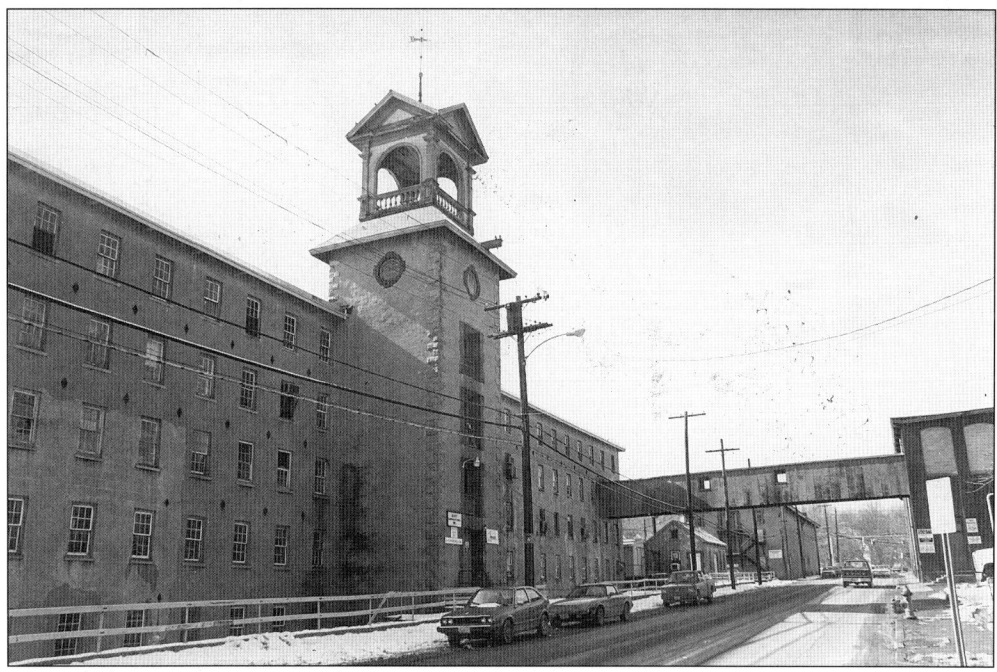

THE PHENIX MILL MAIN BUILDING, BUILT IN 1825. This view illustrates the growth of the textile industry in the 30 years since its founding. Compare the size of this operation to that of the Lippitt Mill.

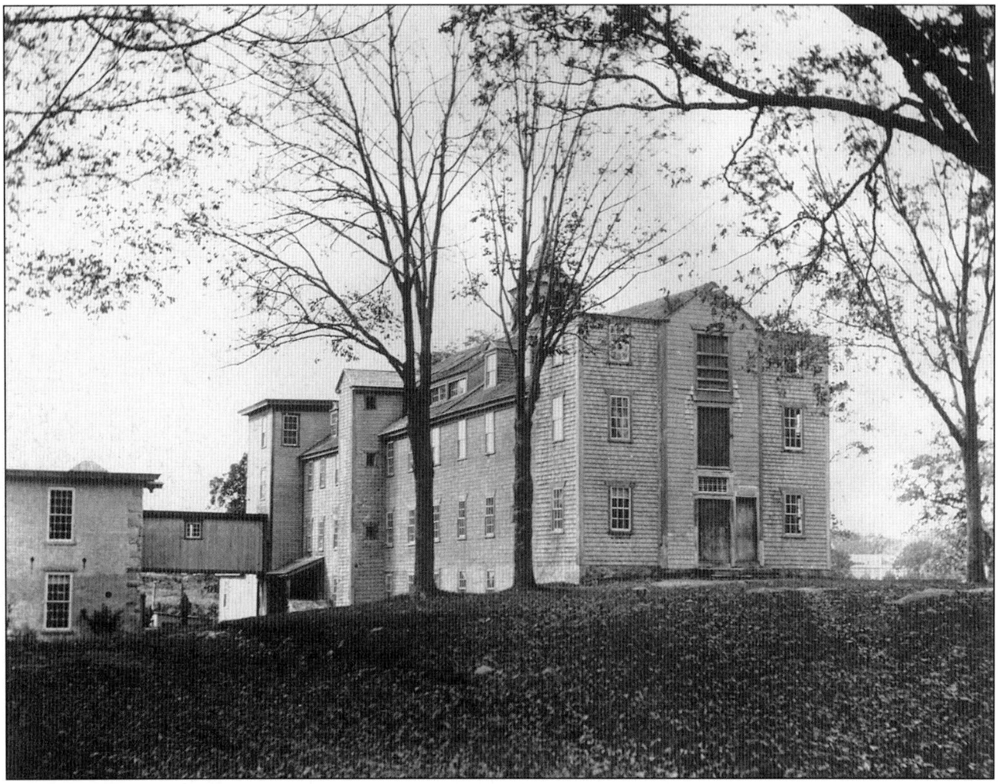

THE FISKEVILLE MILL, C. 1910.

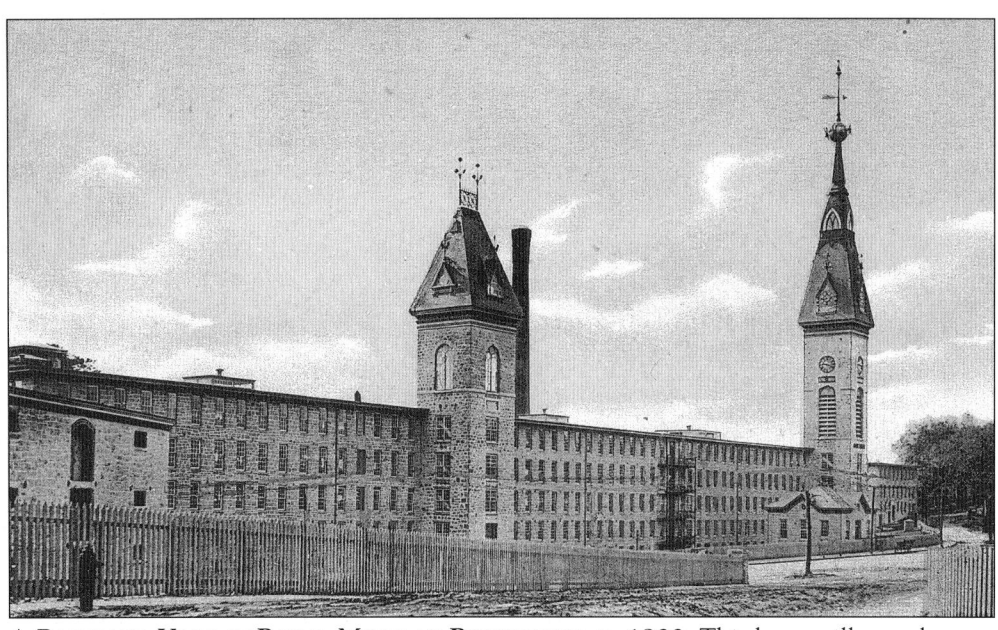

A POSTCARD VIEW OF ROYAL MILLS AT RIVERPOINT, C. 1900. This large mill complex was consolidated by B.B. & R. Knight Company in the 1880s from smaller operations.

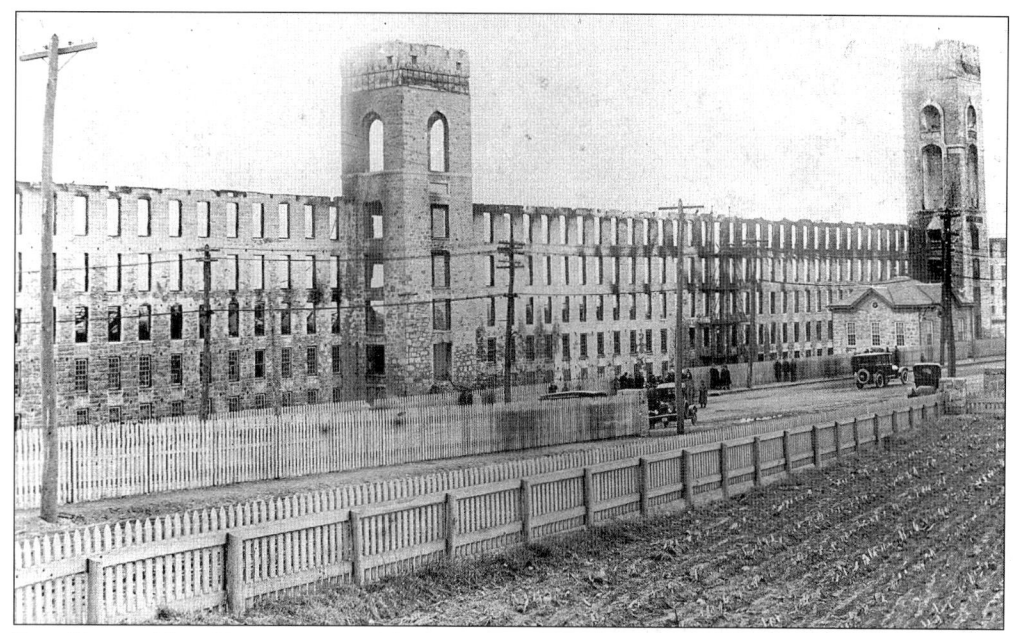

THE ROYAL MILL DESTROYED BY FIRE IN 1919. A massive fire in 1919 destroyed the Royal Mill, but it was rebuilt by 1921. It is an example of the size and profitability of the industry by the late 19th century. Part of the company farm is visible on the right.

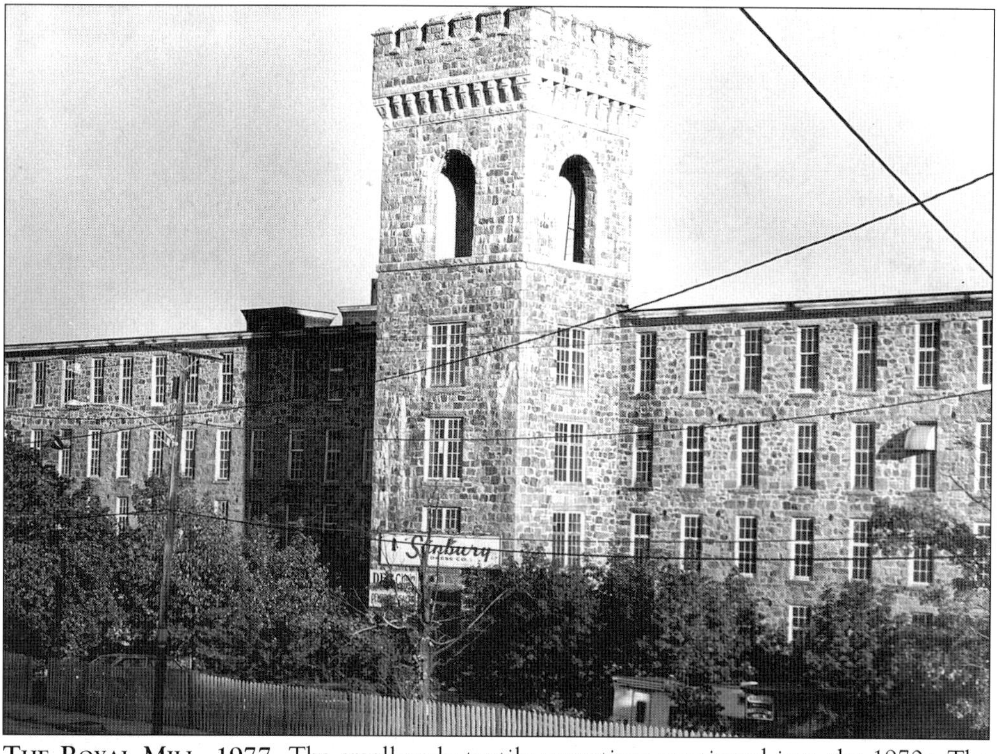

THE ROYAL MILL, 1977. The small-scale textile operations continued into the 1970s. The Great Depression and the companies' attempt to avoid union organization led larger companies to leave the Pawtuxet Valley from the 1920s on.

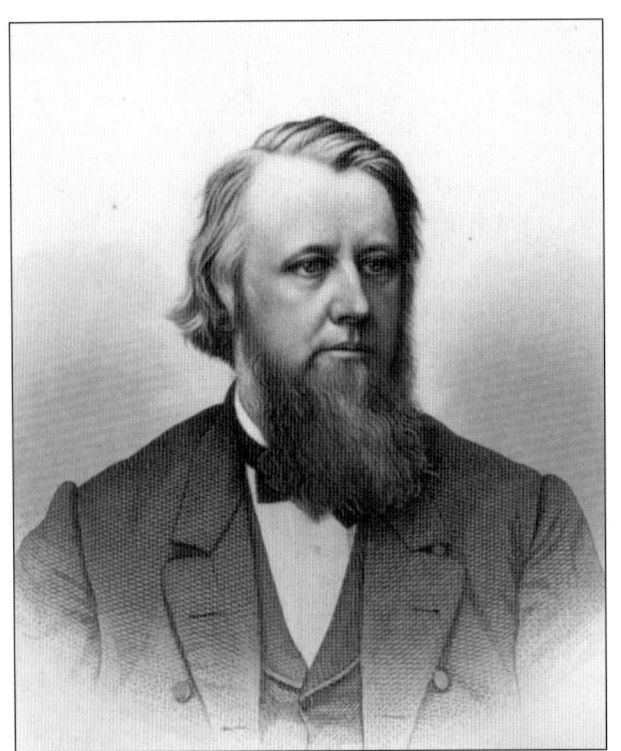

SEN. HENRY B. ANTHONY. Anthony was an important member of the powerful Anthony family that built a textile company on the South Branch of the Pawtuxet River in the 19th century. He was also a key player in the development of the *Providence Journal Bulletin* newspaper as owner and publisher.

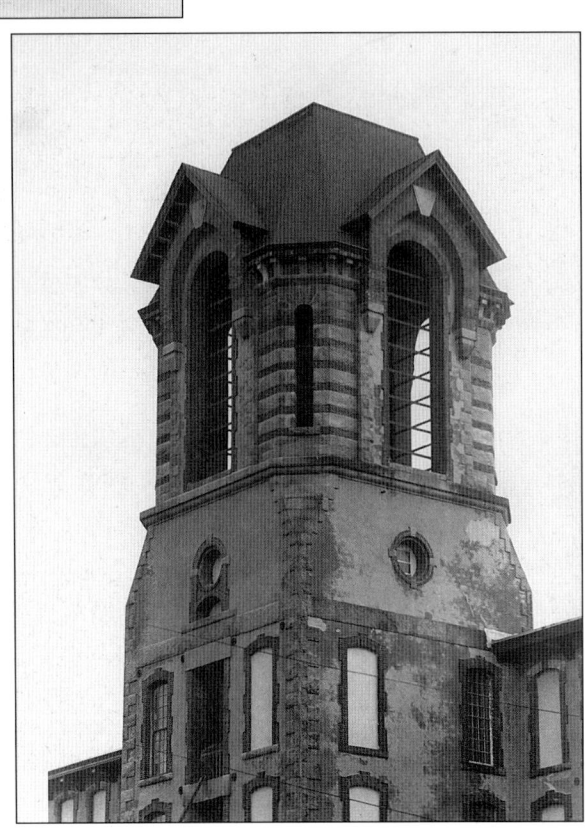

THE ANTHONY MILL TOWER.

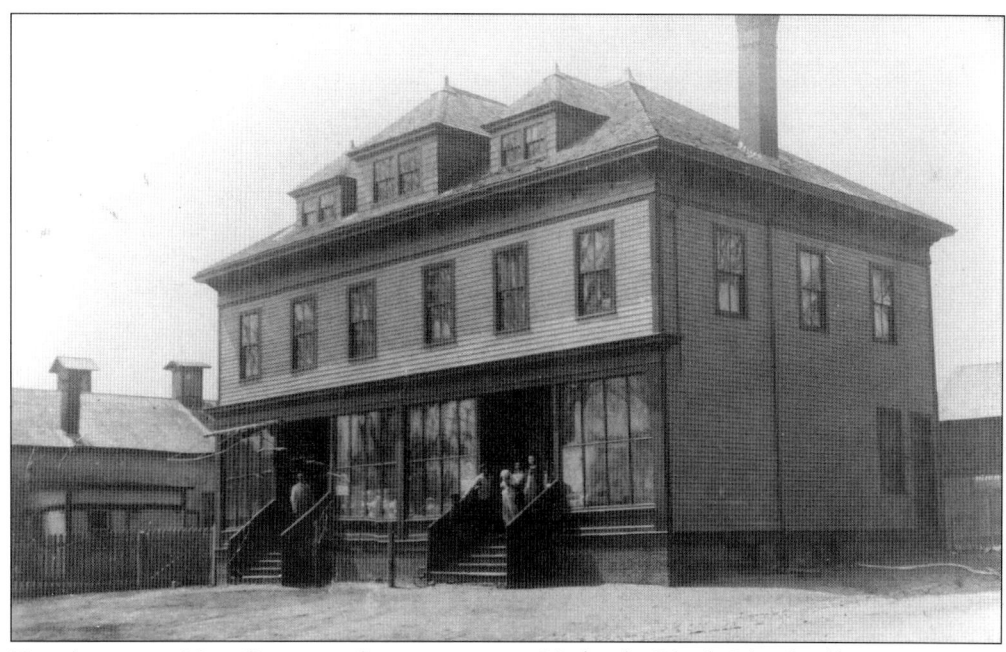

THE ANTHONY MILL COMPANY STORE, C. 1890. Under the Rhode Island Village System, the company owned worker housing, the local store, and the farm that supplied the store. At the height of the system, company scrip was often issued in lieu of U.S. currency. The benefits to the company included a stable workforce and control over the social lives of their employees. The system would break down spectacularly by the early 20th century.

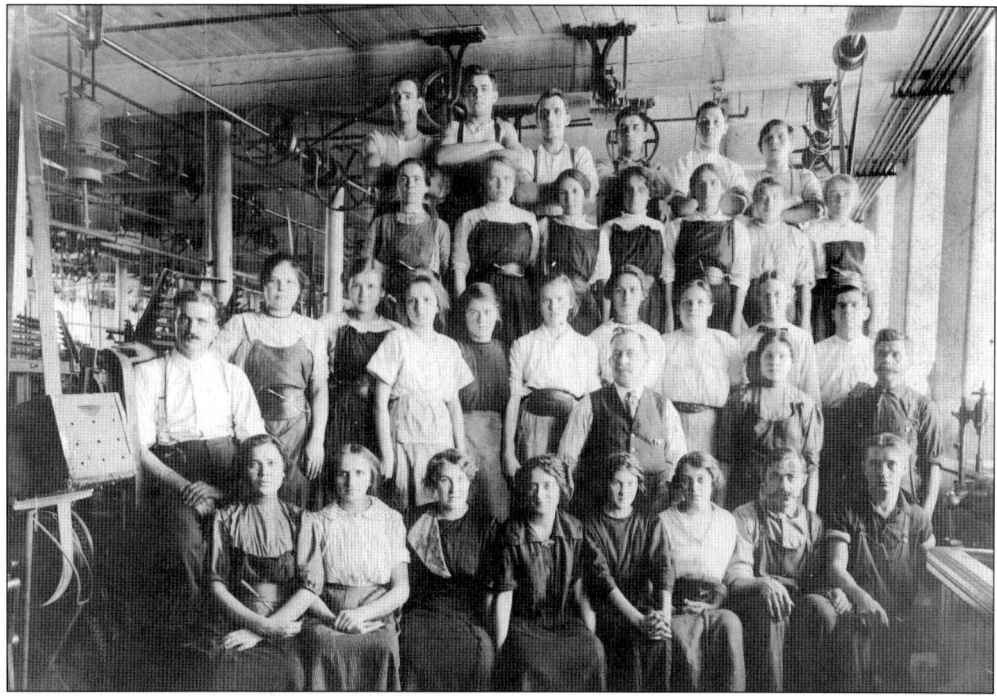

THE WEAVE SHOP OF THE CROMPTON VELVET COMPANY, C. 1920. (Courtesy Bob and Anna Tucker.)

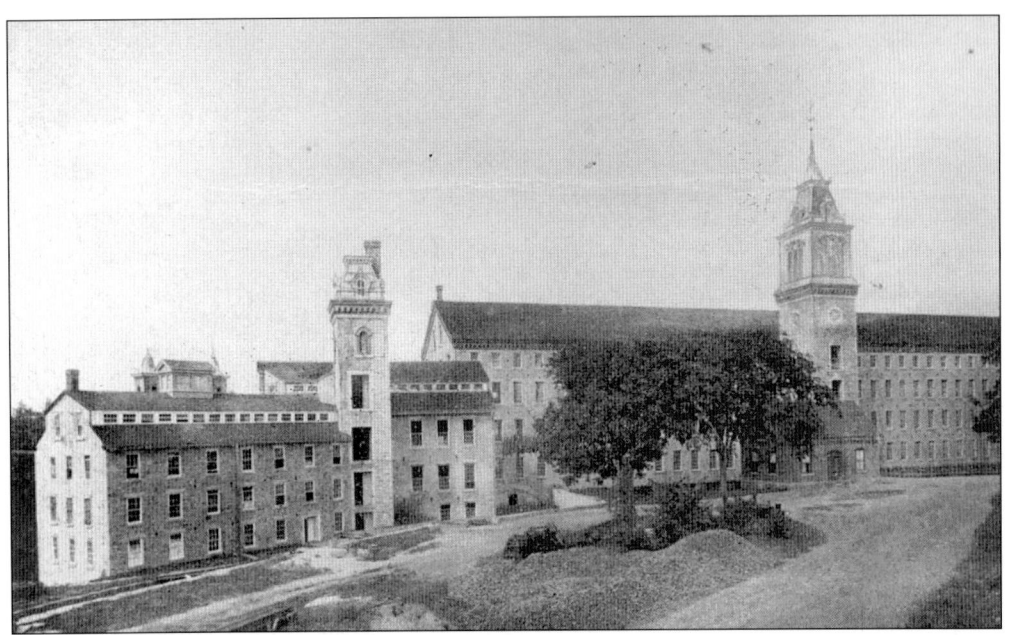

THE CENTREVILLE MILL, C. 1880. Enos Lapham was another of the textile entrepreneurs. Centreville was also the site of the first textile mill in the valley in the 1790s.

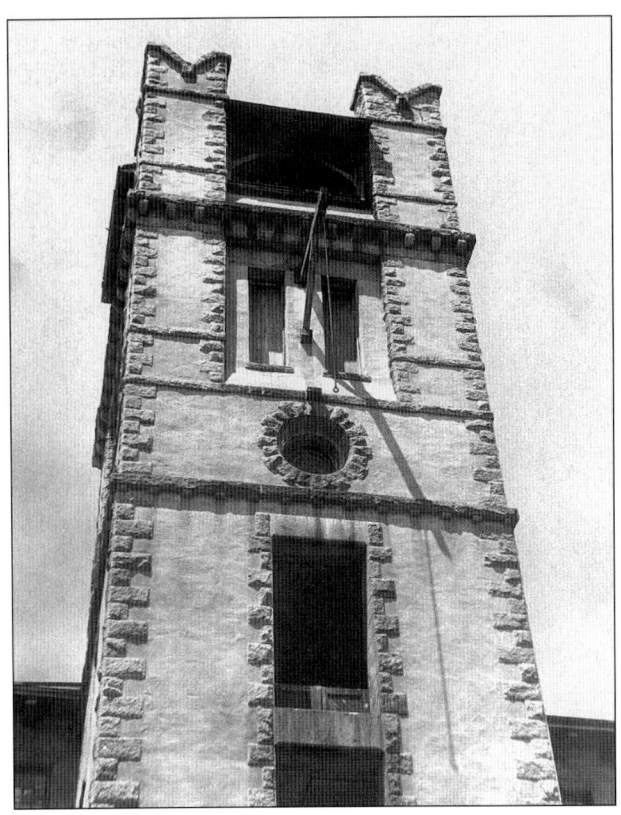

THE CROMPTON COMPANY BELL TOWER. Workers' lives were regulated by the bells in all of the early mill villages. Former agricultural workers, usually daughters of local families, were employed early in the textile era and were not used to the regimented shifts required by industry.

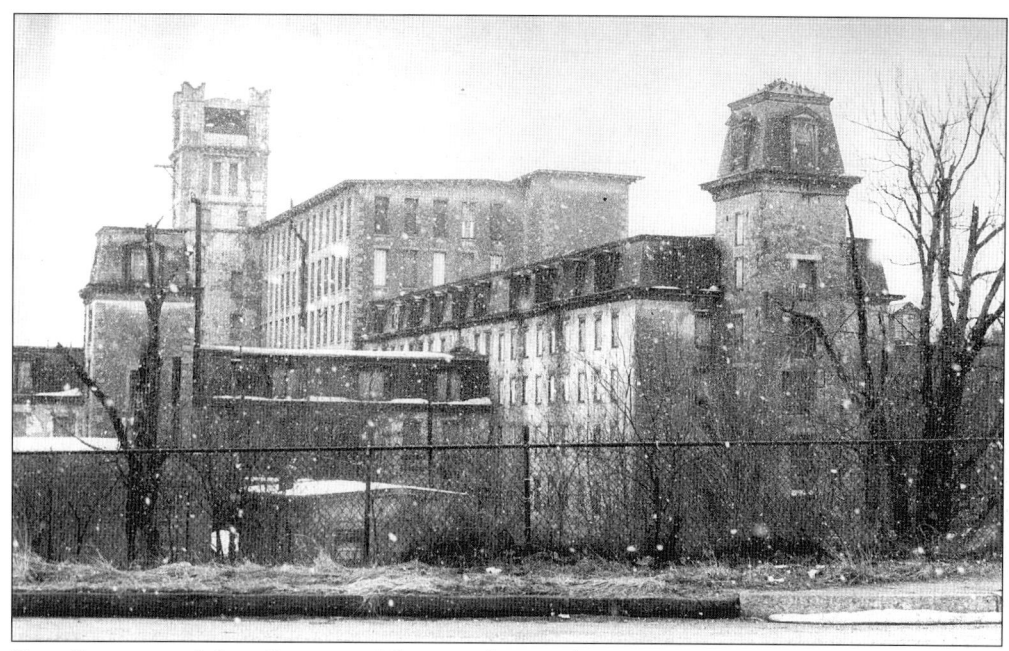

THE CROMPTON MILL COMPLEX. The complex was begun in 1809 and covered both sides of the South Branch of the Pawtuxet River at Crompton. The mill was noted for the manufacture of velvet and corduroy.

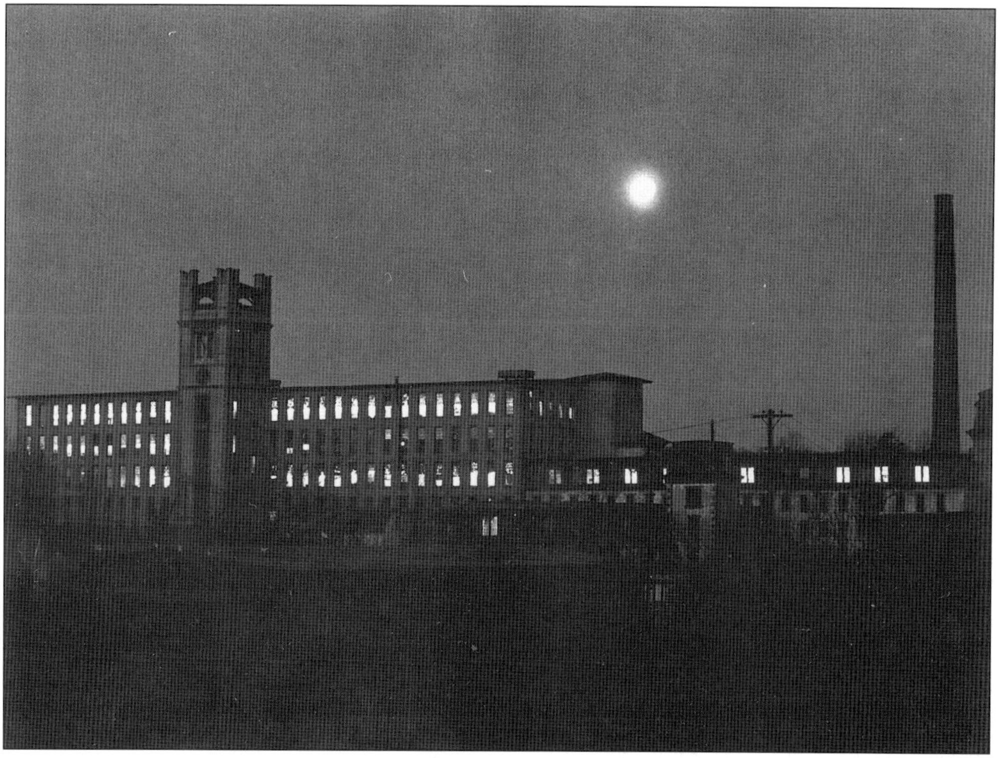

THE CROMPTON COMPLEX AT NIGHT.

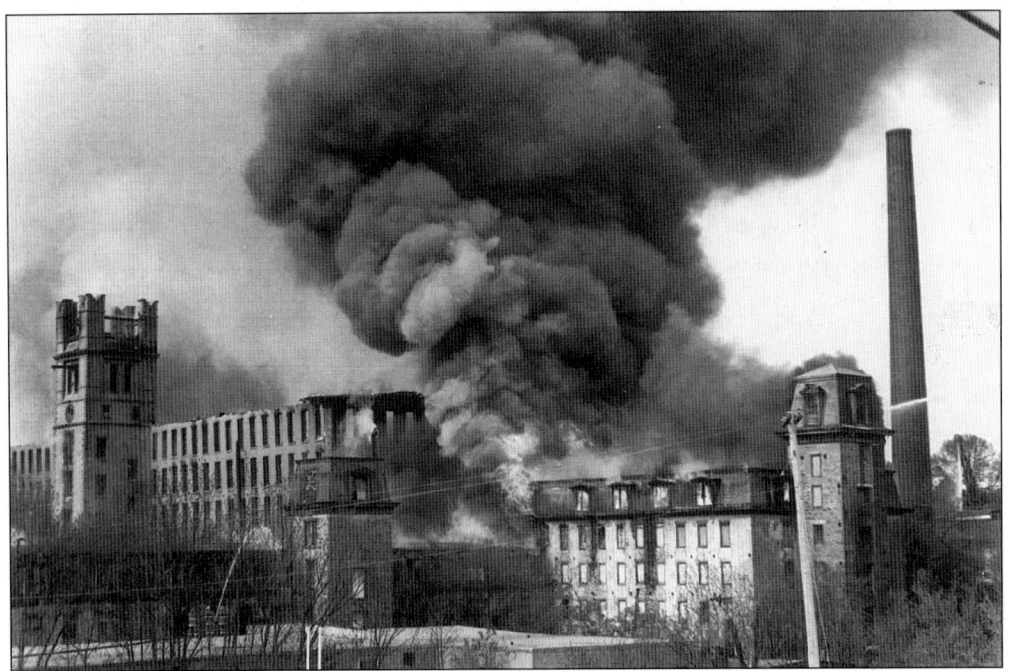

THE 1809 OLD STONE MILL. The main mill buildings were destroyed by fire in 1992, but the 1809 old stone mill survives on the east side of the river.

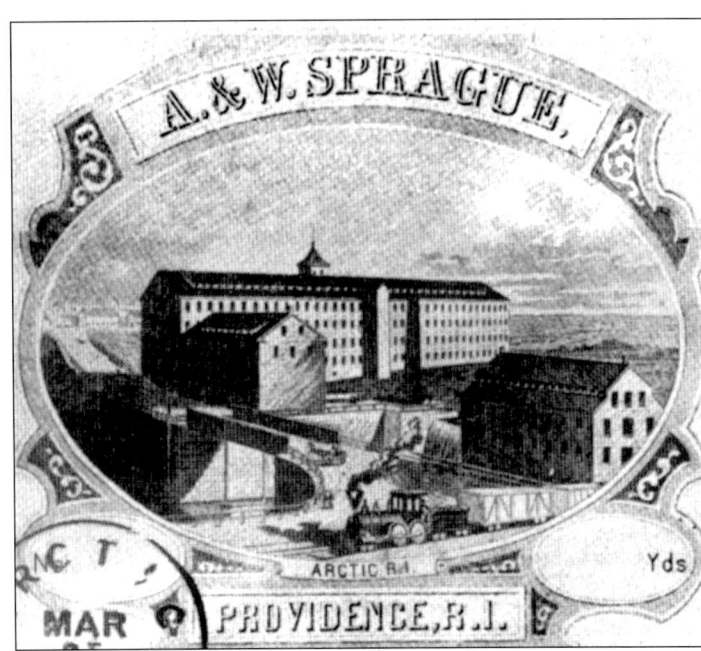

A REPRODUCTION OF THE SPRAGUE-ERA LABEL OF THE ARCTIC MILL. The Sprague textile empire based in Cranston, Rhode Island, survived until the depression of the early 1870s.

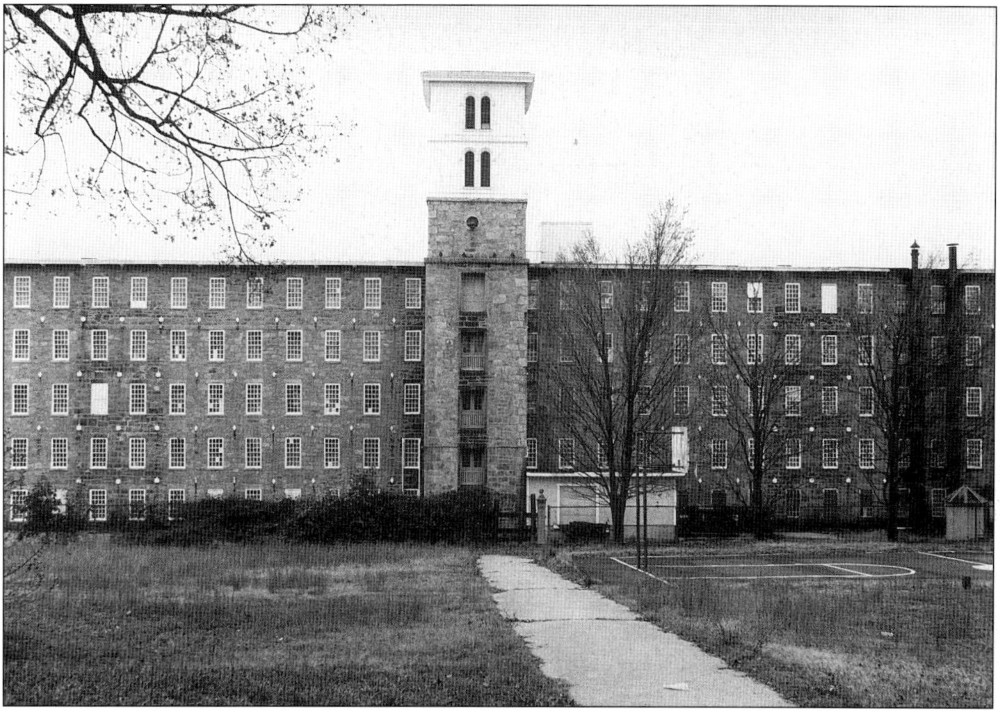

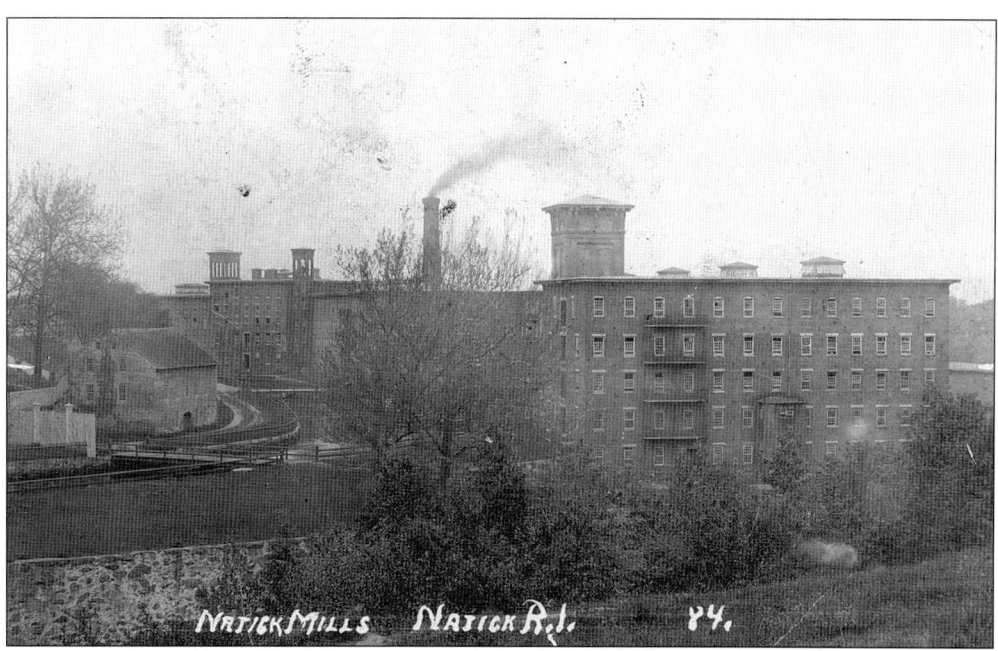

THE FRONT OF THE ARCTIC MILL, BUILT FROM 1834 TO 1865.

THE NATICK MILL FROM THE NATICK BRIDGE, C. 1900. This mill was built from 1852 to 1883 by the Sprague and later by the B.B. & R. Knight Company.

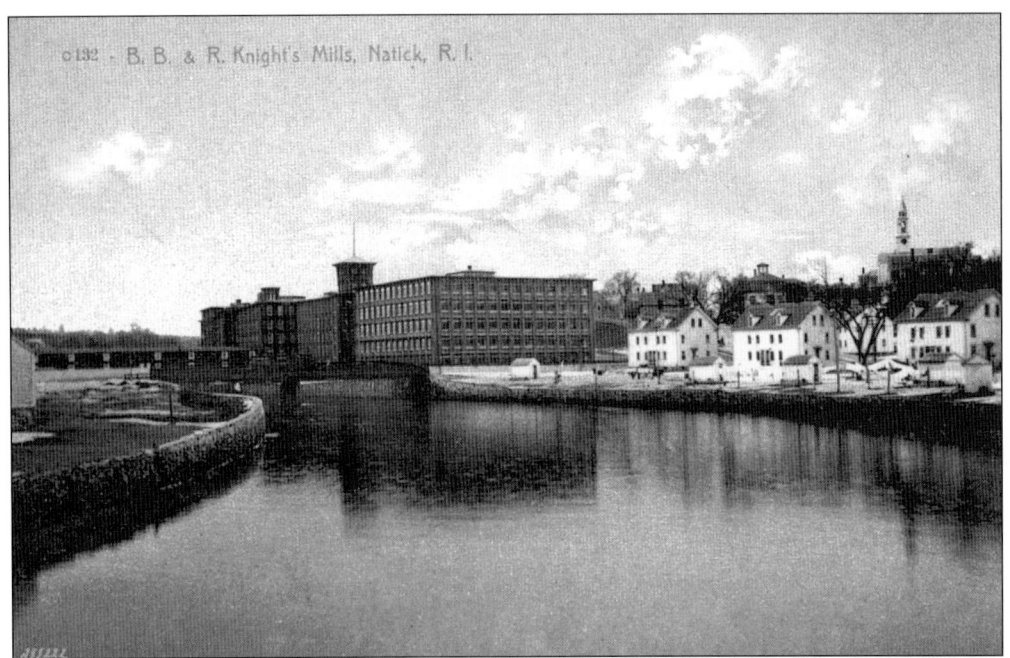

THE NATICK MILL FROM THE OPPOSITE SIDE, C. 1900. A connection of several large mills, it was the biggest in the Pawtuxet Valley. The entire industrial process, from raw cotton delivered by rail to finished cloth goods, could be completed under one roof.

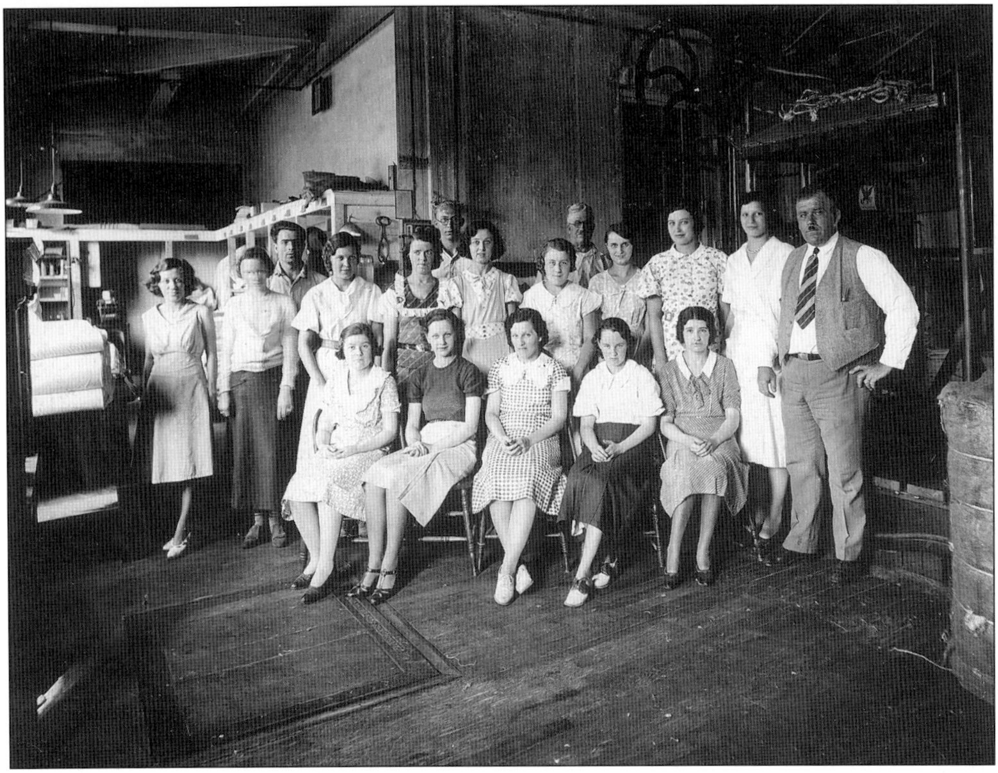

ARCTIC MILL WORKERS, C. 1933.

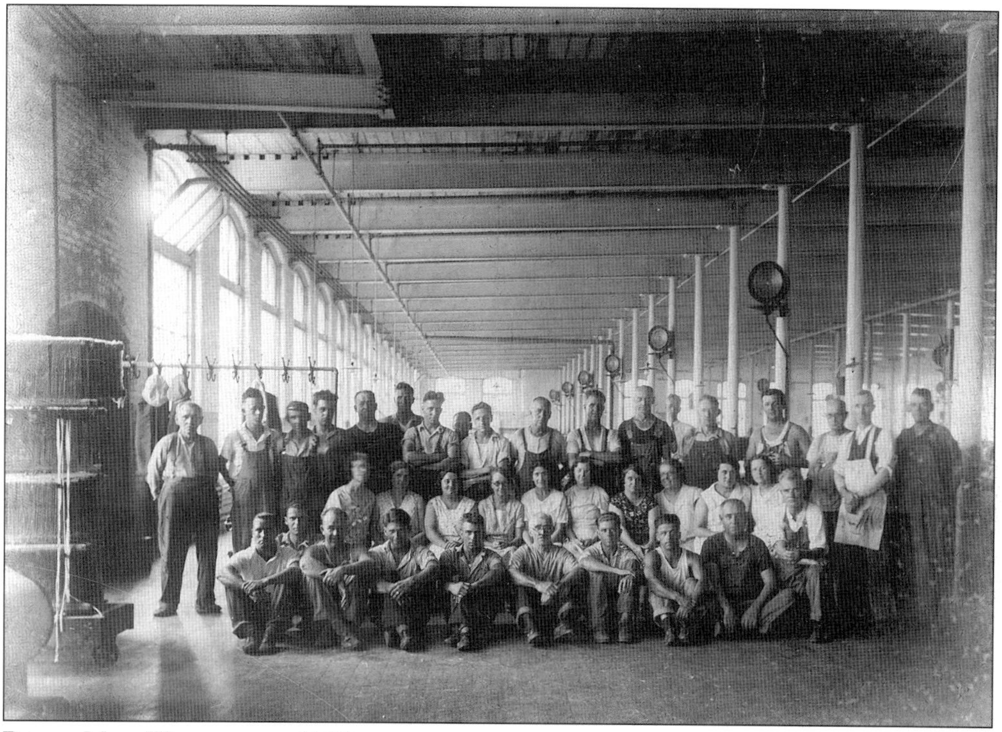

Royal Mill Workers, c. 1930.

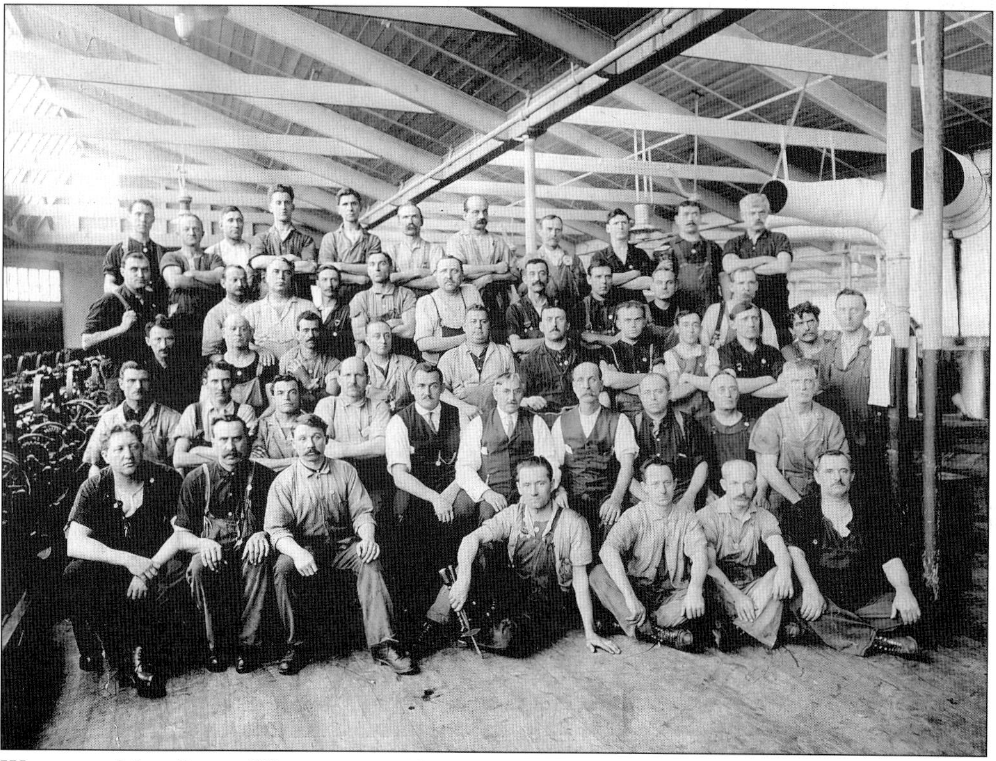

Warwick Mill Loom Workers, c. 1910.

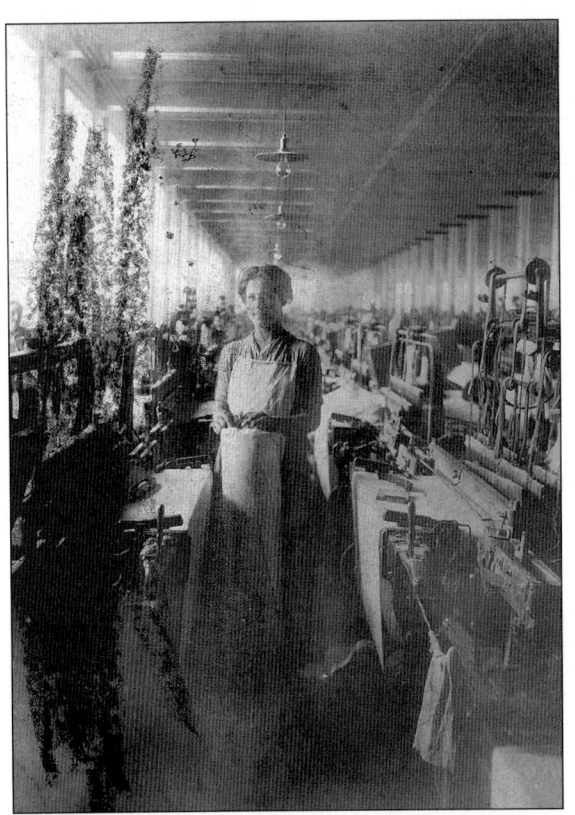

A Weaver at Warwick Mill, c. 1910. The Warwick Mill is located in Centreville.

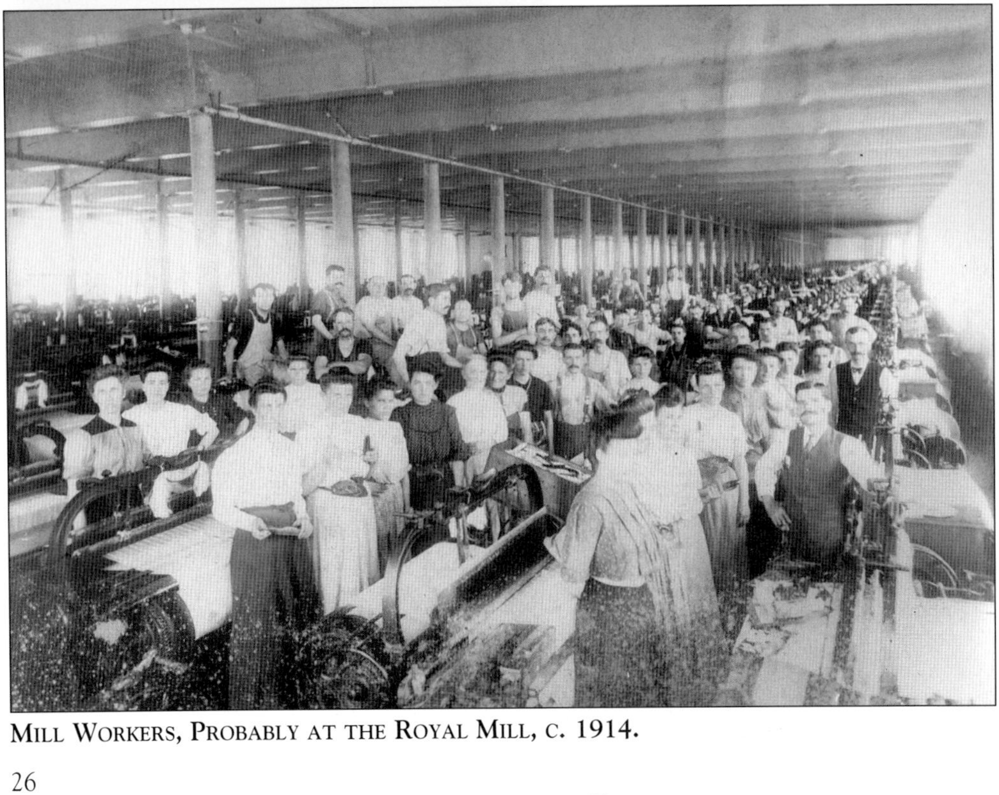

Mill Workers, Probably at the Royal Mill, c. 1914.

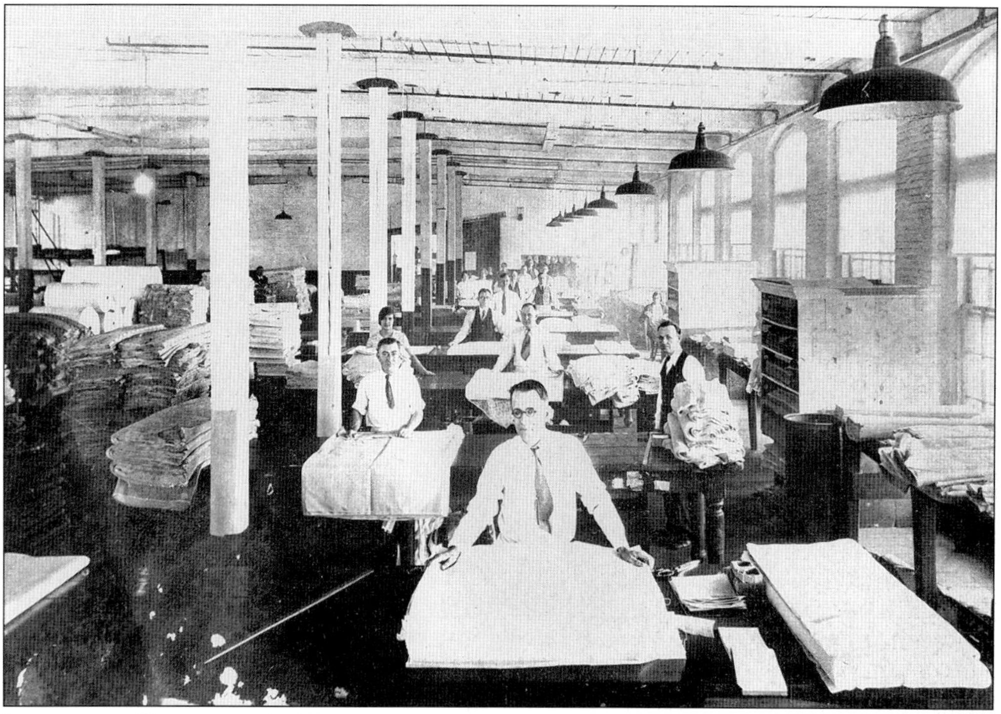

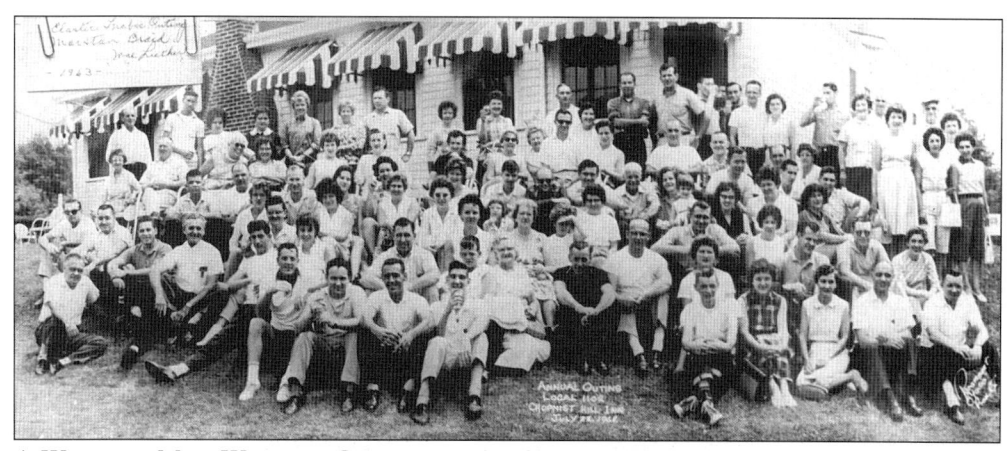

INSPECTING FABRIC, C. 1928.

A WARWICK MILL WORKERS OUTING AT THE CHOPMIST HILL INN, 1963.

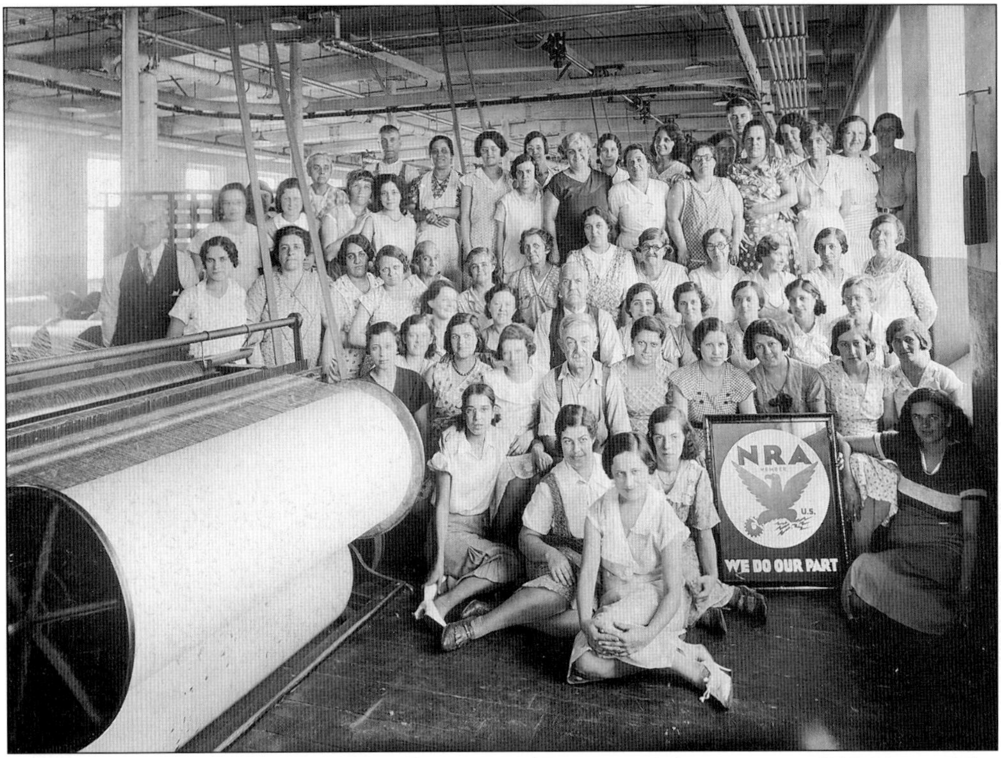

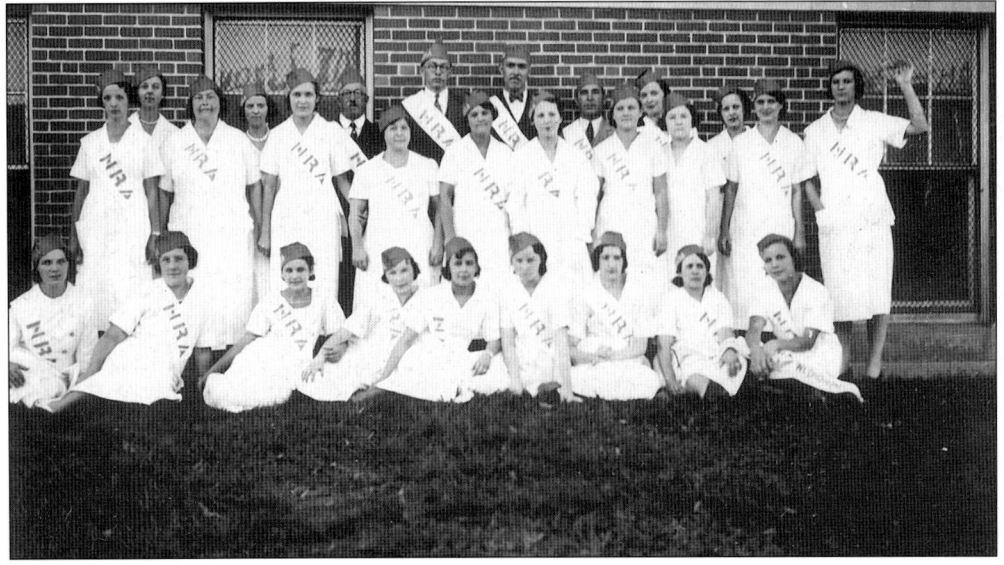

ARCTIC MILL WORKERS, 1933. Note the National Recovery Administration (NRA) sign. The NRA was a wage- and price-control scheme designed to combat the Great Depression.

THE NRA PARADE AT THE ARCTIC MILL, 1933.

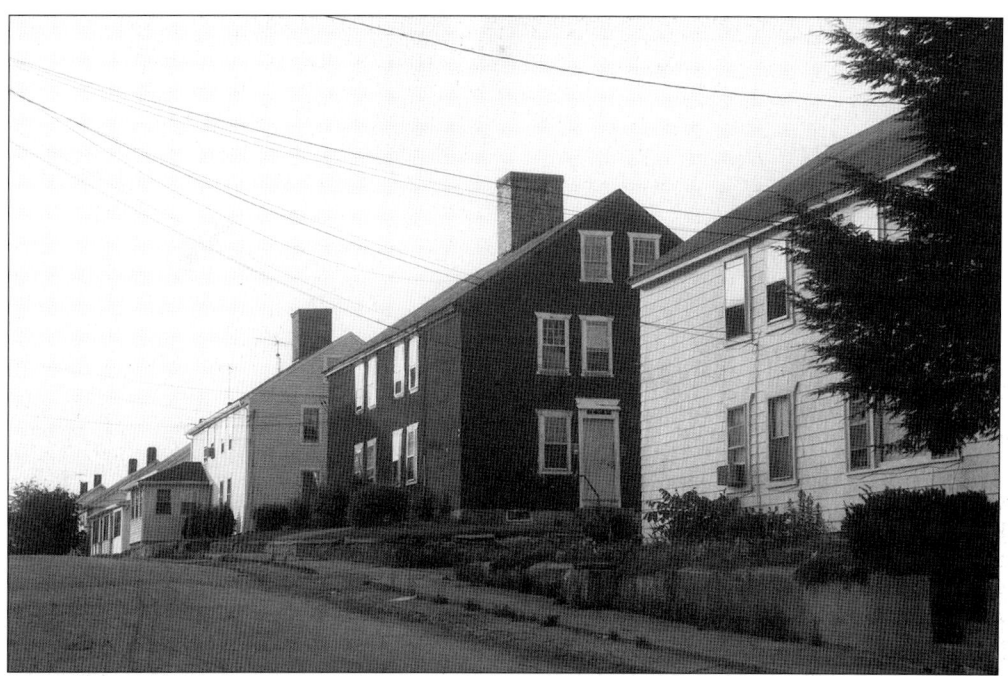

MILL HOUSING. This is a typical multiple-family mill house. Boardinghouses were also provided for single men, some with specific skills who often moved from village to village.

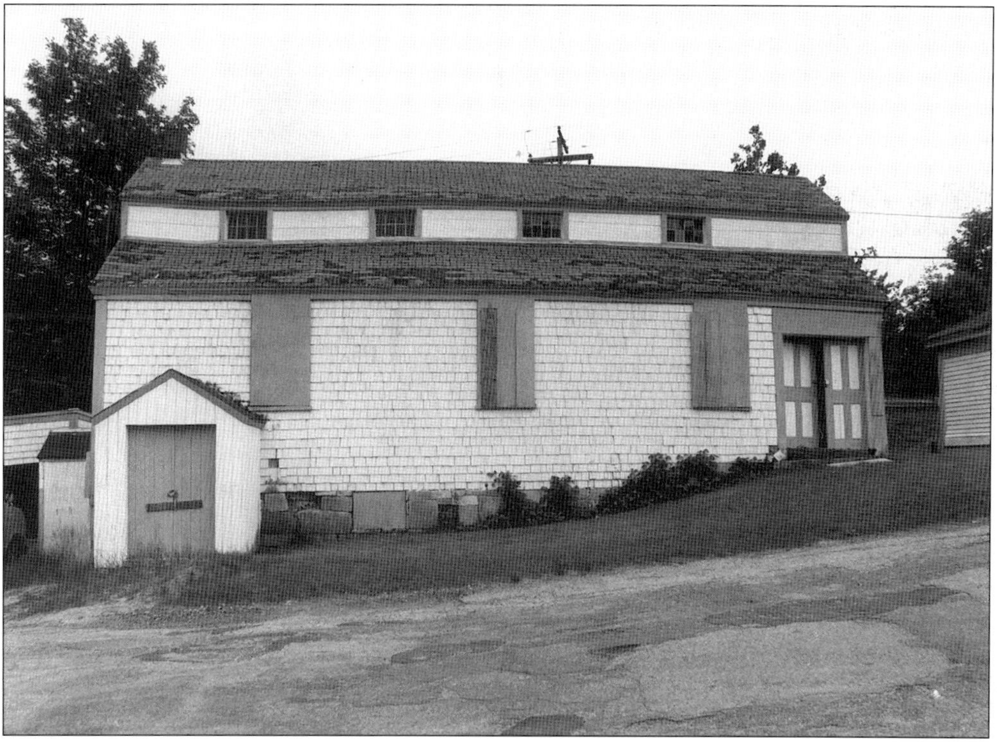

AN EARLY PART OF THE HOPE MILL COMPLEX, THE PICKER ROOM.

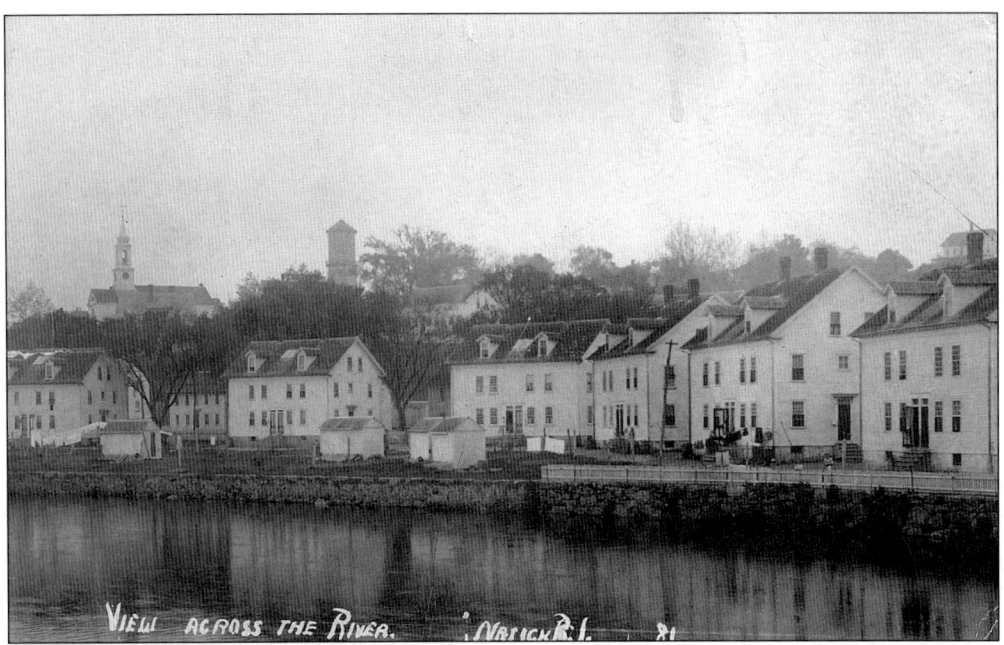

NATICK MILL VILLAGE HOUSING, C. 1910. The water tower on the hill supplied the mill complex and also supported a sprinkler system for fire safety.

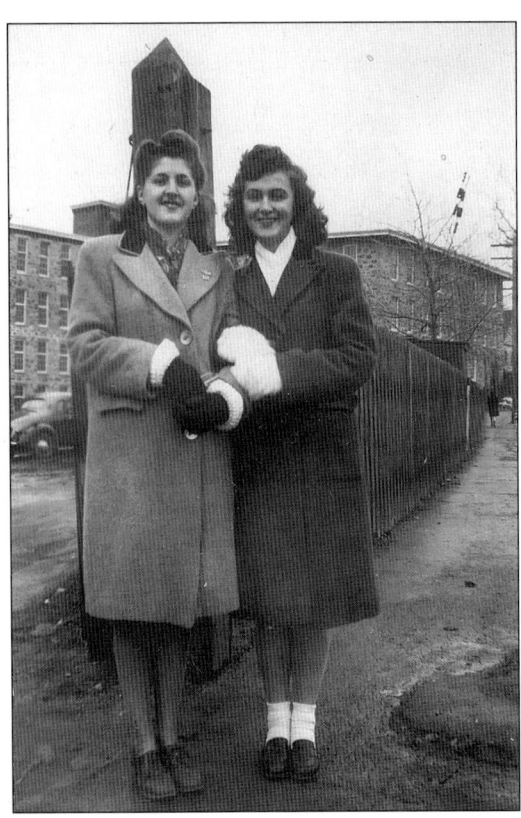

MARY JUSCZYK AND FRIEND, C. 1950. These workers are posing at the Royal Mill gate before their shift.

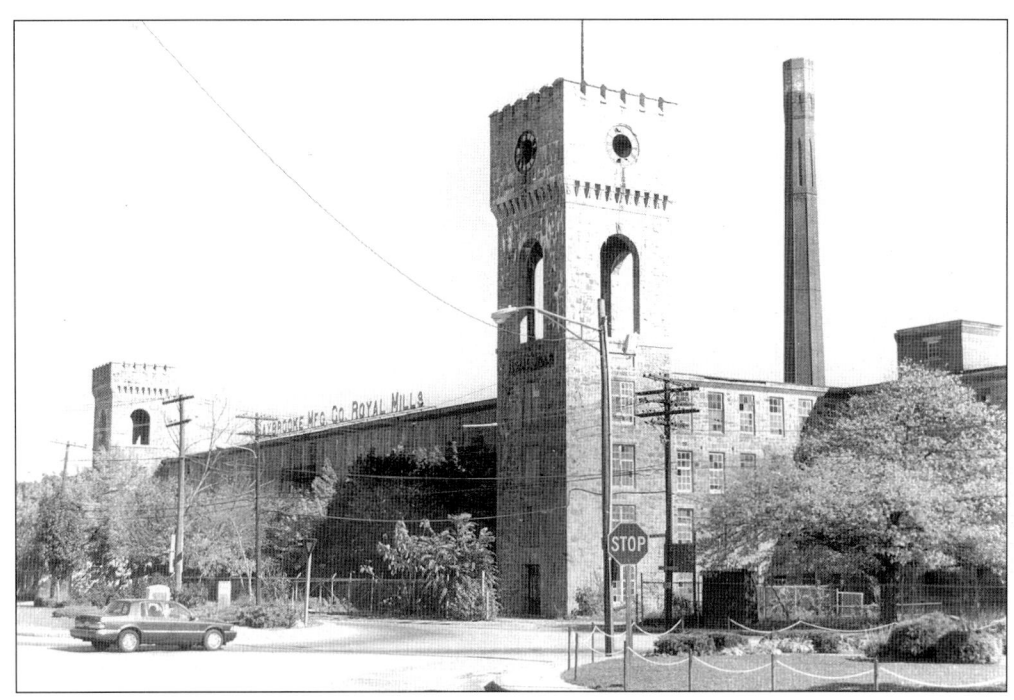

THE ROYAL MILL TODAY.

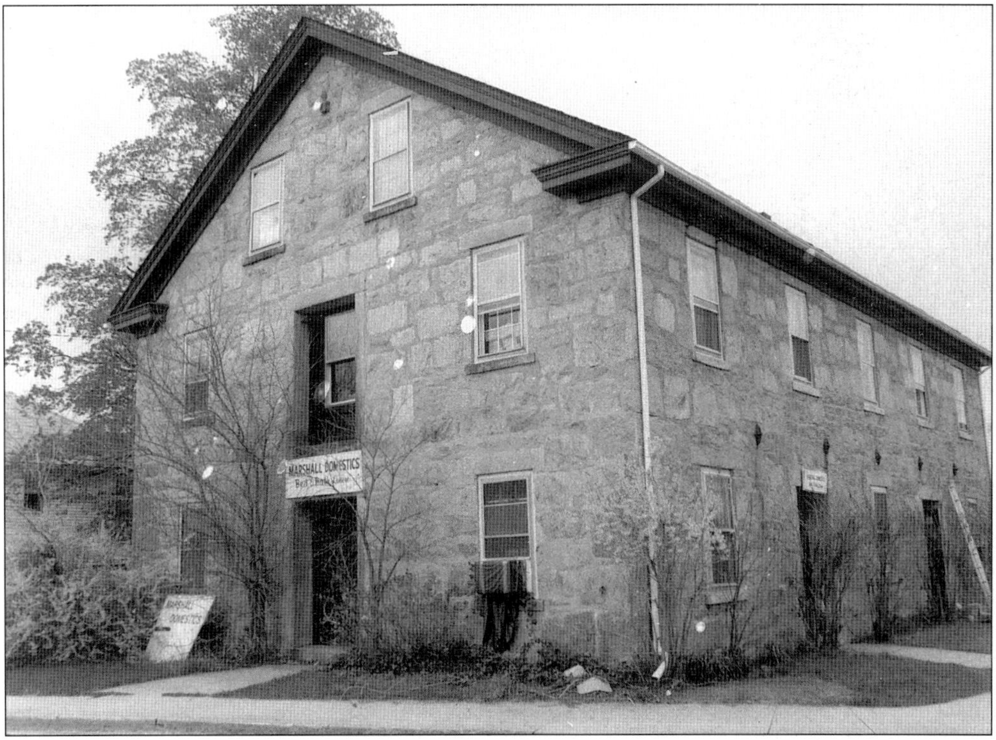

THE ARCTIC COMPANY STORE BUILDING.

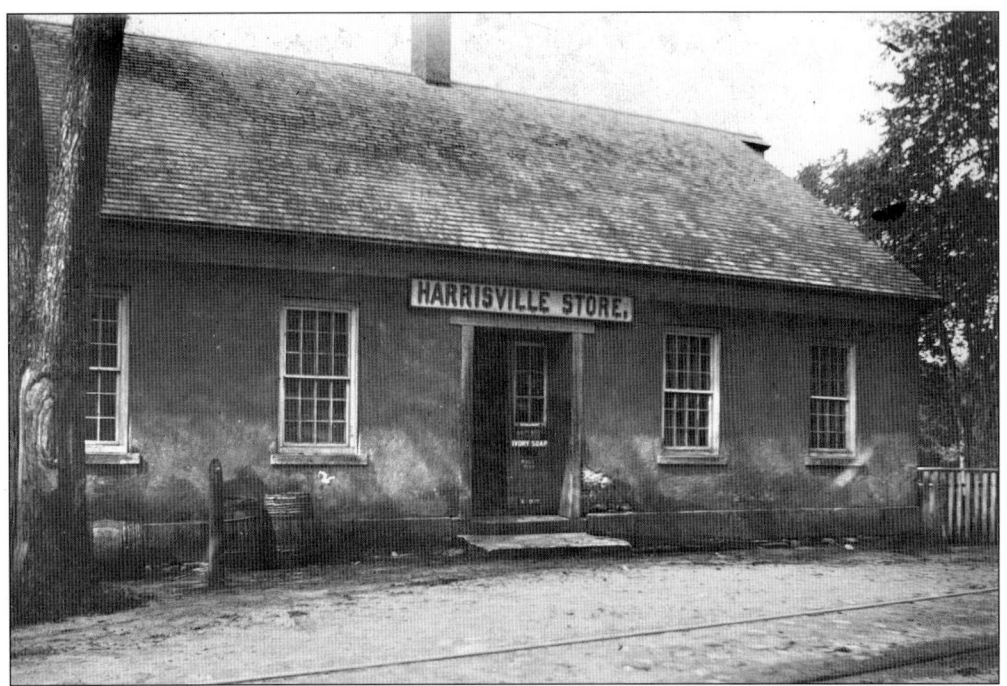

THE HARRIS COMPANY STORE BUILDING, C. 1890. Harris Village was also called Harrisville in the 19th century.

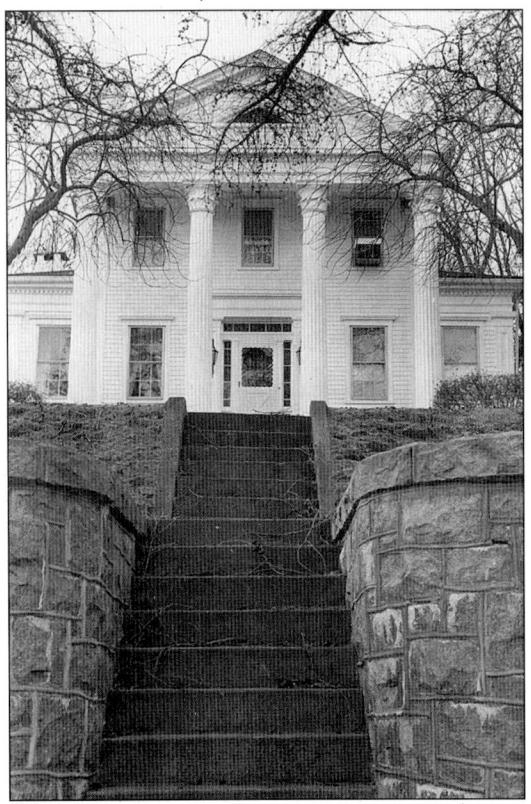

THE WILLIAM B. SPENCER HOUSE, PHENIX. Built in 1847, this house is a superb example of Greek Revival architecture. Many mill owners, officials, and business people built large homes in the latest styles on hills overlooking the valley.

Two
THE RURAL AND COLONIAL VALLEY

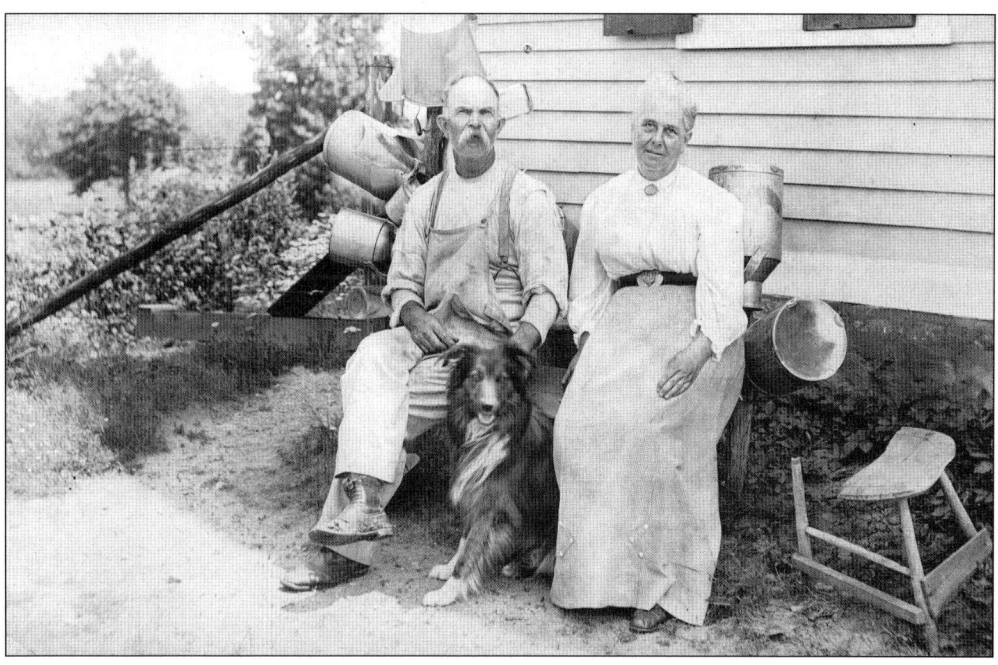

WILLIAM AND ELLA POWELL, c. 1890. William and Ella Powell are seen here at their farm off Blackrock Road in Coventry between Anthony and Harris Villages.

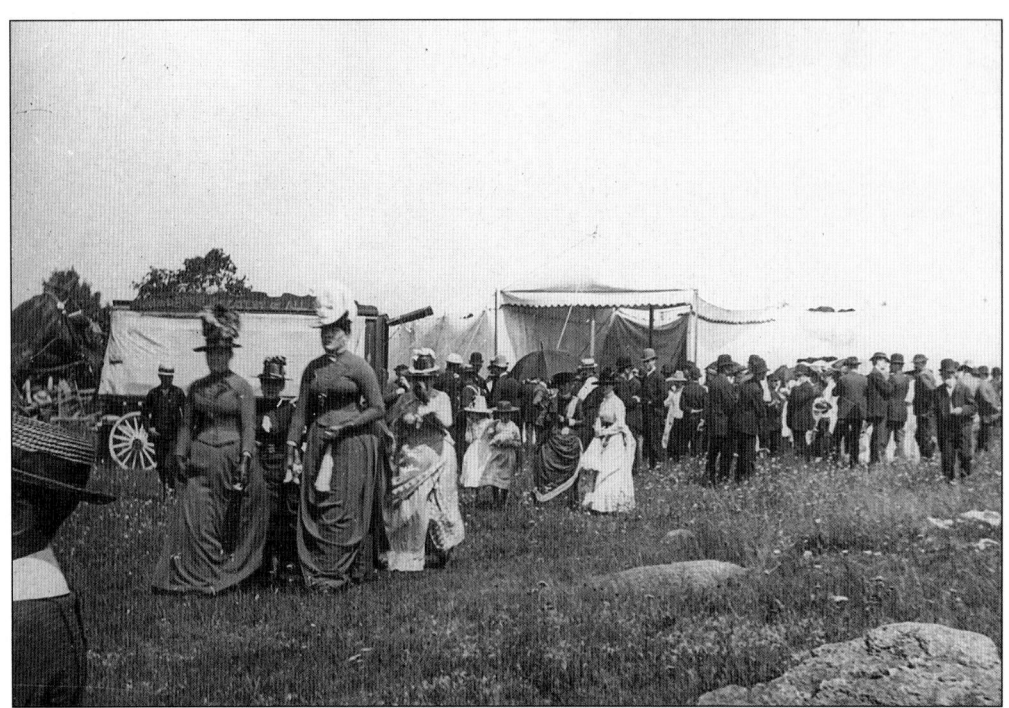

THE PAWTUXET VALLEY AGRICULTURAL FAIR, C. 1882. The fairgrounds were located near Phenix. John L. Sullivan, noted boxer and sometime valley resident, is set up to display his skill.

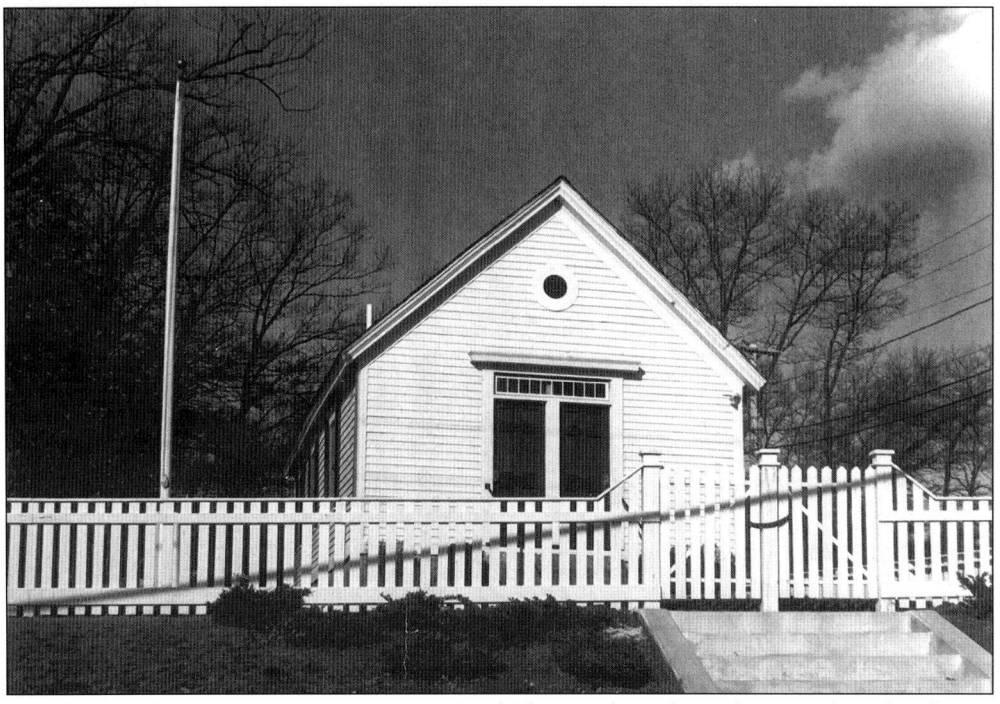

THE READ SCHOOLHOUSE, COVENTRY. Typical of many throughout the area, this schoolhouse is now a museum of the Coventry Historical Society.

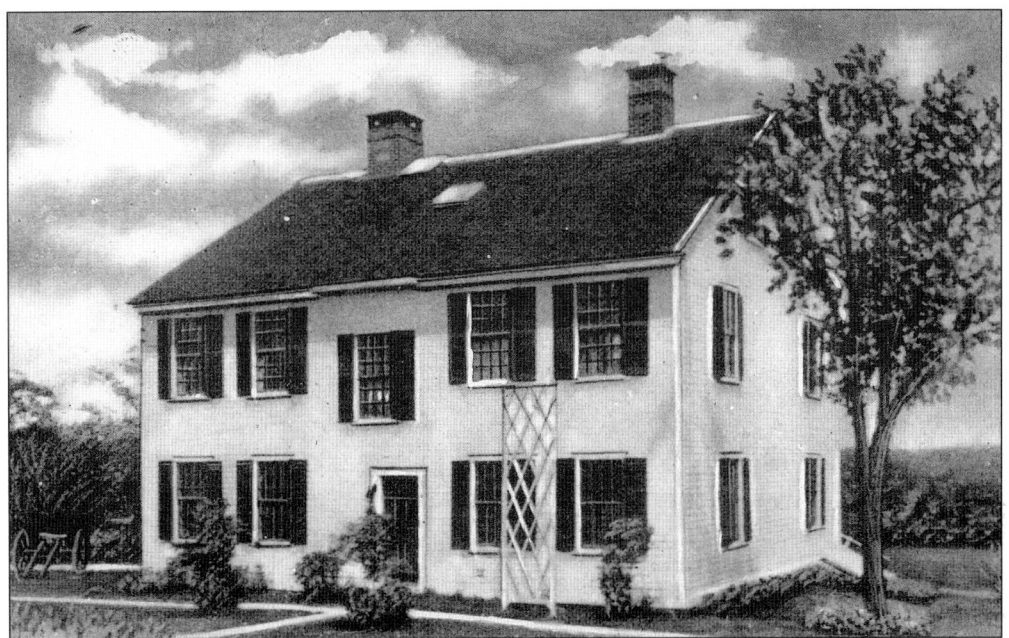

THE NATHANAEL GREENE HOMESTEAD, C. 1930. This was the home of Maj. Gen. Nathanael Greene, who, besides being a Revolutionary War luminary, was an important farmer and industrialist in the valley. Remains of his forge are located on this property along the Pawtuxet River in Quidnick.

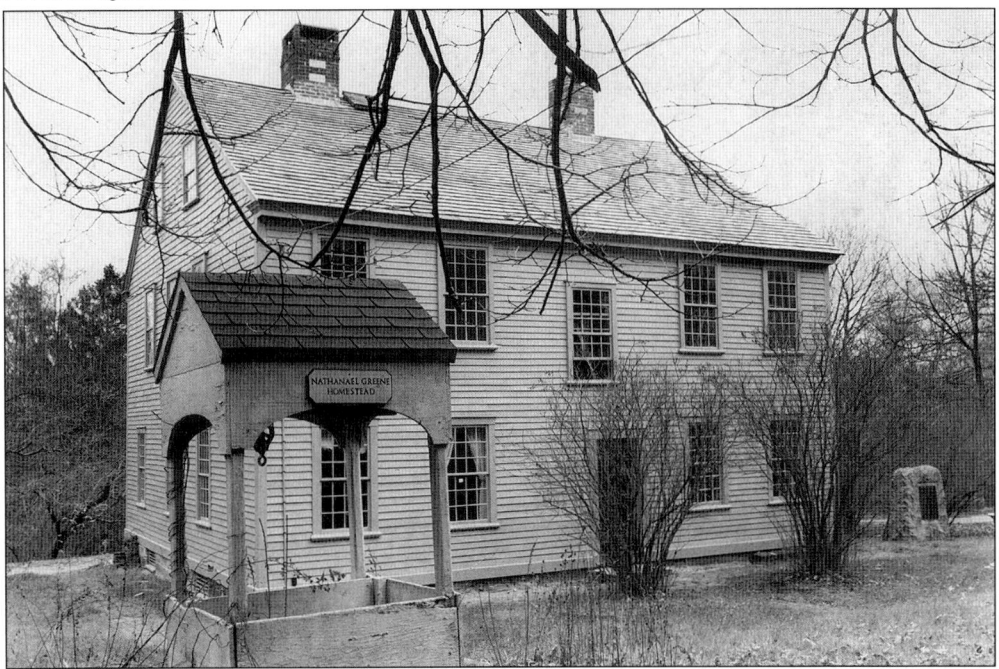

THE NATHANAEL GREENE HOMESTEAD, C. 1975. The homestead is now a museum under the care of the Daughters of the American Revolution and the Nathanael Greene Association. Greene did not return to Coventry after the war but settled in Georgia, where he was given a plantation in recognition of his achievement in driving the British from the South.

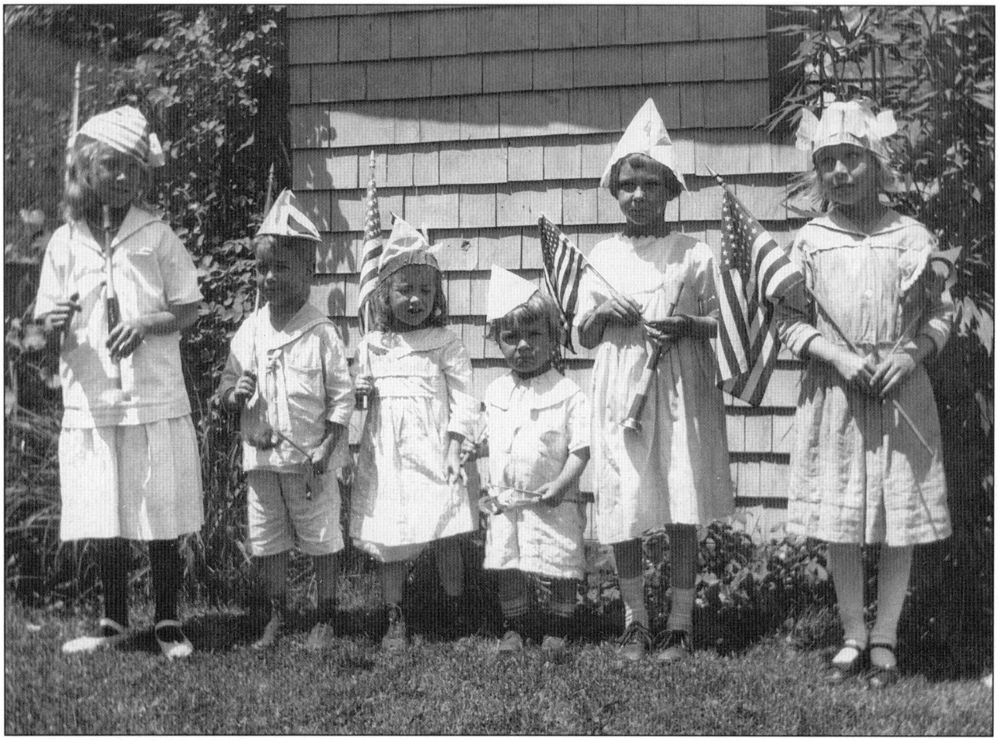

The Hudson Family Celebrating the Fourth of July, c. 1920.

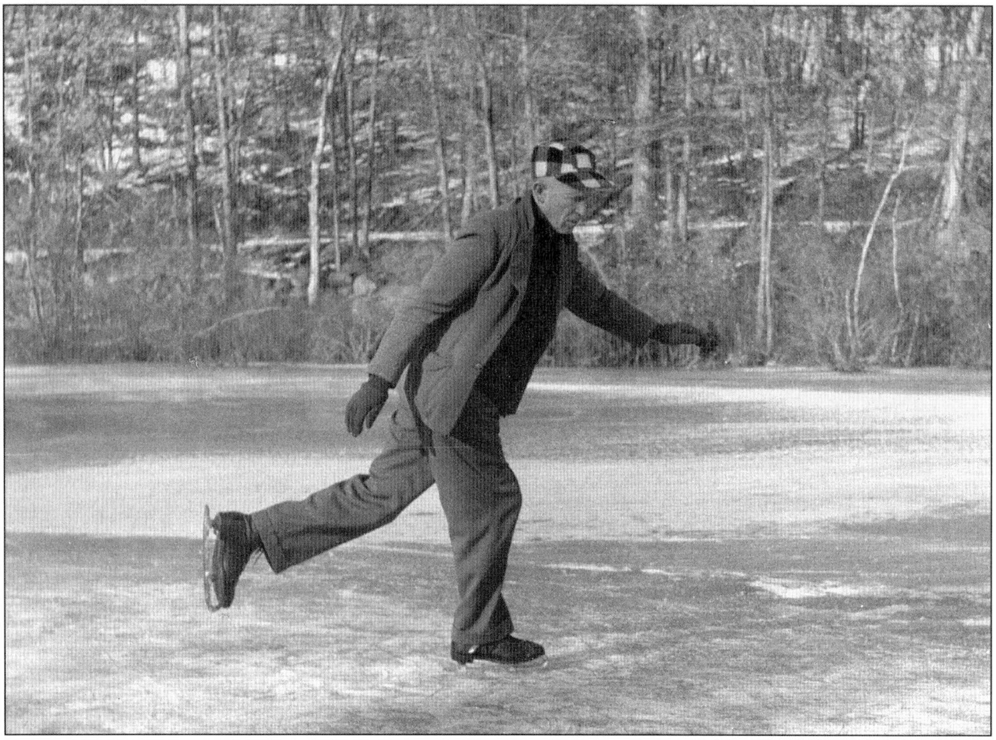

Skater Leo Hudson on Pearce's Pond, Harris Village, 1957.

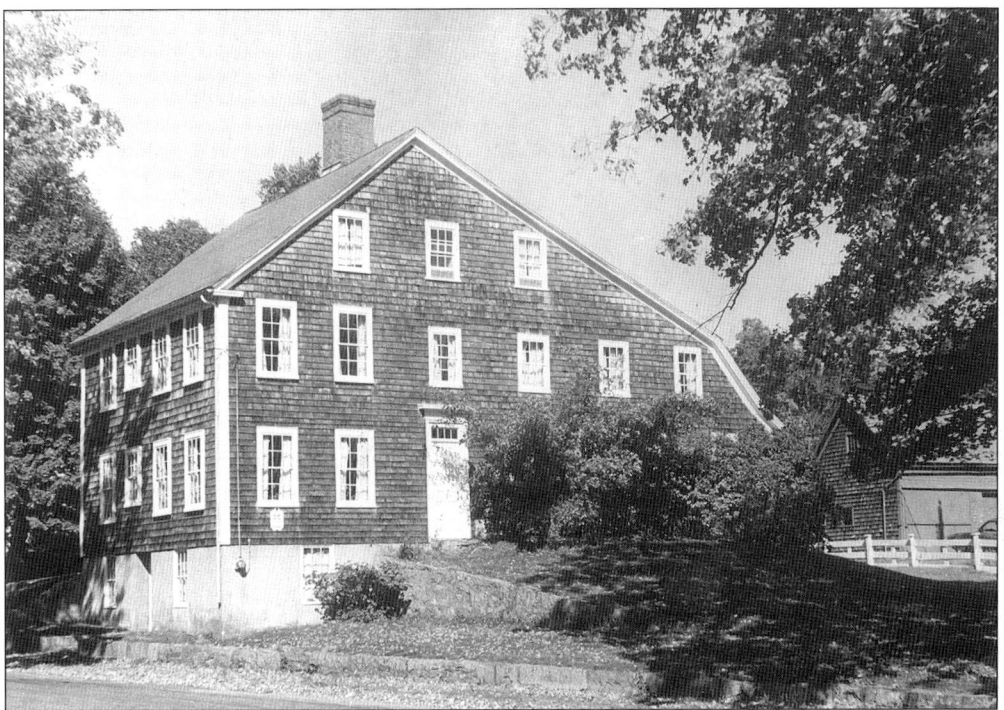

THE PAINE HOUSE, WASHINGTON VILLAGE. A former tavern and farmhouse dating from the late 1600s, the house is now a museum run by the Western Coventry Civic & Historical Society. Its exhibits include many unique artifacts and documents of early Pawtuxet Valley life.

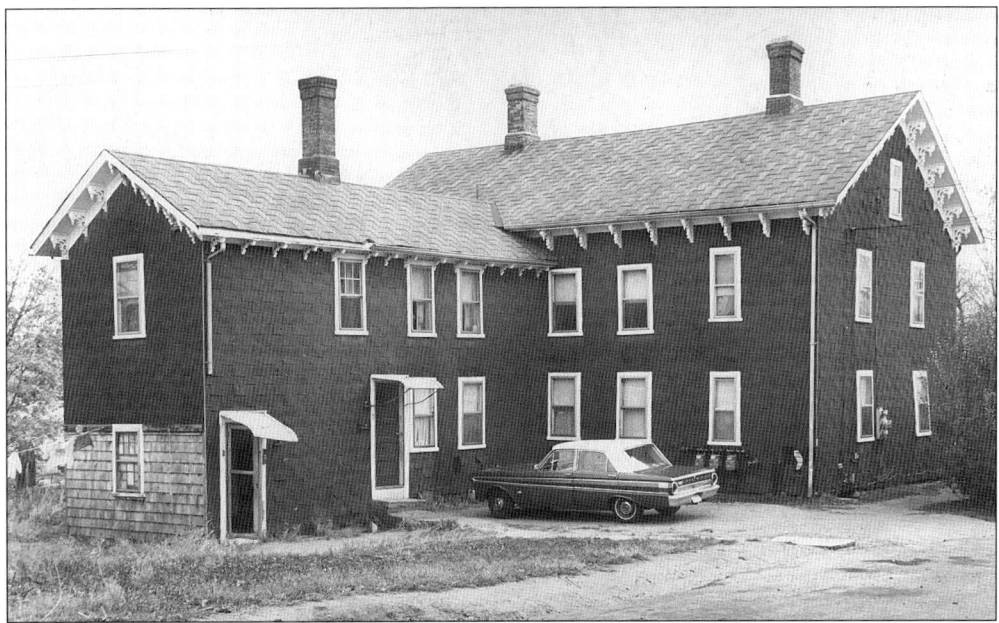

A FARMHOUSE. When the industrial valley overtook the agricultural valley in the 19th century, many farmhouses were converted to other uses. This example, on what is now West Warwick Avenue, became a multifamily tenement. It was also the home in the 1880s of boxer John L. Sullivan and his family.

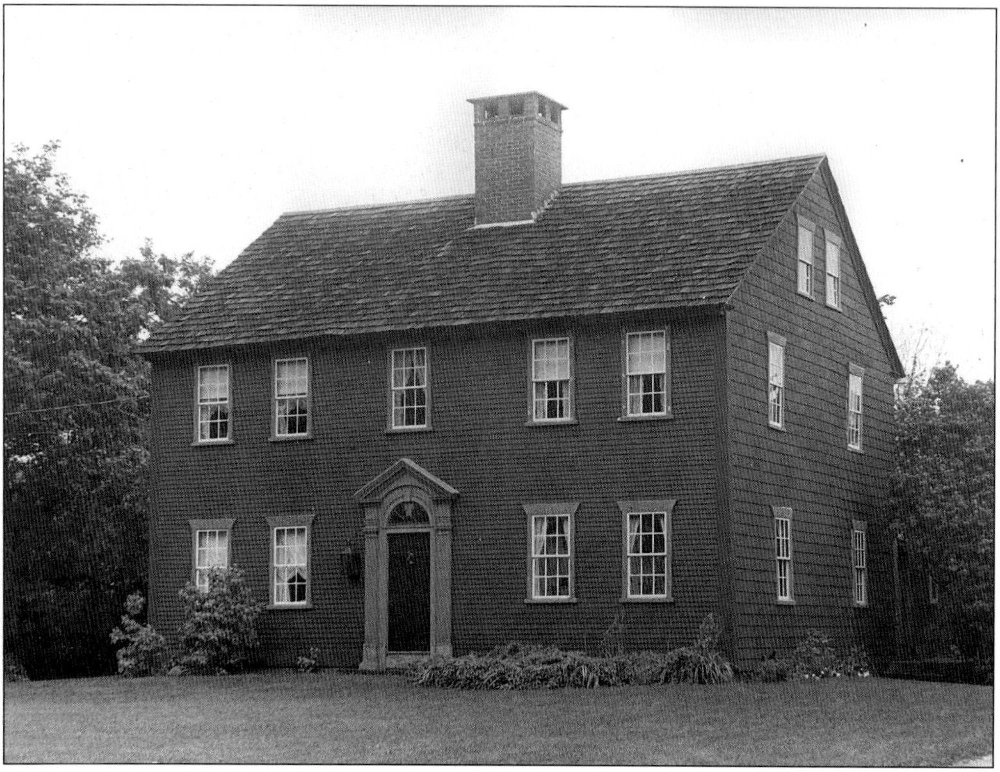

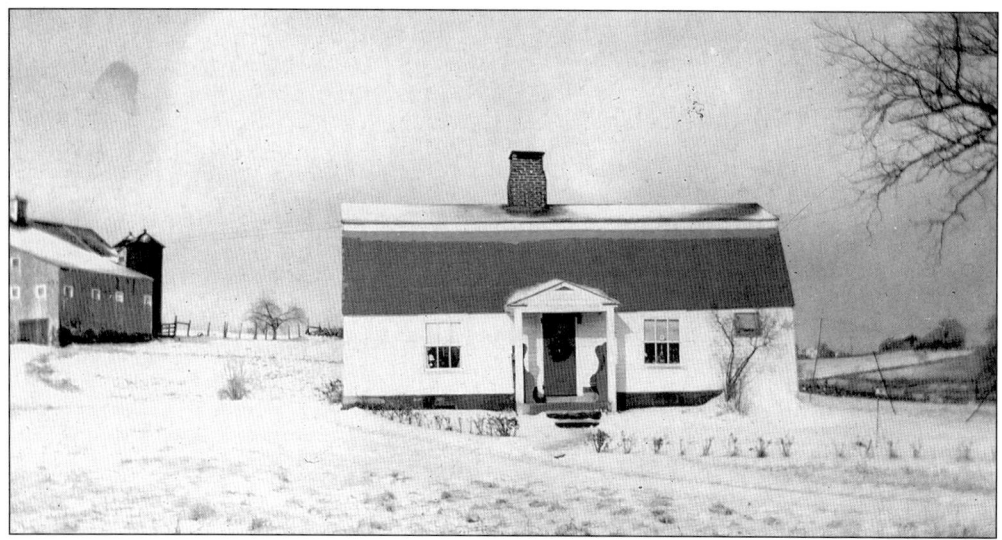

THE SILAS CLAPP HOUSE. Located on East Greenwich Avenue in West Warwick, this house is listed on the National Register of Historic Places as a significant example of a Federal-era dwelling. It was built in 1804.

THE REMINGTON FARM HOMESTEAD, C. 1938. This is the original building of what became a well-known dairy operation in the valley. It was located in the village of Hope.

AN ADVERTISEMENT FOR
REMINGTON'S DAIRY, 1963. Home
delivery of fresh milk products was a
feature of local life until the 1970s.
Remington's was the last surviving
valley business of this kind.

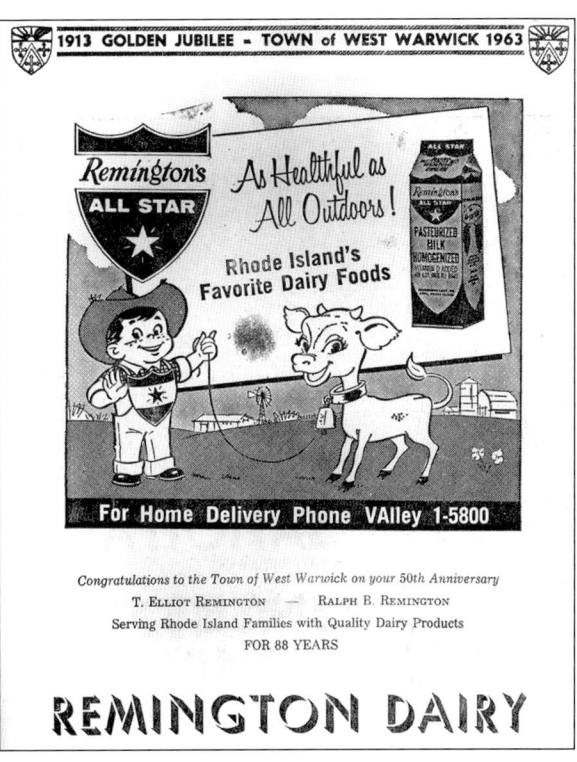

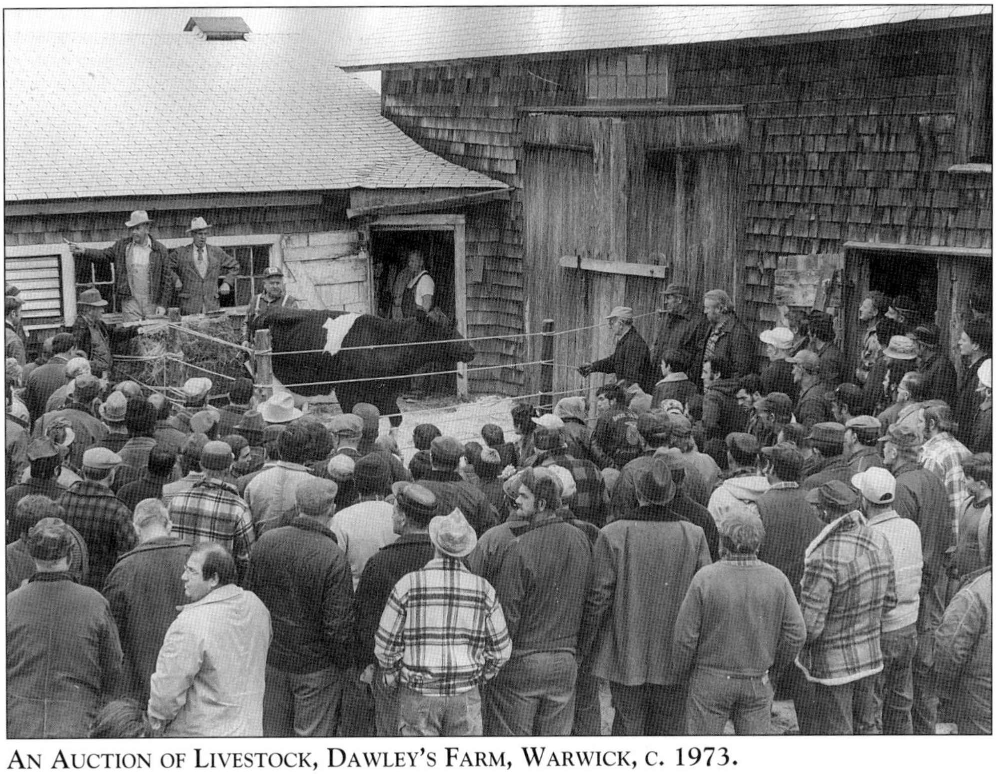

AN AUCTION OF LIVESTOCK, DAWLEY'S FARM, WARWICK, C. 1973.

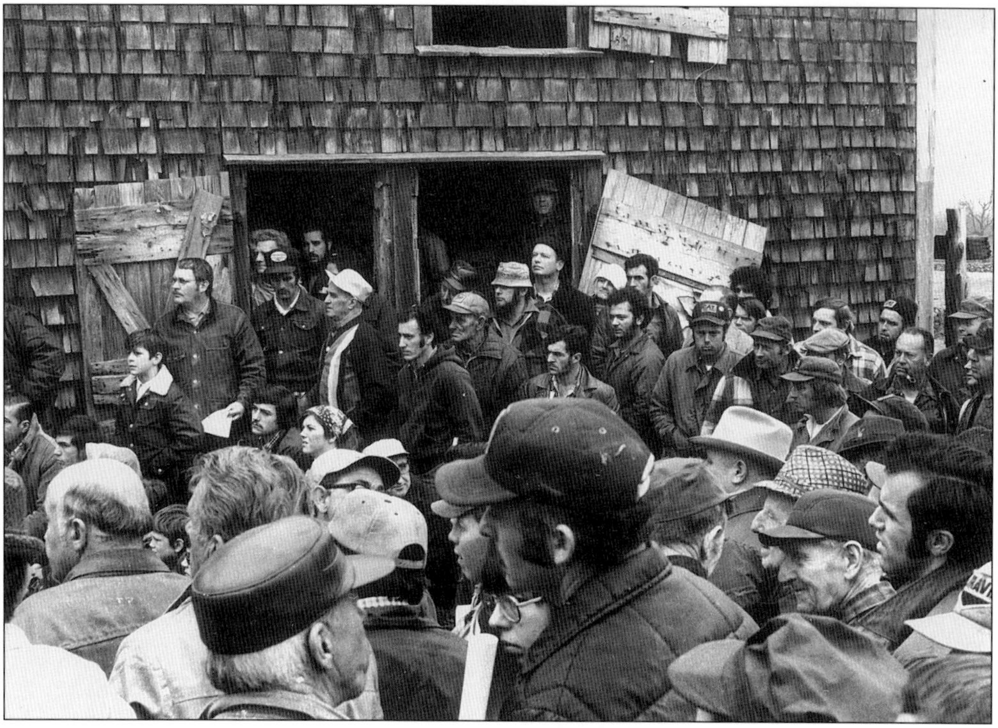

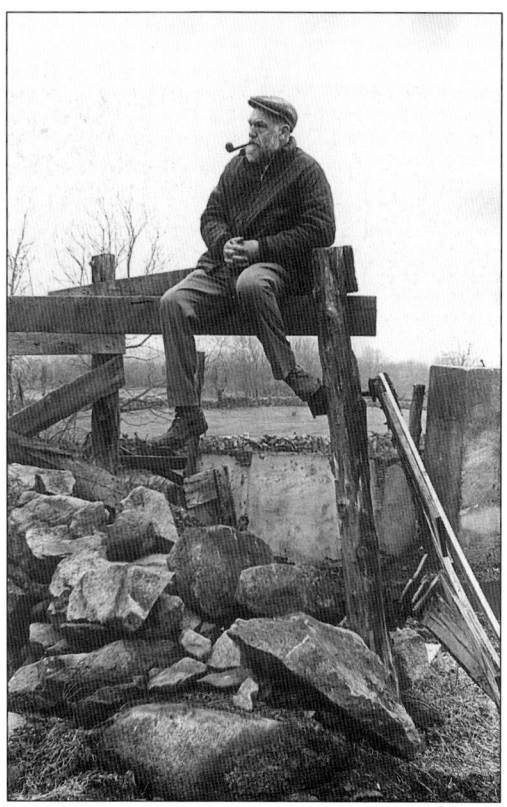

THE AUCTION OF DAWLEY FARM. The auction of Dawley Farm in the mid-1970s is evocative of the slow death of agriculture in the Pawtuxet Valley area. Located in Warwick on what is now the main business route of central Rhode Island, Route 2, the Dawley Farm was sold to make way for a suburban corporate park of the Metropolitan Life Insurance Company.

Three
THE IMMIGRANTS: STARTING A NEW LIFE

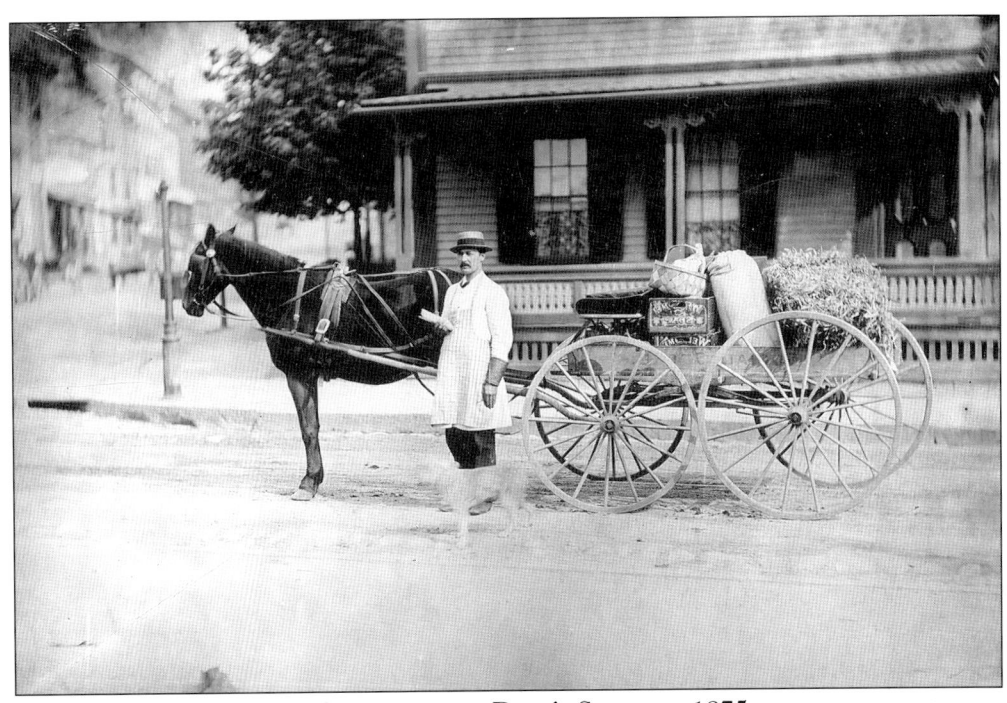

PIERRE SOUCY DELIVERING GROCERIES FOR DION'S STORE, C. 1875.

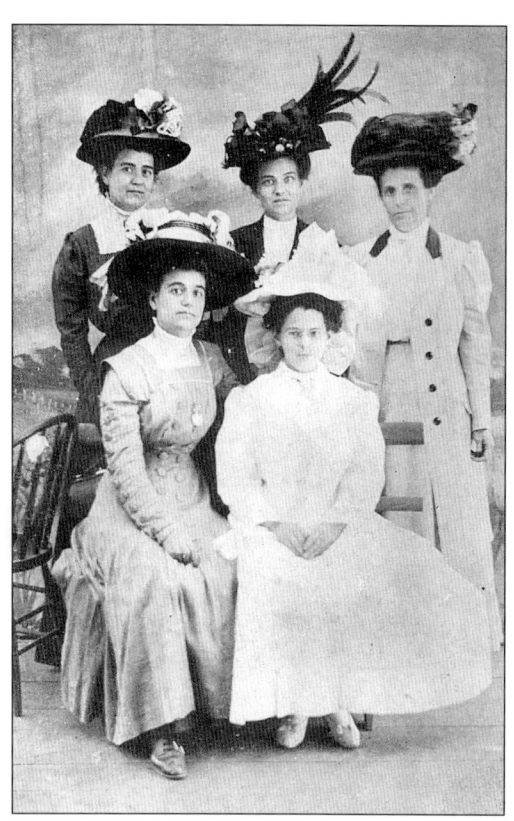

THE MINEAU SISTERS KEEP UP WITH FASHION, NATICK, C. 1900.

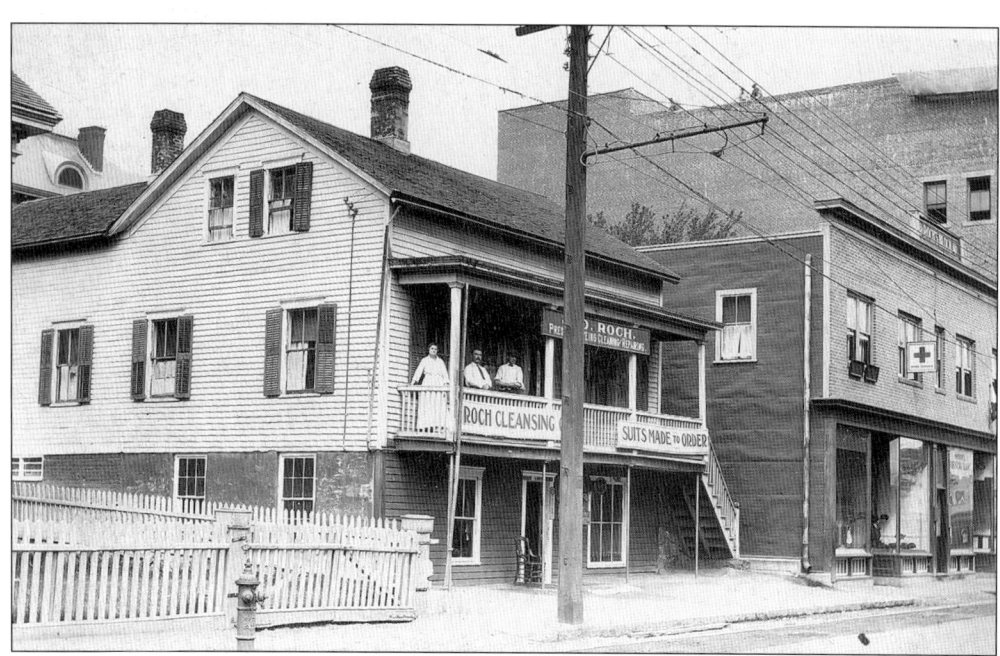

THE ROCH TAILOR SHOP, ARCTIC CENTER, C. 1920. Joseph Roch came from Quebec, opened his shop in 1885, and slowly built up his business and holdings. Roch is shown here with his wife and son Albert. He also owns the building next door.

Son Elphege Roch and Grandson Norman, Robert Street in Arctic, 1978. Norman Roch still runs a tailoring business at that location.

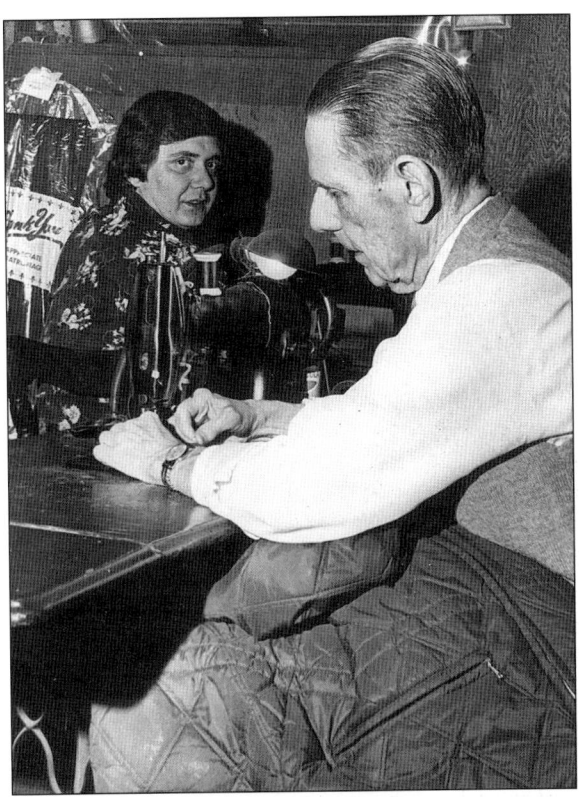

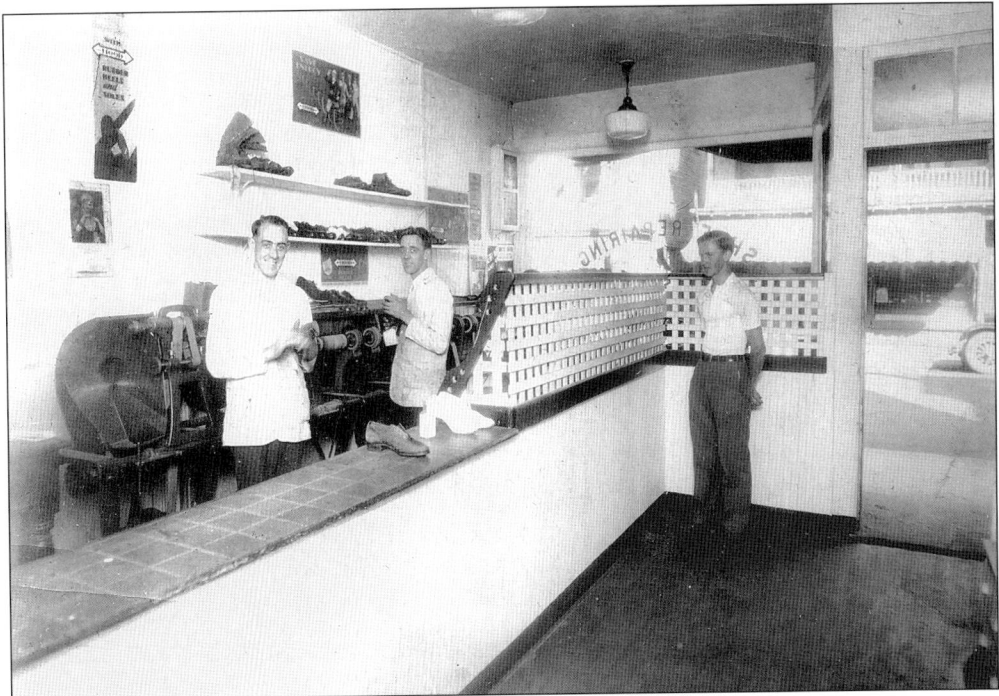

The Cayouette Family Shop, c. 1925. The Cayouette family opened this shoe-repair business in Arctic.

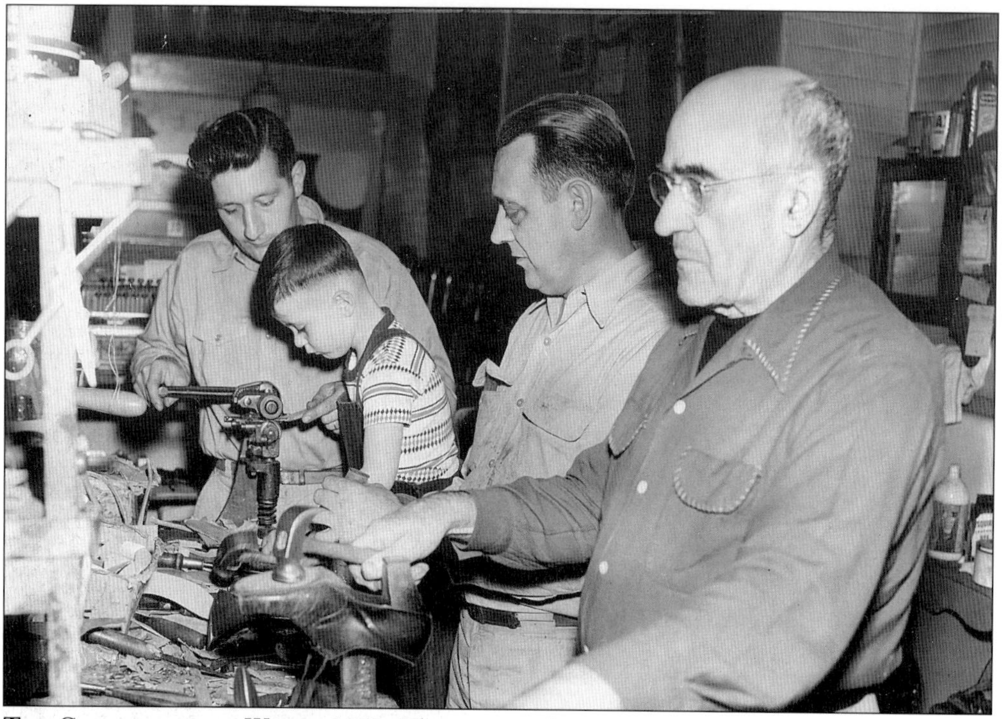

THE CAYOUETTES AT WORK, 1950. This picture shows several generations of Cayouettes at work in their shop on Archambault Avenue. They are still in business today.

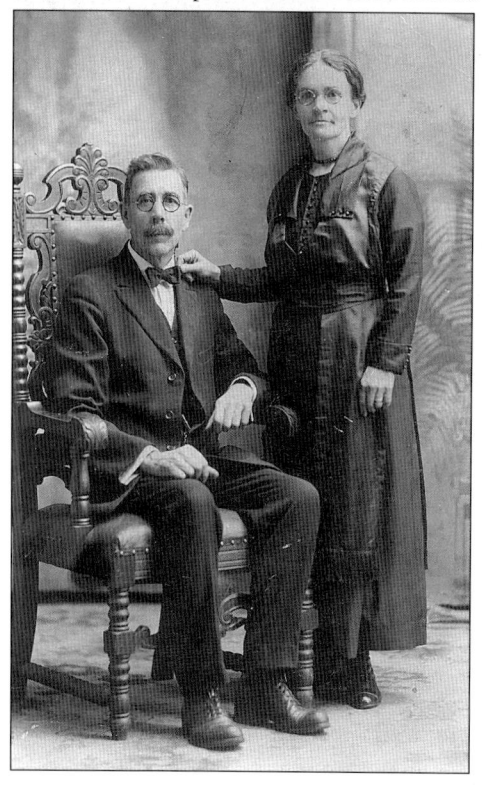

THE LEVEILLEES SITTING FOR A FORMAL PORTRAIT, 1900.

First Communion, Arctic, c. 1910.

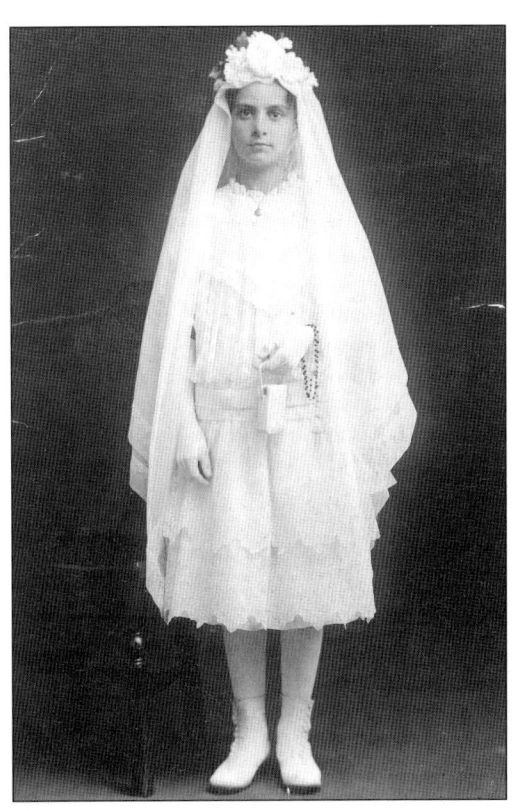

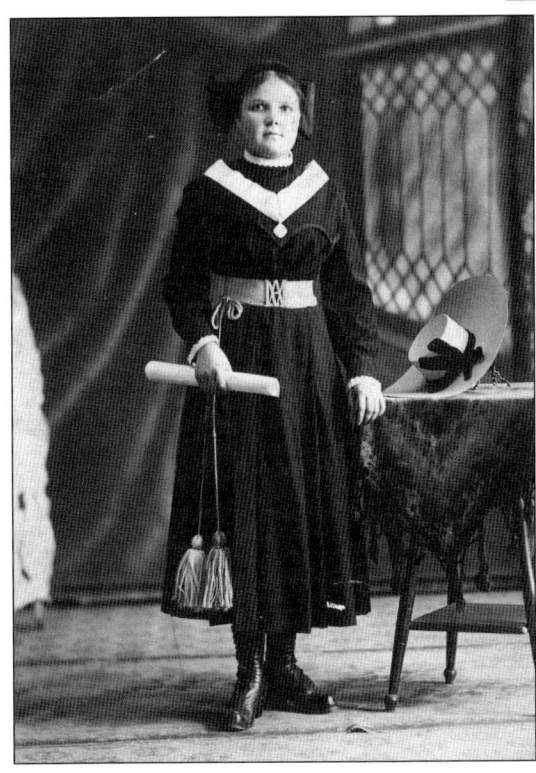

A Parochial School Graduate, Arctic, c. 1905. Any major event was an occasion for a photographic portrait.

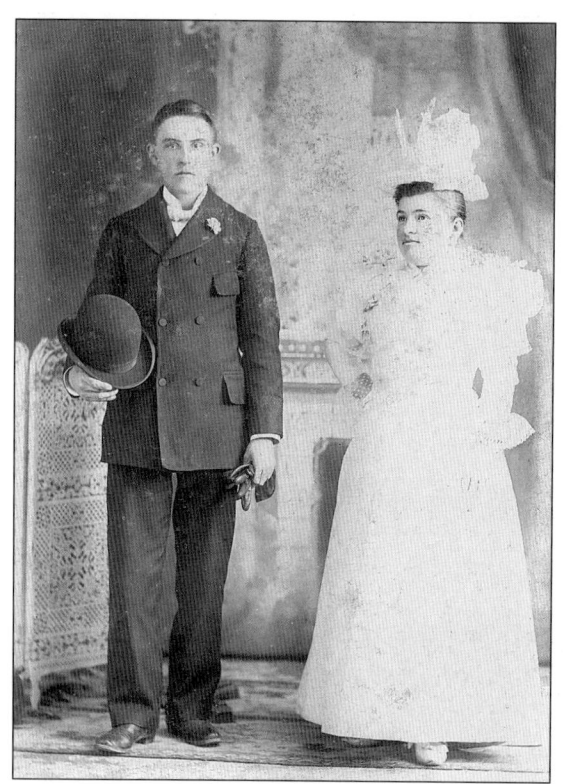

NEWLYWEDS. These Franco-American newlyweds were photographed at Geoffroy's Studio across from St. John the Baptist Church in Arctic.

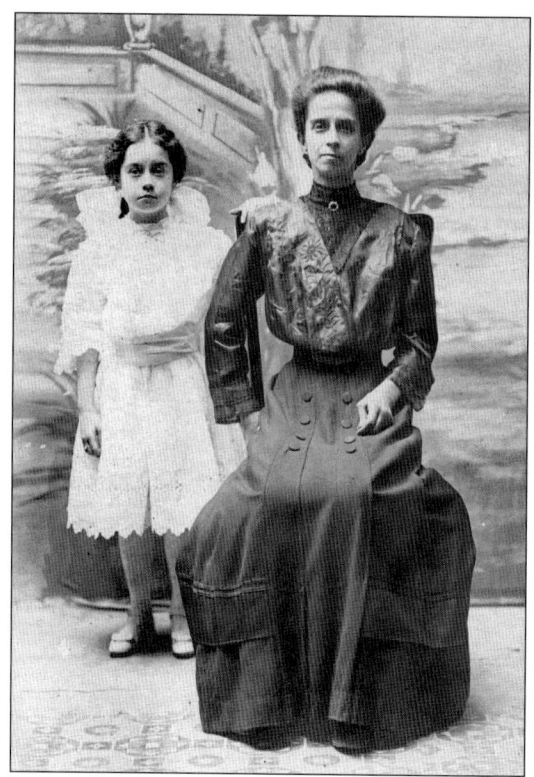

A FRENCH CANADIAN MOTHER AND CHILD, C. 1900. Immigrants from Quebec arrived in large numbers after 1865 to work in the mills and settled especially in Arctic, Phenix, Natick, and Centreville.

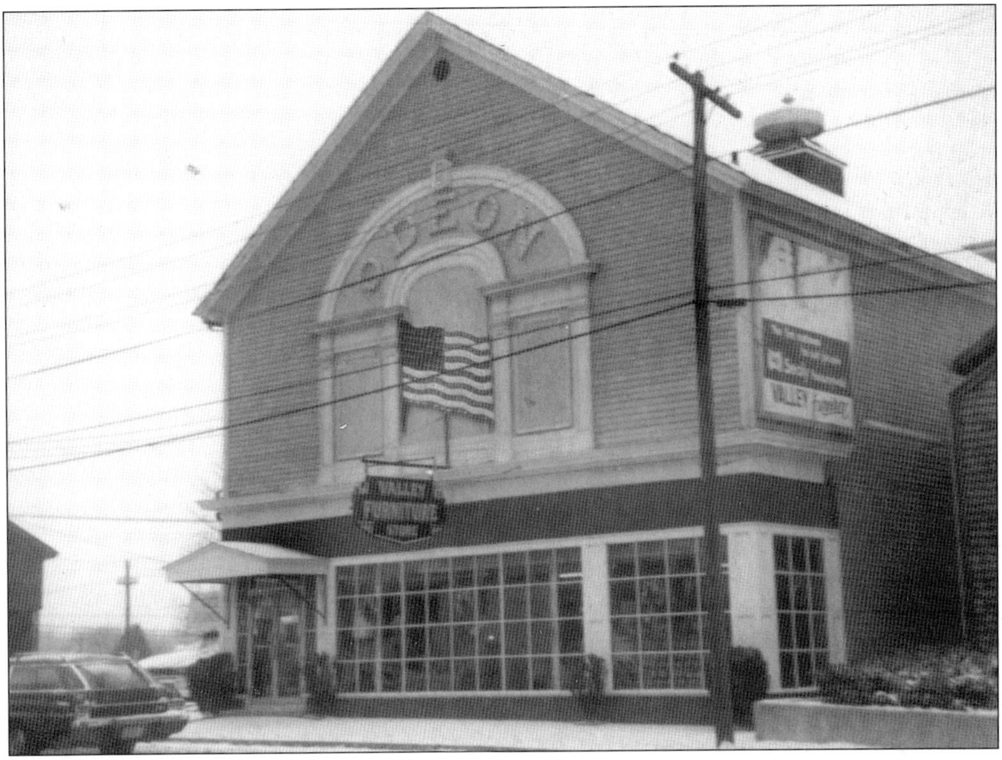

THE ODEON THEATRE, 1976.

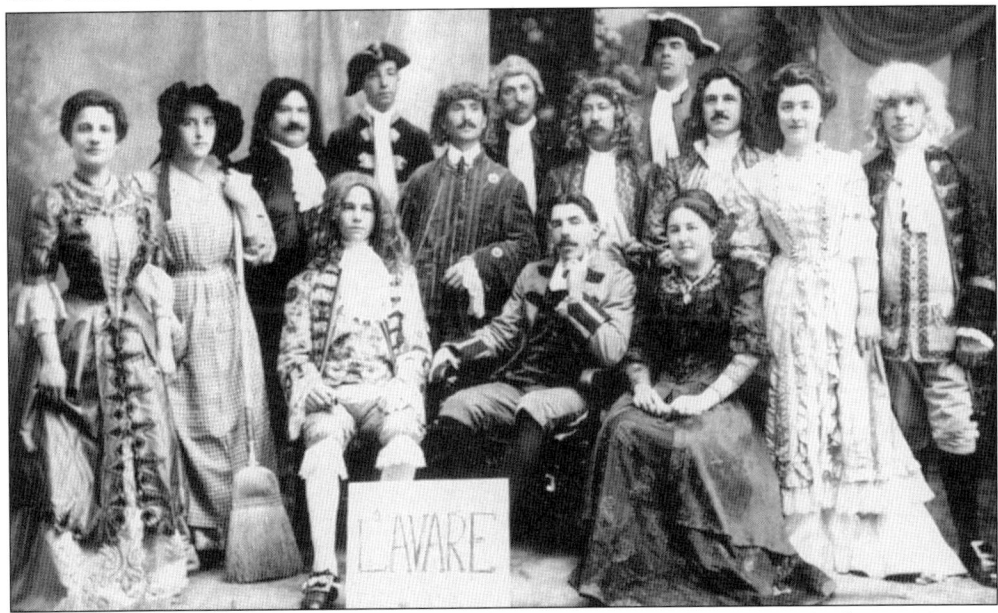

A PRODUCTION FROM THE ODEON THEATRE, C. 1918. The theater was built in 1909 as a showcase of French cultural life by Father Bourgeois of St. John the Baptist parish. It was located on Robert Street in Arctic Center and featured traveling French vaudeville shows, as well as more serious plays and local productions. This production of a Moliere play featured Toussaint Parenteau. (Courtesy St. John the Baptist Church.)

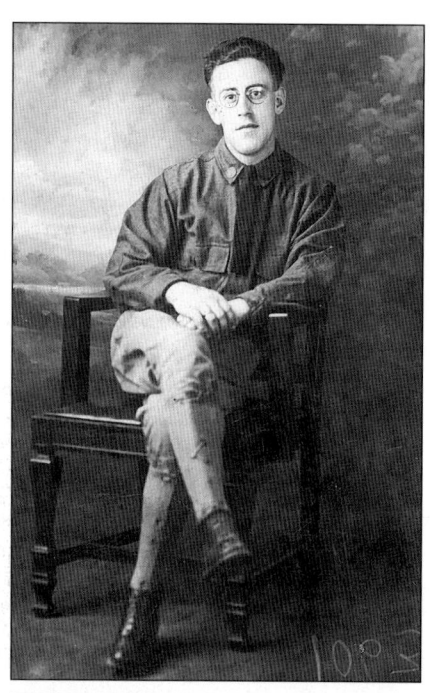

A 1918 Postcard. A French World War I veteran sent this postcard home to the valley in 1918. Like many other immigrant groups, the French Canadians were quick to volunteer for the armed forces during times of war.

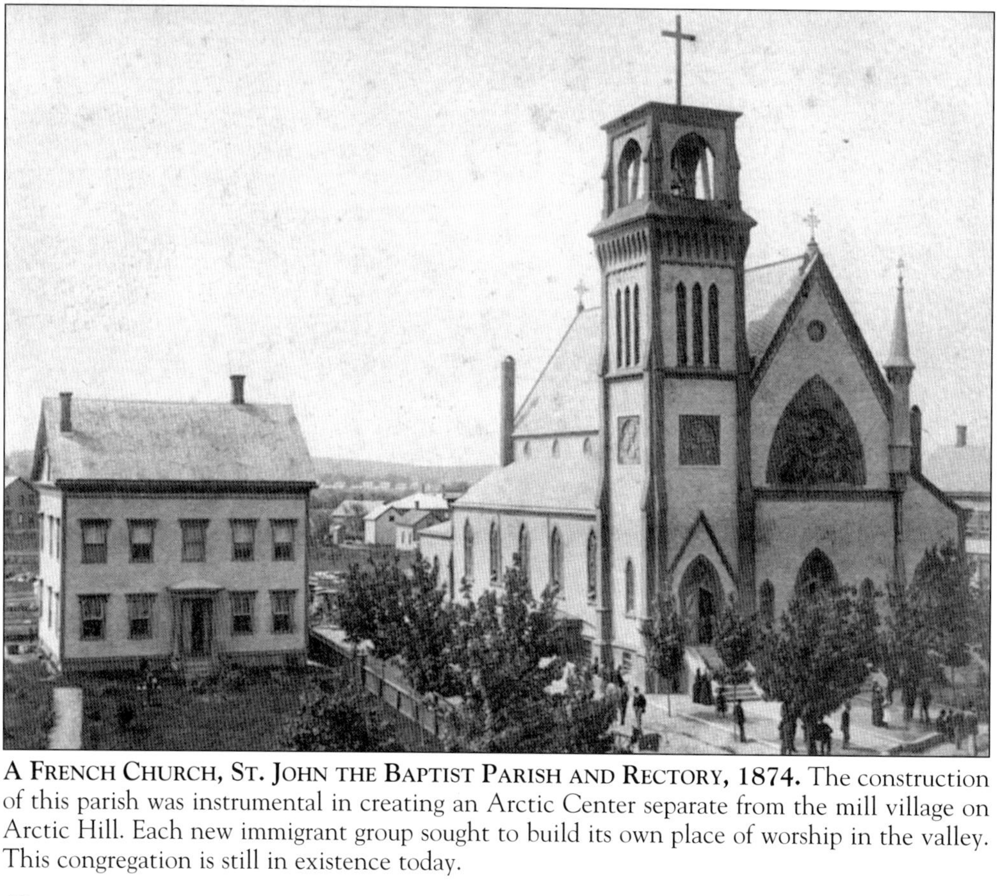

A French Church, St. John the Baptist Parish and Rectory, 1874. The construction of this parish was instrumental in creating an Arctic Center separate from the mill village on Arctic Hill. Each new immigrant group sought to build its own place of worship in the valley. This congregation is still in existence today.

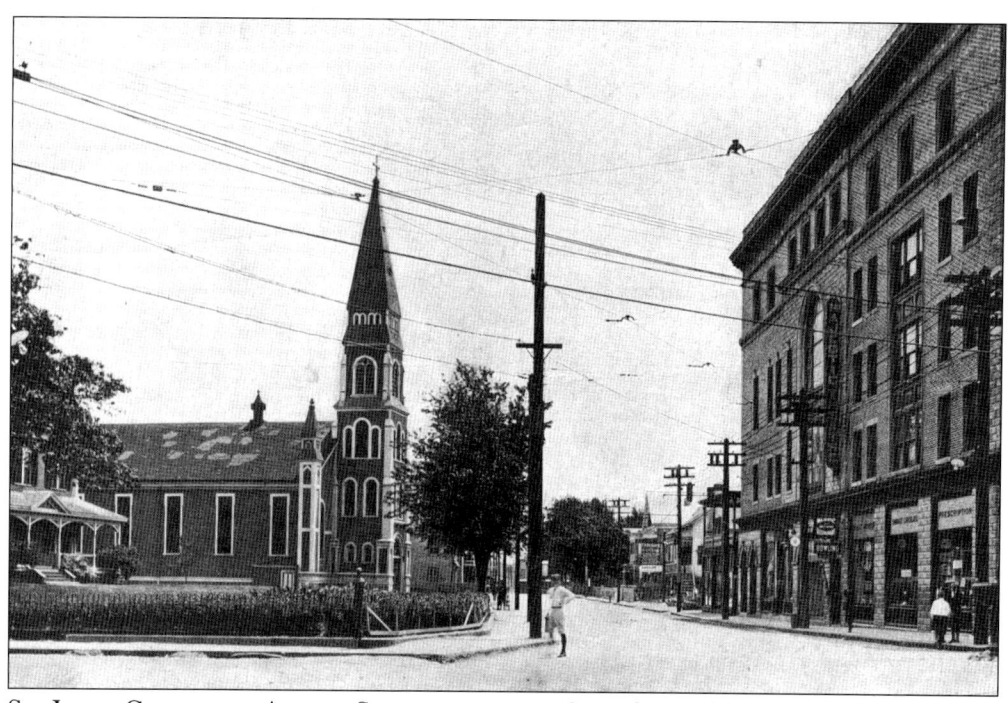

ST. JAMES CHURCH IN ARCTIC SQUARE, C. 1913. One of several Irish Catholic parishes set up in the valley beginning in the 1840s.

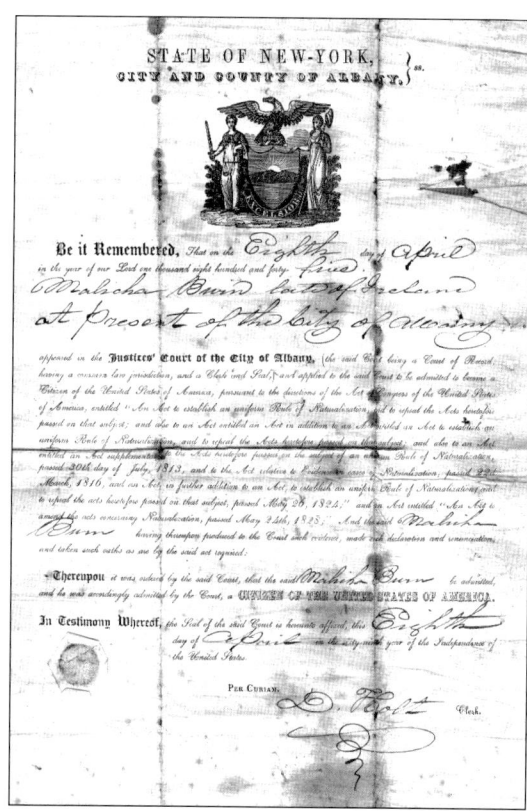

NATURALIZATION PAPERS FOR MALACHY BURNS. Burns followed a typical route for Irish immigrants to the valley—via Canada and upstate New York in the 1840s. Famine in Ireland and job opportunities in the Pawtuxet Valley led to a heavy Irish presence in places like Crompton, Clyde, and Arctic.

ST. MARY'S CATHOLIC CHURCH IN CROMPTON. Another Irish parish, it is the oldest Catholic church building in use in Rhode Island. It was built in 1844–1845.

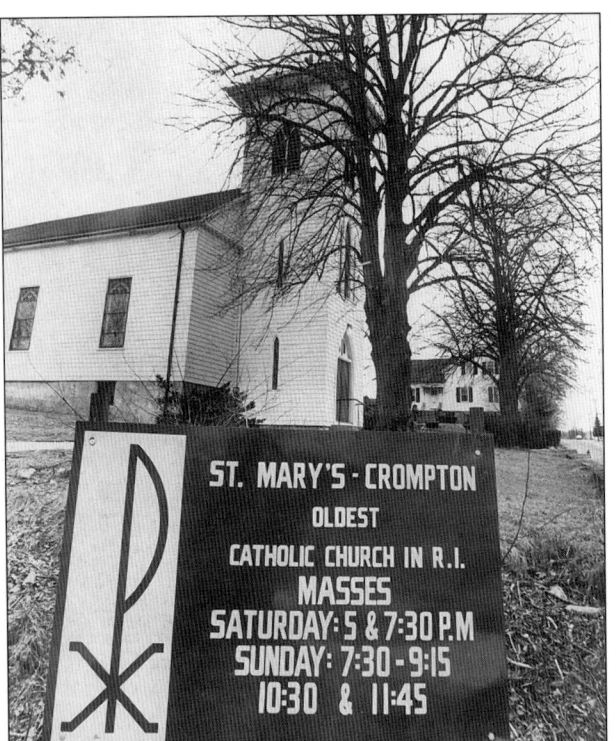

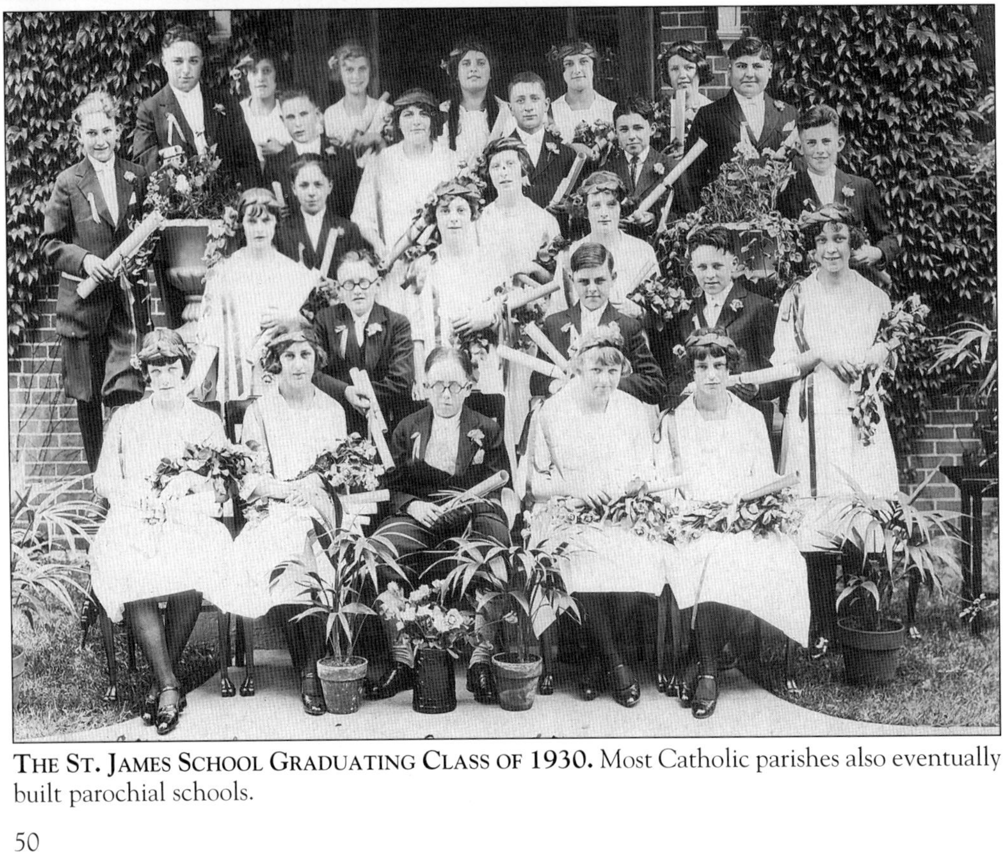

THE ST. JAMES SCHOOL GRADUATING CLASS OF 1930. Most Catholic parishes also eventually built parochial schools.

VOLUNTEER NATICK FIREMAN WILLIAM HENRY BURNS, C. 1880.

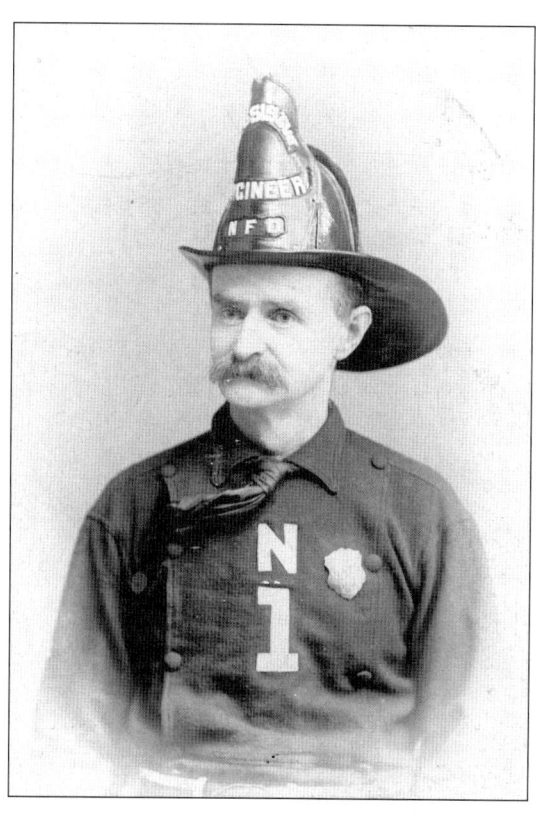

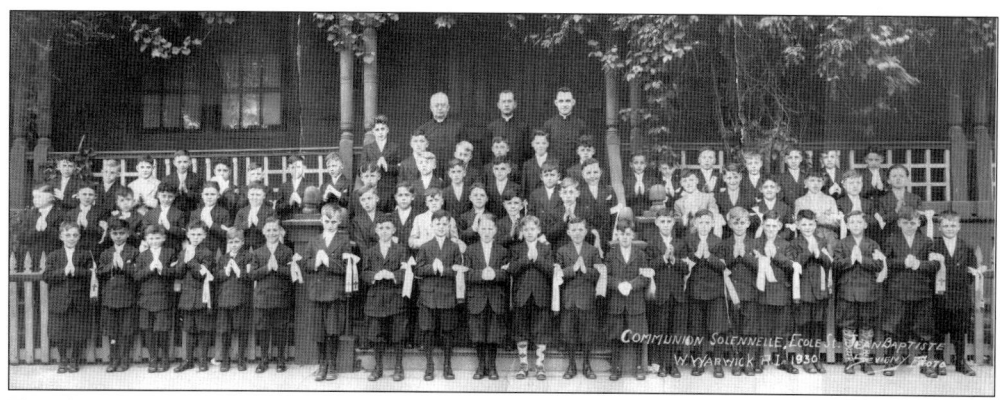

THE ST. JOHN THE BAPTIST SCHOOL GRADUATING CLASS OF 1930.

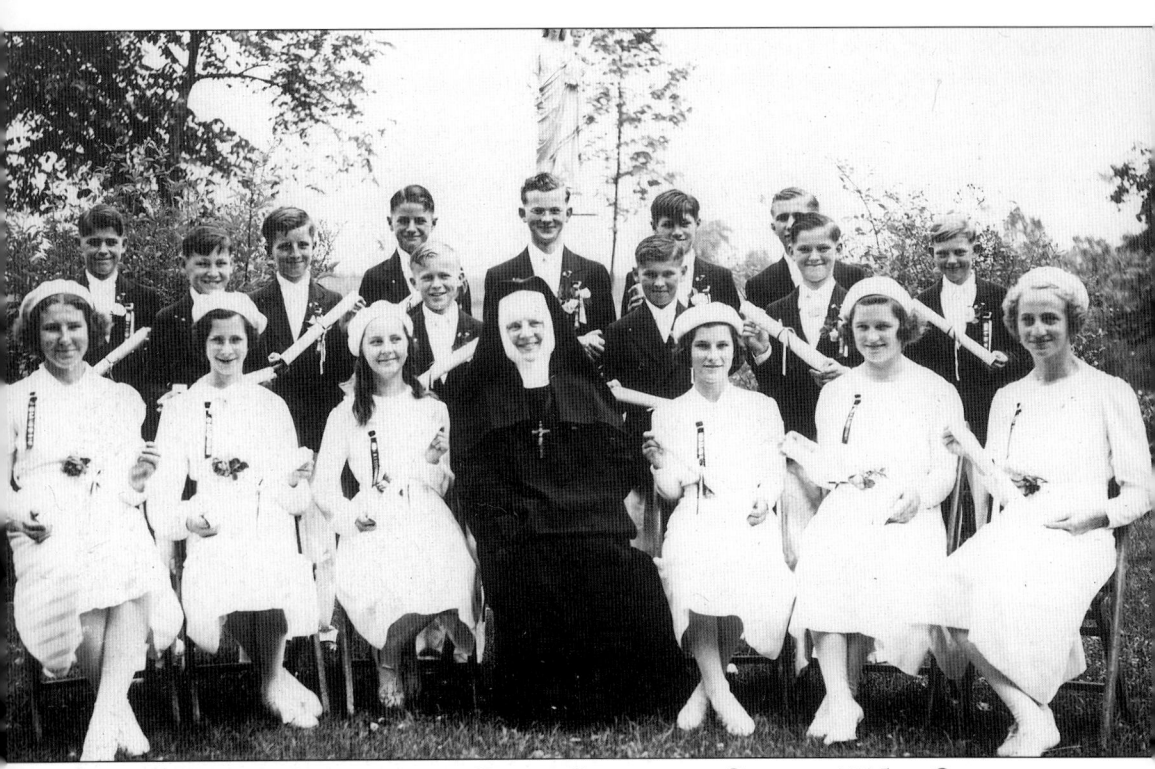
The Our Lady of Czenstochowa School Graduating Class of 1935 in Quidnick.

A PERRY FAMILY PORTRAIT, 1948. The Perrys are one of many families of Portuguese origin in the valley.

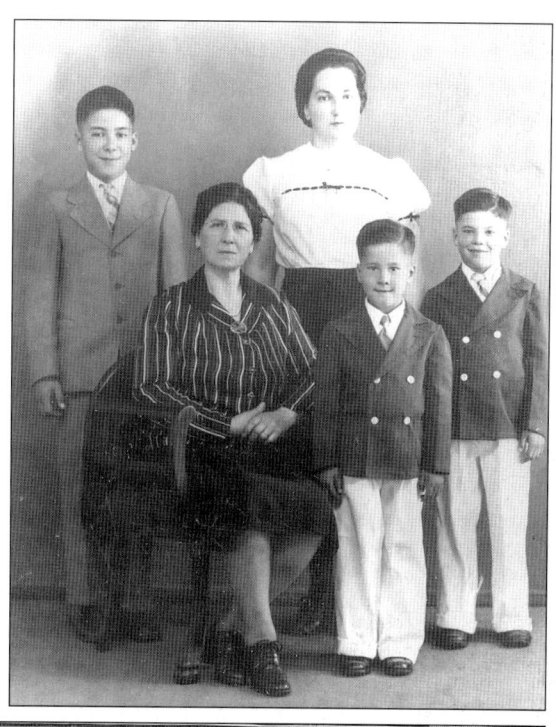

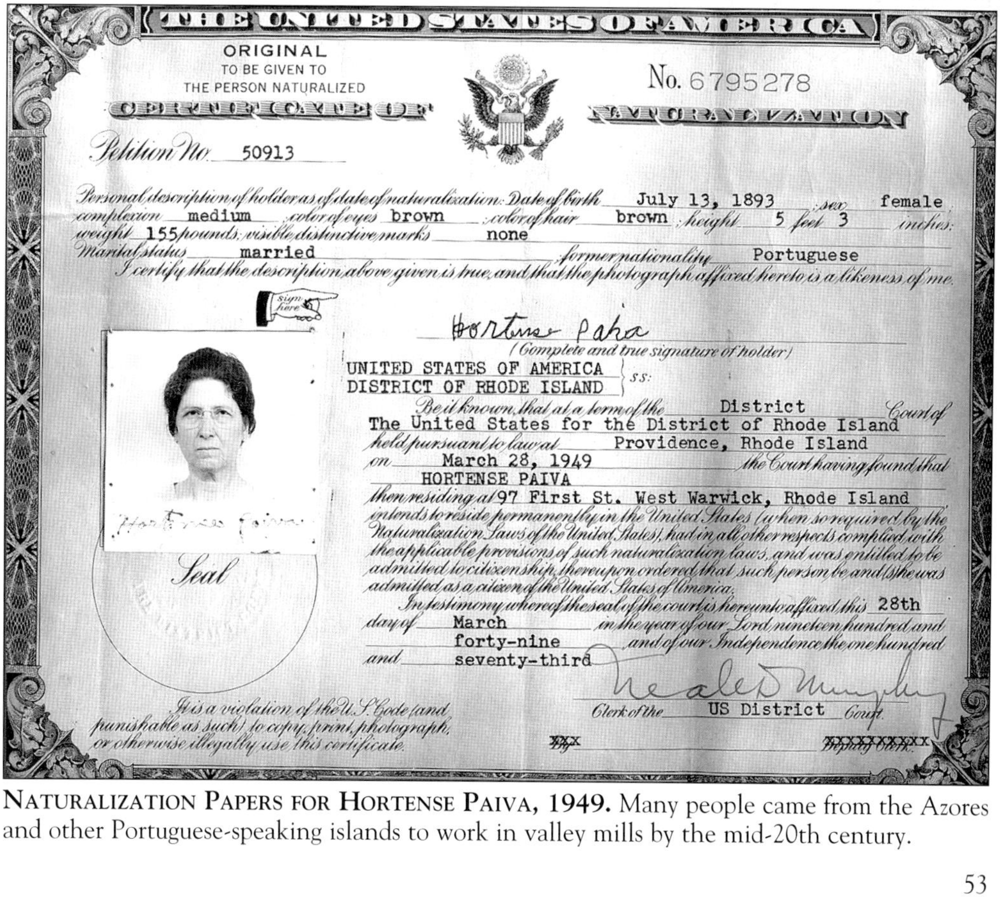

NATURALIZATION PAPERS FOR HORTENSE PAIVA, 1949. Many people came from the Azores and other Portuguese-speaking islands to work in valley mills by the mid-20th century.

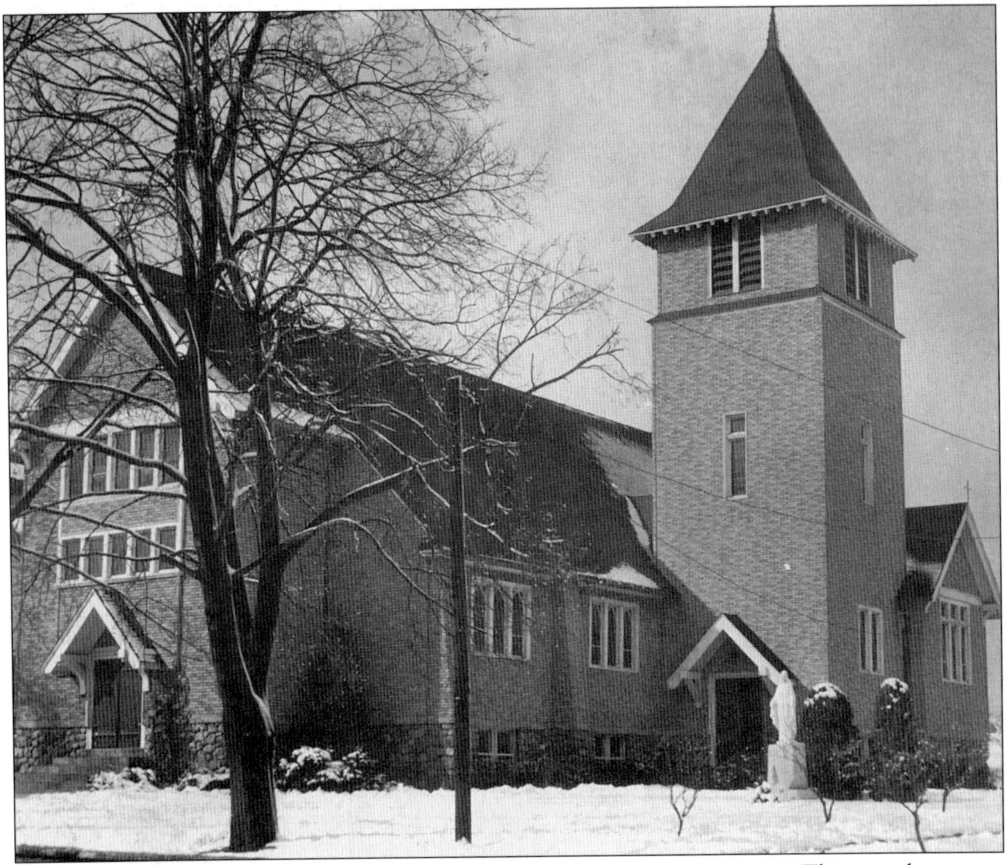

A Polish Church, Our Lady of Czenstochowa in Quidnick, 1957. This was the center of Polish immigrant activity in the valley. Polish immigrants began arriving in the late 19th century and settled in villages like Quidnick, Crompton, and Arctic Hill.

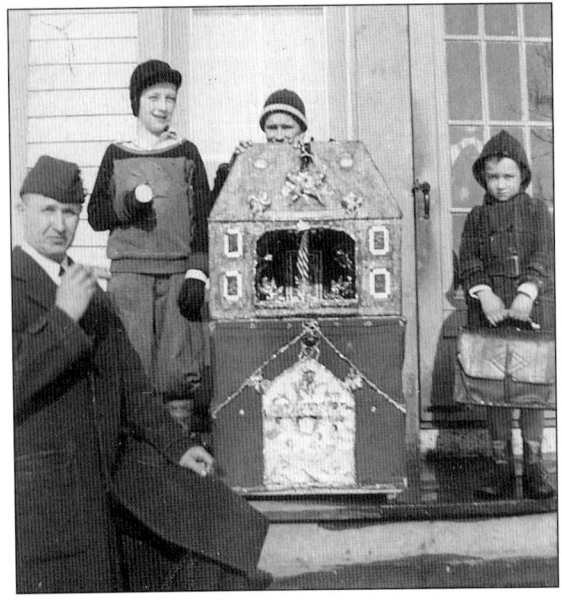

Christmas in the Arctic Hill Mill Village, 1940. Stanislaus Kos and family are shown at a traditional Polish nativity puppet show. It would be taken door to door in the village, similar to the Anglo-American tradition of caroling.

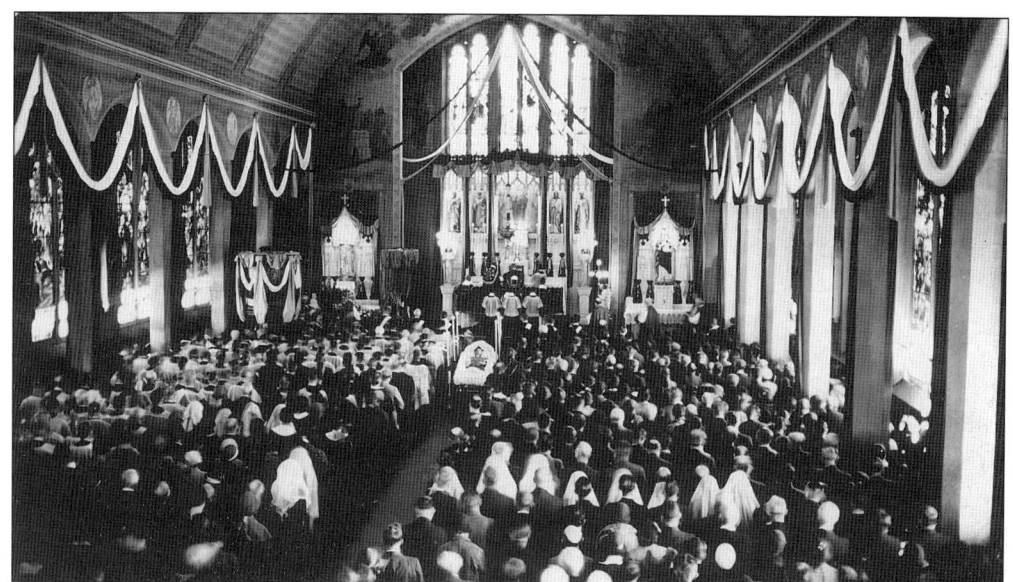

A POLISH FUNERAL, 1955.

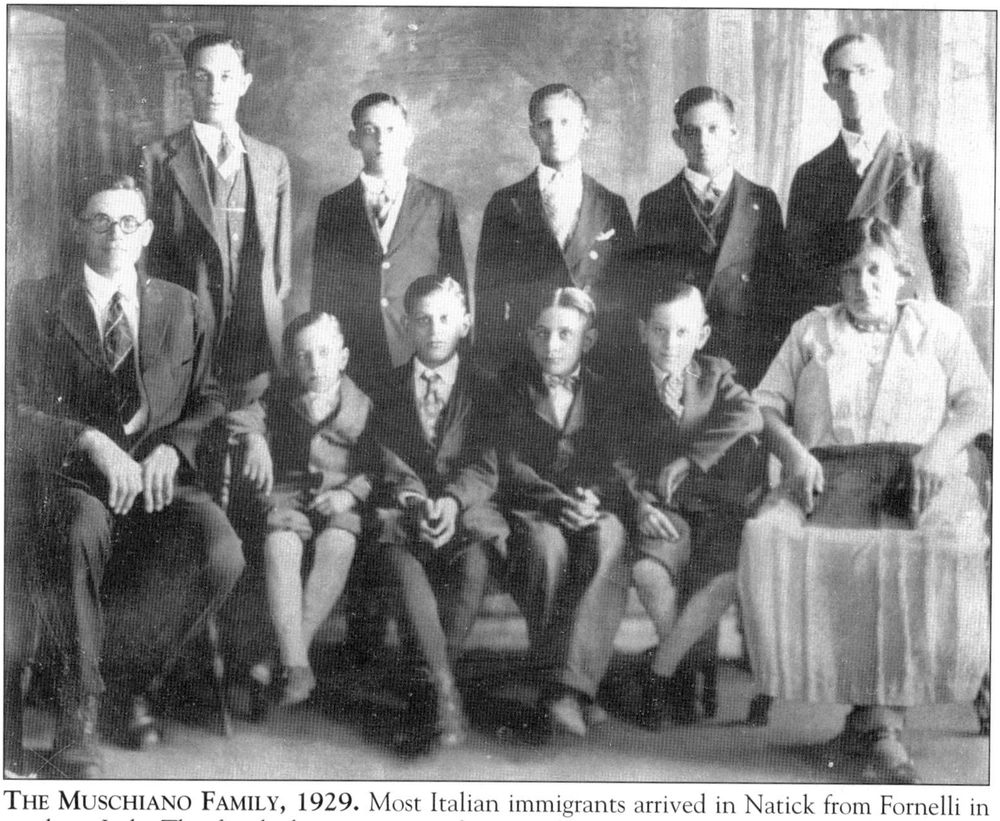

THE MUSCHIANO FAMILY, 1929. Most Italian immigrants arrived in Natick from Fornelli in southern Italy. This family, however, came from Naples. The Sacred Heart Catholic parish was set up to serve this growing community in 1929. The Muschiano family members shown here are, from left to right, as follows: (front row) Corraidno, Olindo, Joseph, Nicola, Vincent, and Antonia; (back row) Carmine, Ugo, Al, Victor, and Tony.

ST. JOSEPH'S CHURCH IN NATICK. Built in 1873, this was the Catholic church that originally served a French- and English-speaking congregation.

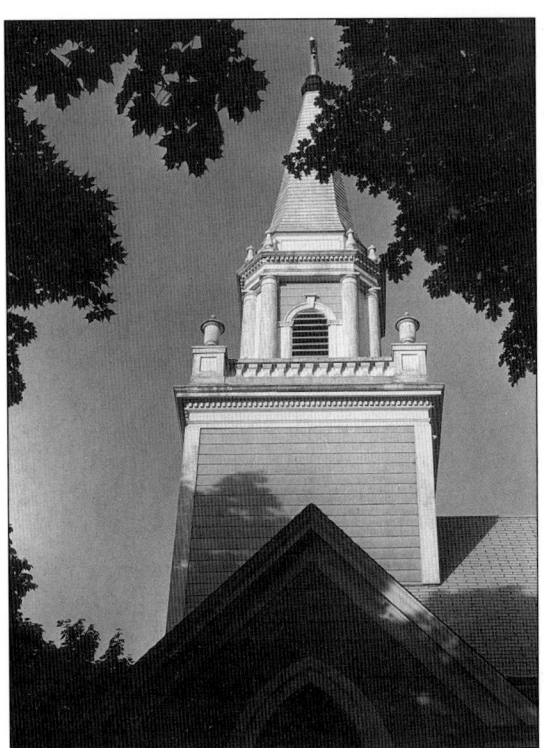

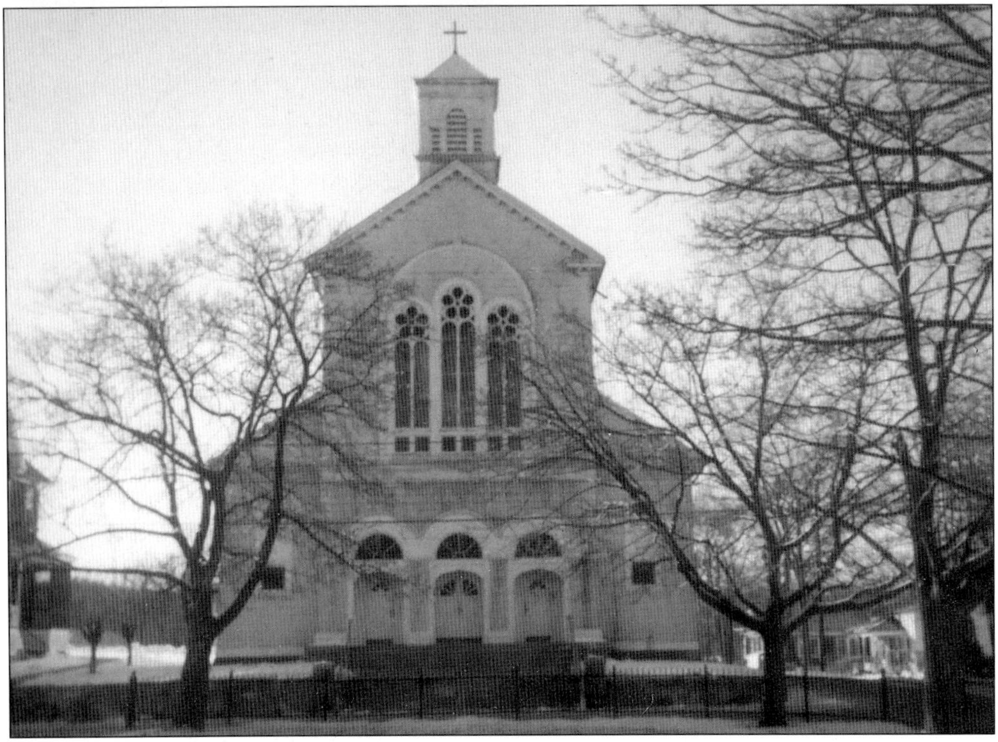

NOTRE DAME DU BON CONSIEL IN PHENIX. Built in 1903, it served the French Catholics of that area.

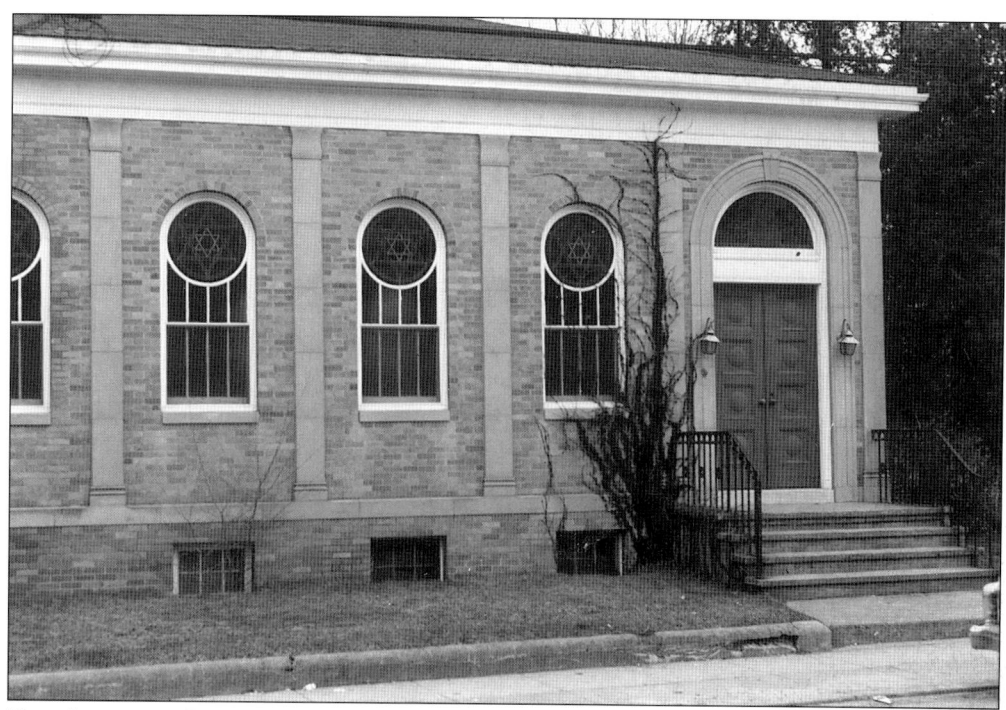

THE AHAVATH SHALOM SYNAGOGUE. The valley's small Jewish community continued to use this building, built in 1919, until the 1970s.

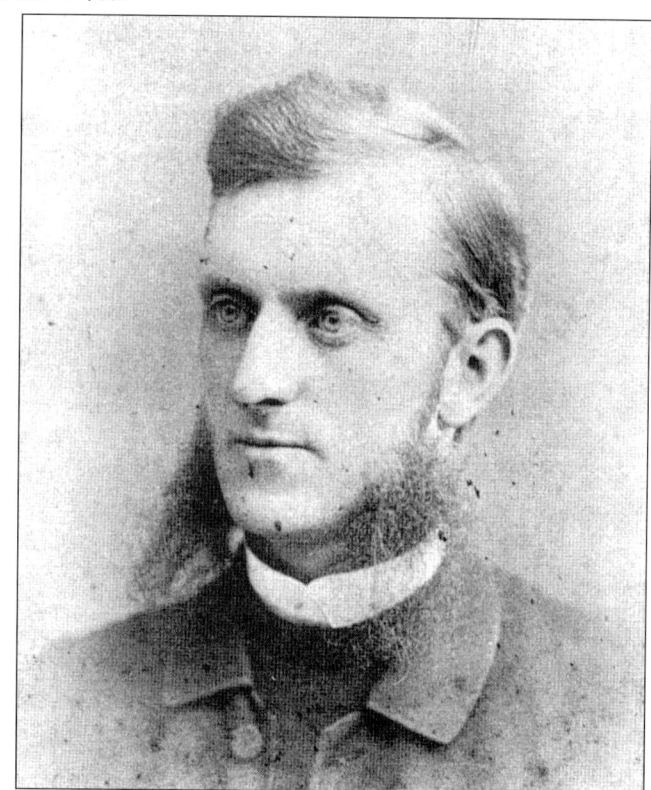

REV. W.A. COCROFT OF THE FIRST RECTOR ST. ANDREWS EPISCOPAL CHURCH IN HARRIS, 1880. There were many English immigrants in the 19th century, and they gravitated to the Episcopal and Methodist churches throughout the valley.

ST. ANDREWS CHURCH, C. 1900.

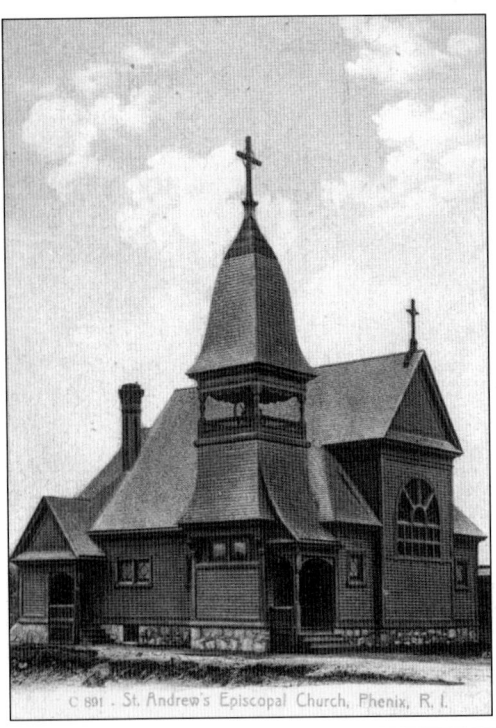

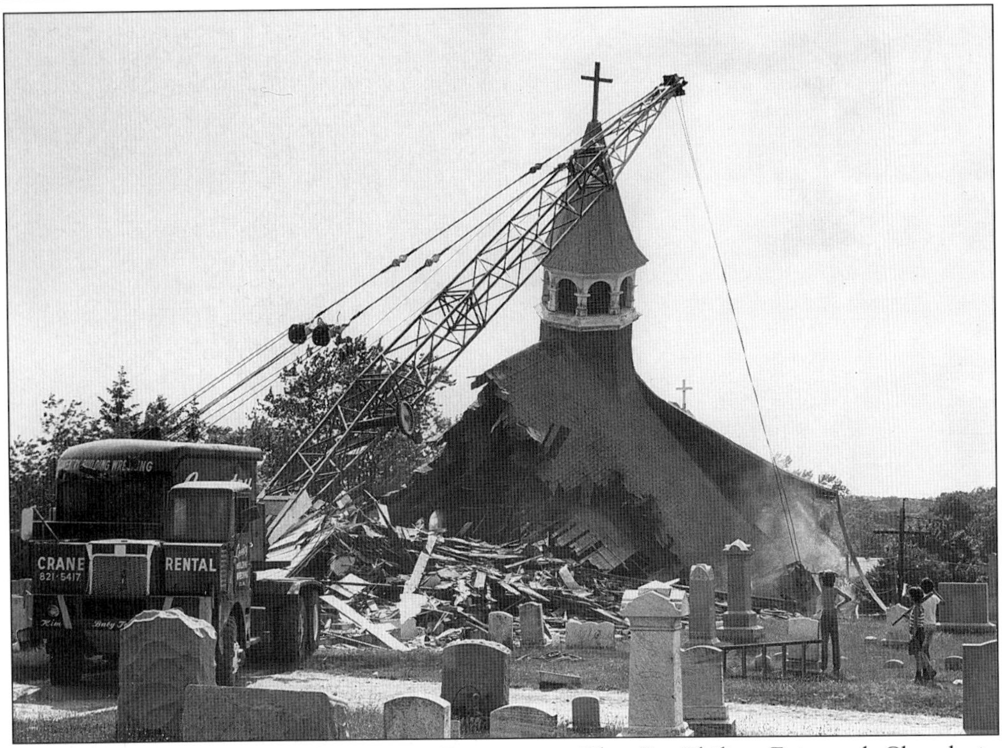

ST. PHILIPS EPISCOPAL CHURCH IN CROMPTON. The St. Philips Episcopal Church in Crompton was demolished in 1972. St. Andrews and St. Philips were merged in the 1970s, and a new church was built on Fairview Avenue in Phenix.

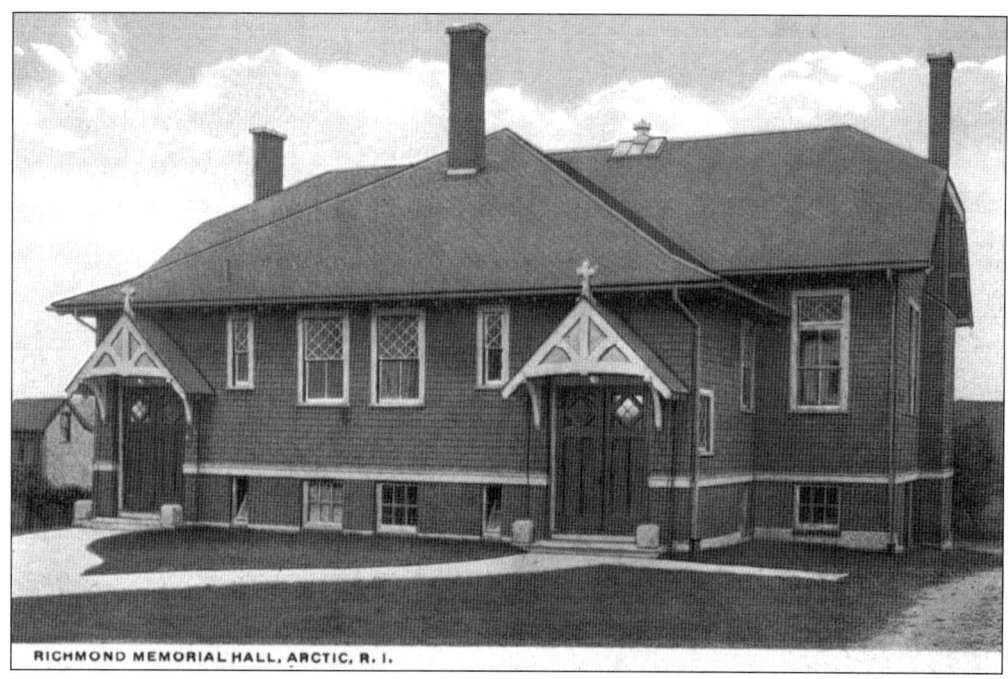

RICHMOND HALL IN CROMPTON, C. 1910.

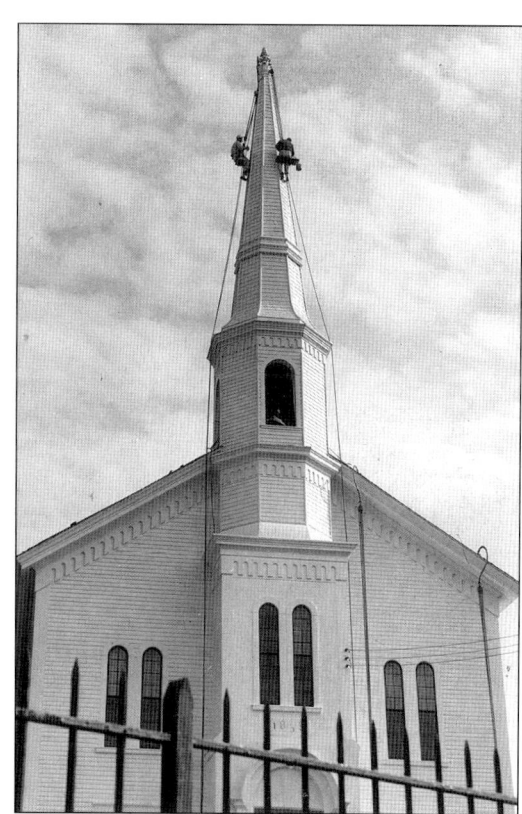

THE PHENIX METHODIST CHURCH, 1959. The Phenix Methodist Church was built in 1859 and was supported by many of the mill owners of the North Branch of the Pawtuxet River.

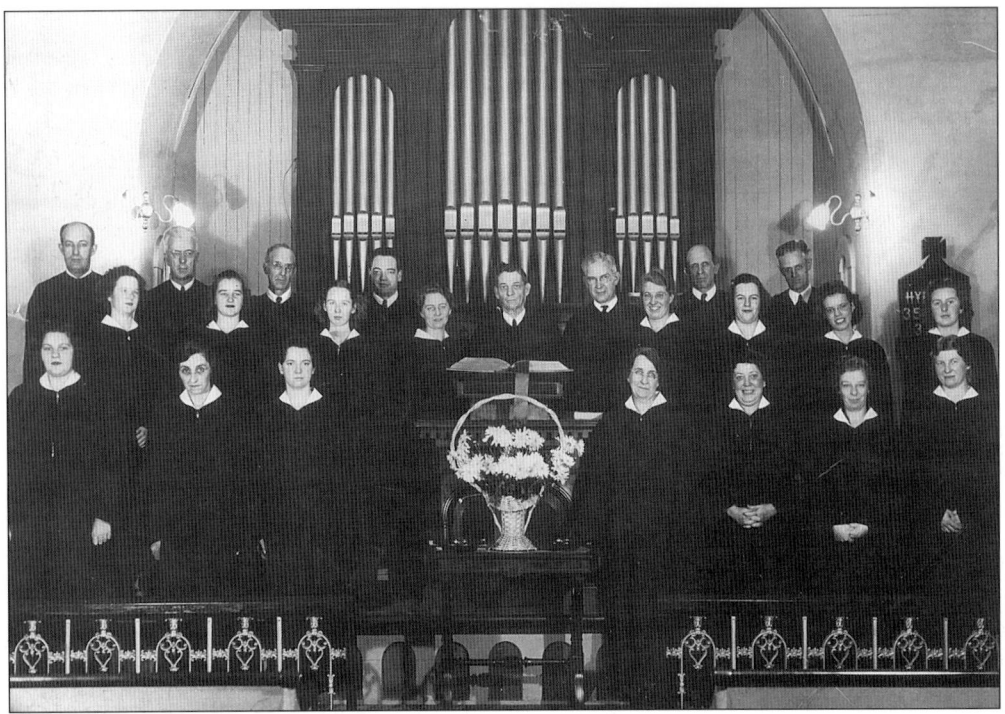

THE CHOIR AT THE PHENIX METHODIST CHURCH, 1940.

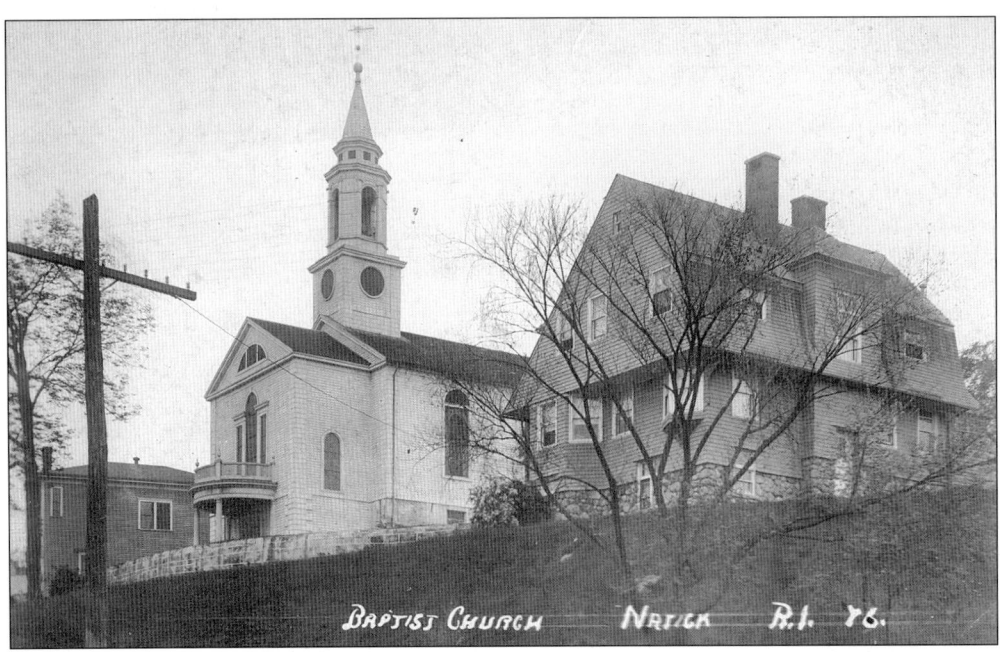

THE NATICK BAPTIST CHURCH AND PARSONAGE, C. 1900. The Natick Baptist Church was built in 1839 and expanded in 1891. This church was supported by mill owner William Sprague and was part of the concept of the company village. Mill owners often set up congregations in the villages to provide a place of worship for employees.

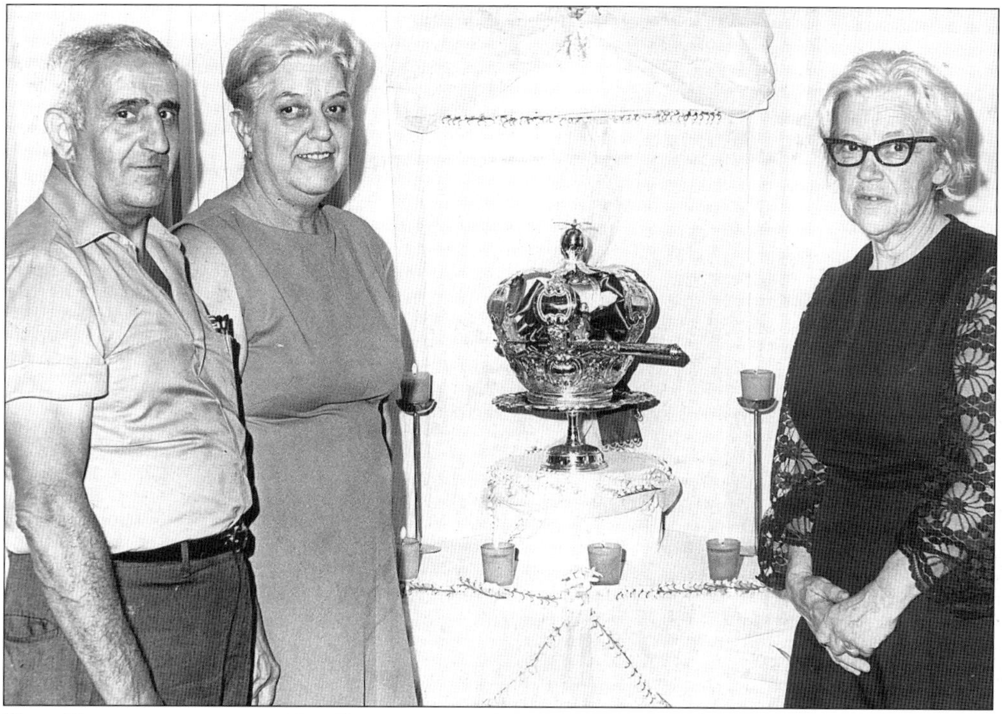

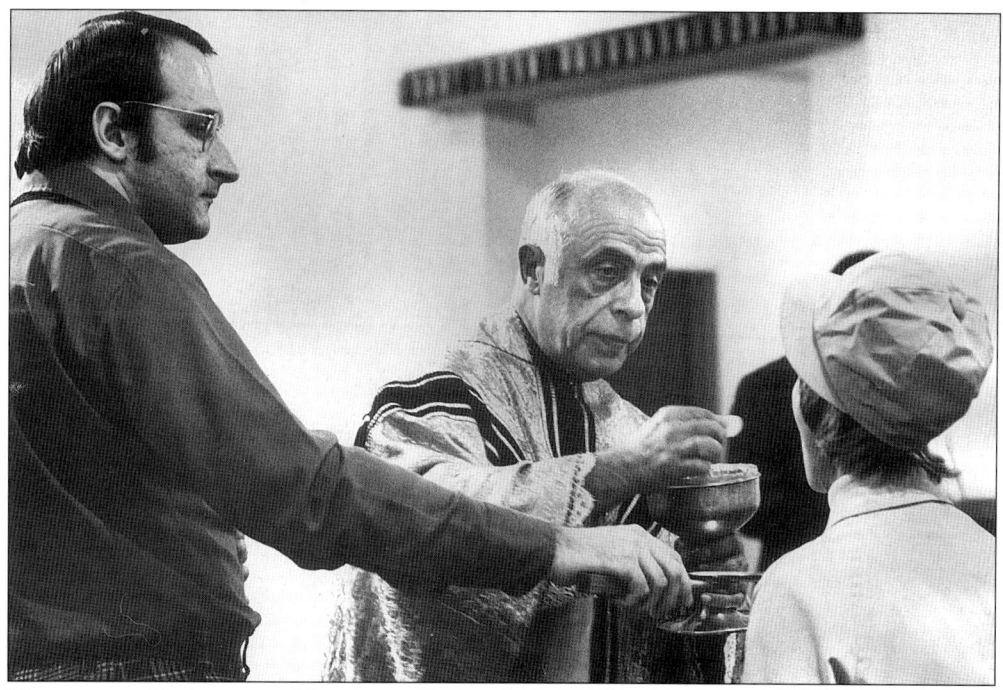

THE CROWN AT THE 1971 PORTUGUESE FESTIVAL. Pictured are Mr. and Mrs. Albert Mariorenzi and Bessie Fleury.

MONSIGNOR DEANGELIS. Monsignor DeAngelis was a longtime pastor of the Sacred Heart Church in Natick. In the 1980s, he sponsored major public-housing projects in Natick that bear his name.

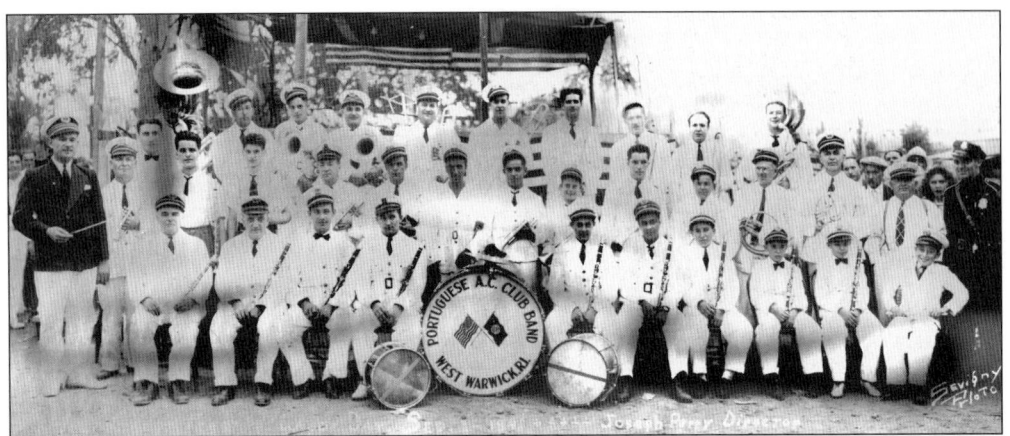

THE PORTUGUESE INDEPENDENT BAND AT THE PORTUGUESE HOLY GHOST FESTIVAL BAND, LABOR DAY 1941. Leader Joseph Perry, a native of Madeira, was a trained musician and composer. Many of his marches, including the one shown below, are still performed every year during the Holy Ghost Festival. Perry died shortly after this photograph was taken at age 38.

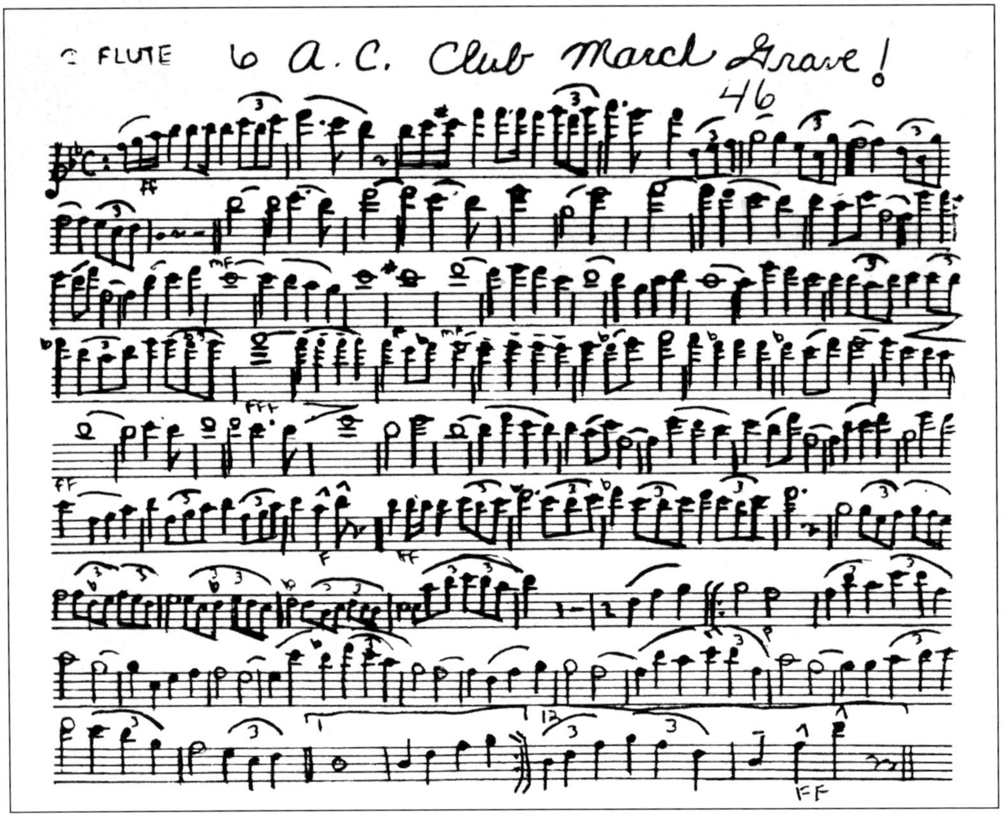

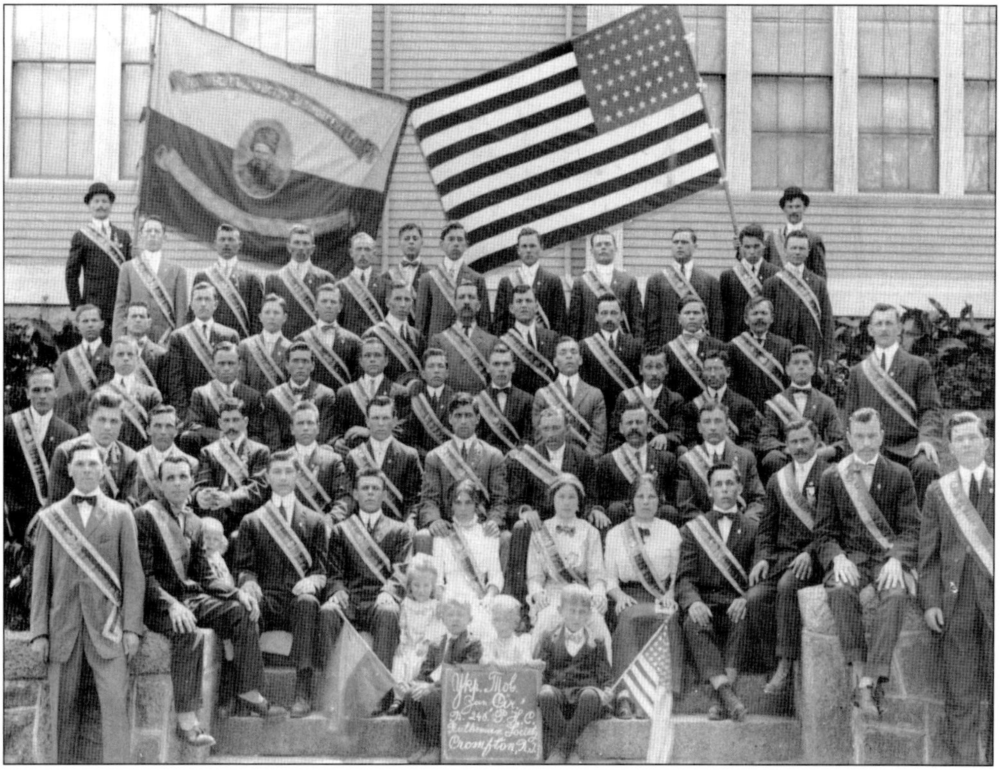

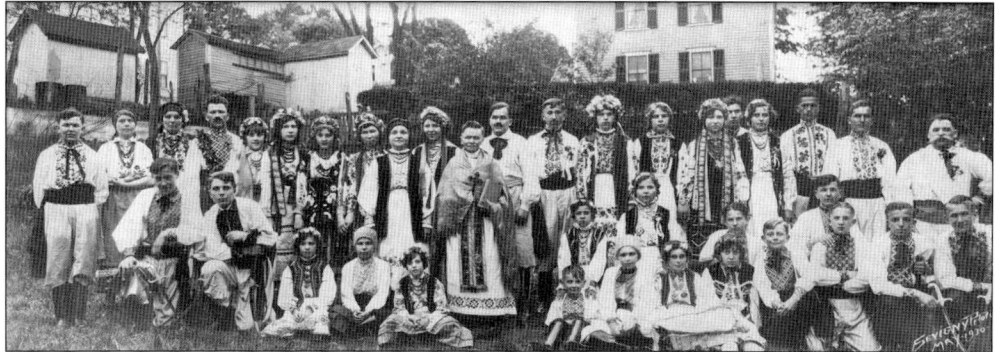

THE UKRAINIAN NATIONAL SOCIETY MEETING AT COWESETT ELEMENTARY SCHOOL, c. 1822. Many Ukrainians moved into the Crompton area to work in the velvet mills c. 1900. Like many other immigrant groups, Ukrainians formed societies to maintain old-world culture while easing the transition to American life. (Courtesy Bob and Anna Tucker.)

A MOCK UKRAINIAN WEDDING CEREMONY, ODD FELLOWS HALL, CROMPTON, MAY 1930. Ukrainian folk and other events were common in the area in the 1920s and 1930s. (Courtesy Bob and Anna Tucker.)

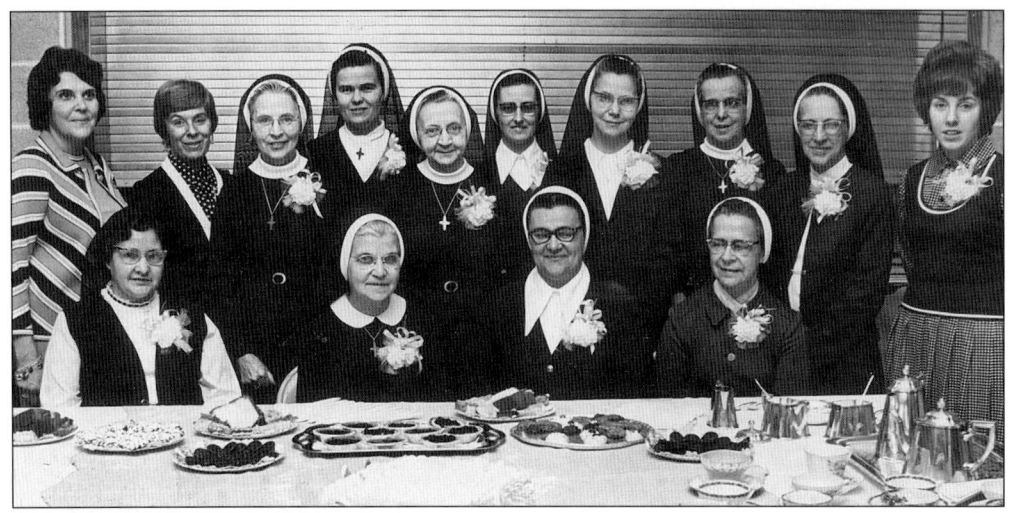

THE SISTERS OF THE PRESENTATION OF MARY, 1974. The Sisters of the Presentation of Mary are shown celebrating at the St. John the Baptist parish in Arctic. This order served the parish as teachers until the 1990s.

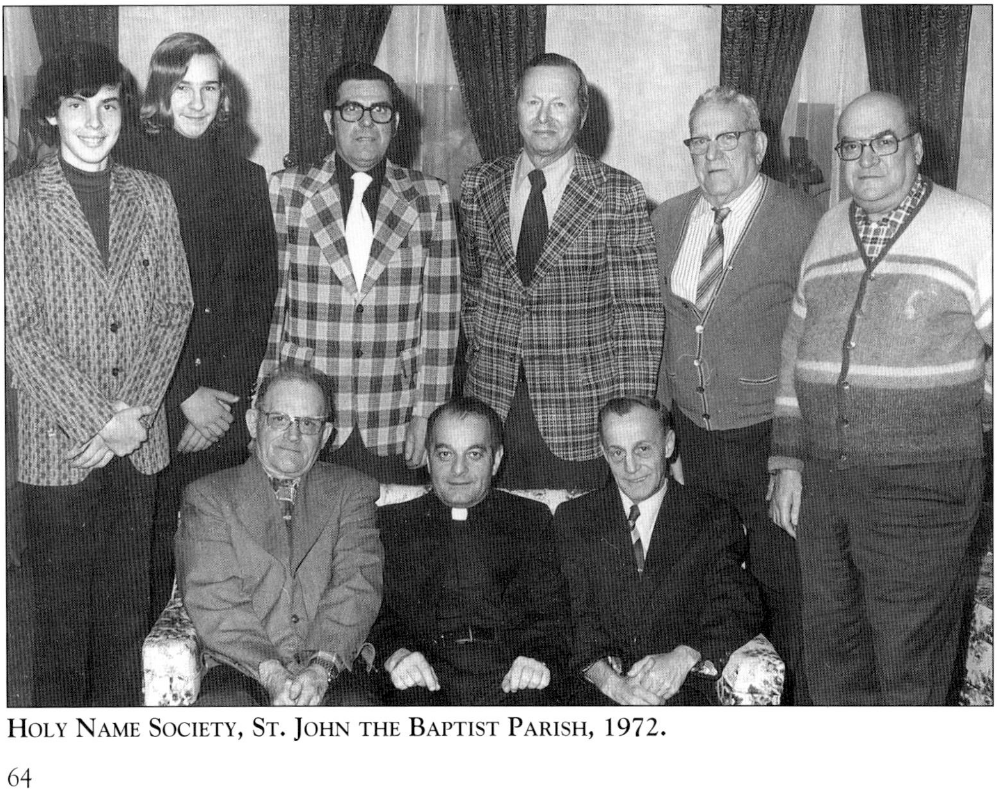

HOLY NAME SOCIETY, ST. JOHN THE BAPTIST PARISH, 1972.

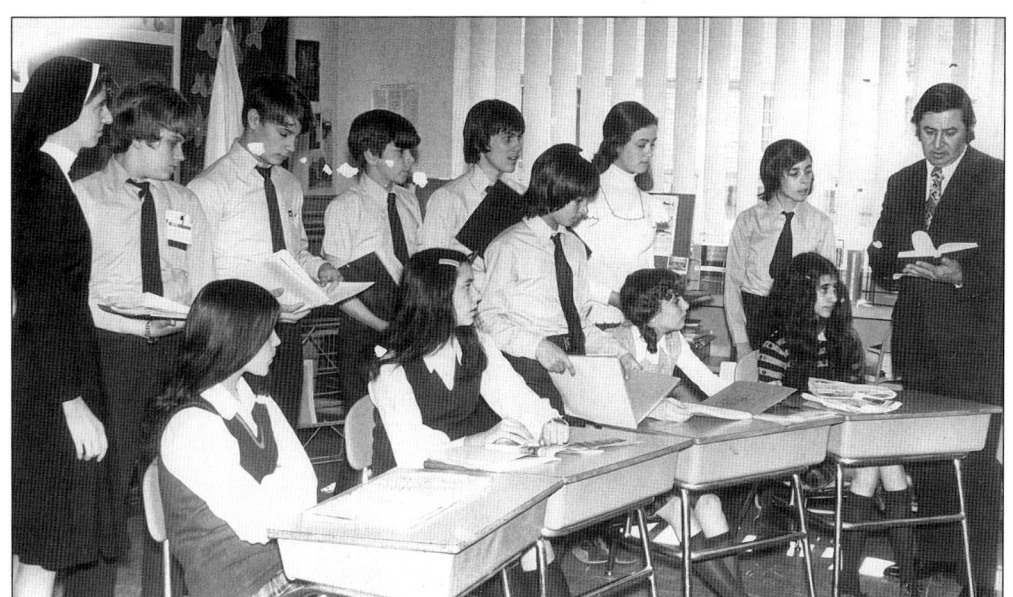
ST. JOSEPH'S SCHOOL CLASS OF 1973.

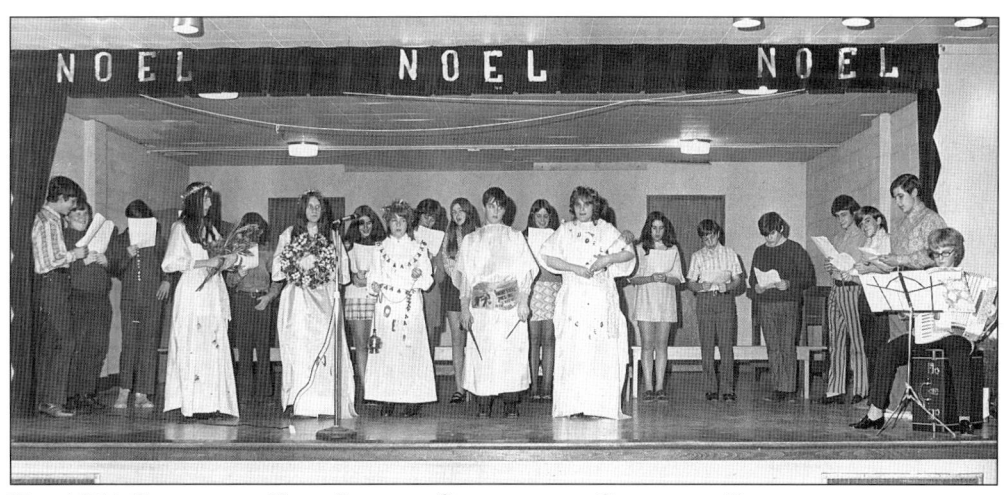
THE 1971 CHRIST THE KING SCHOOL, CENTREVILLE, CHRISTMAS PROGRAM.

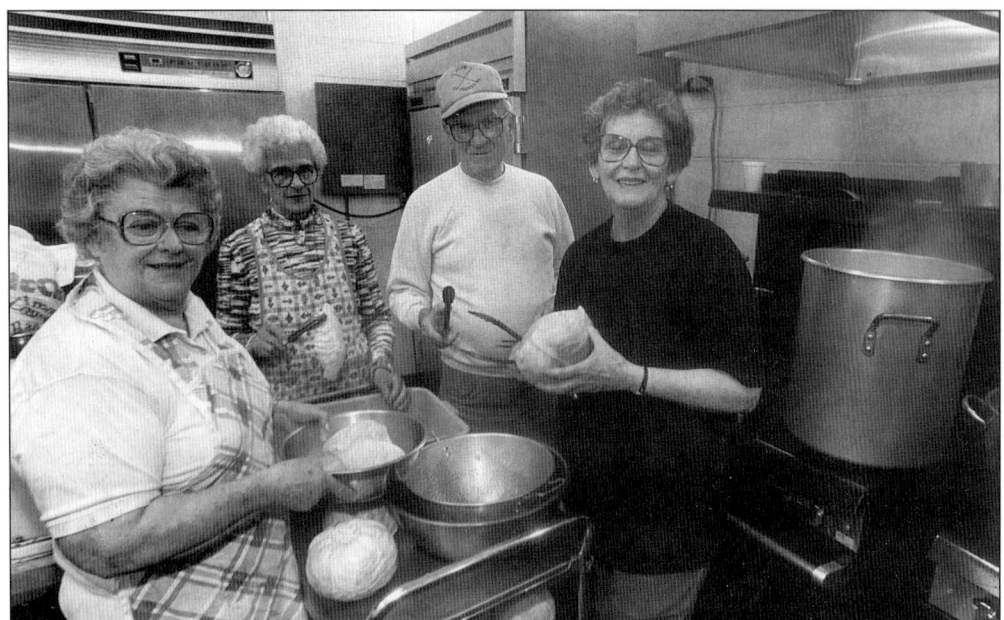

THE POLISH FESTIVAL AT OUR LADY OF CZENSTOCHOWA, 1990. Here we see members of the festival committee preparing the cabbage. This yearly summer festival of Polish food and music brings the whole Polish community together.

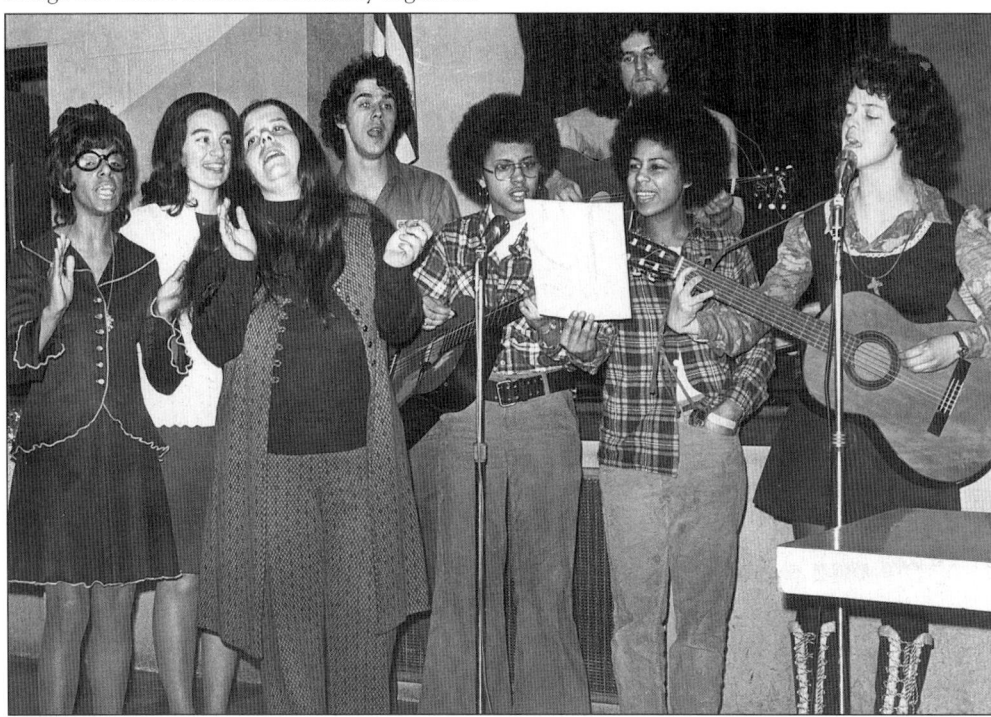

A FOLK MASS, CHRIST THE KING CATHOLIC CHURCH, CENTREVILLE, 1973. From left to right are the following: (front row) Barbara Wright, Sr. Carmelia LaCascio, Janice Luongo, Walter Burke, Charlene Andrade, Priscilla SanBento, and Sarah Burke; (back row) Nelson DeCouteau.

Four
BUSINESS

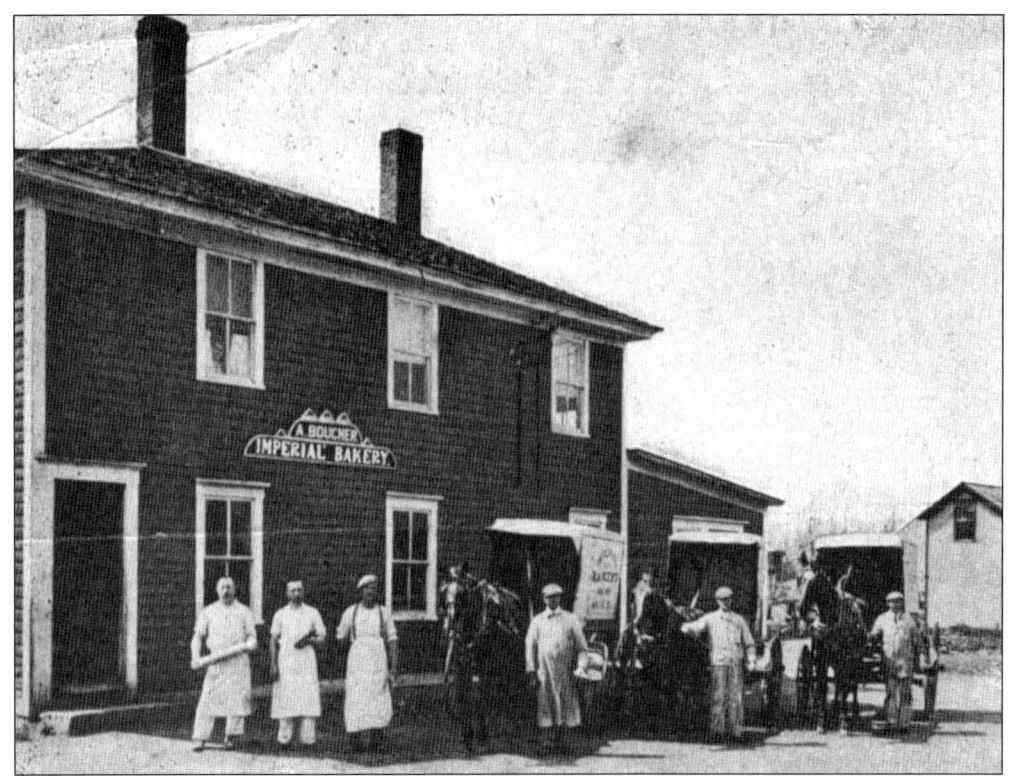

THE IMPERIAL BAKERY ON READ AVENUE, 1913.

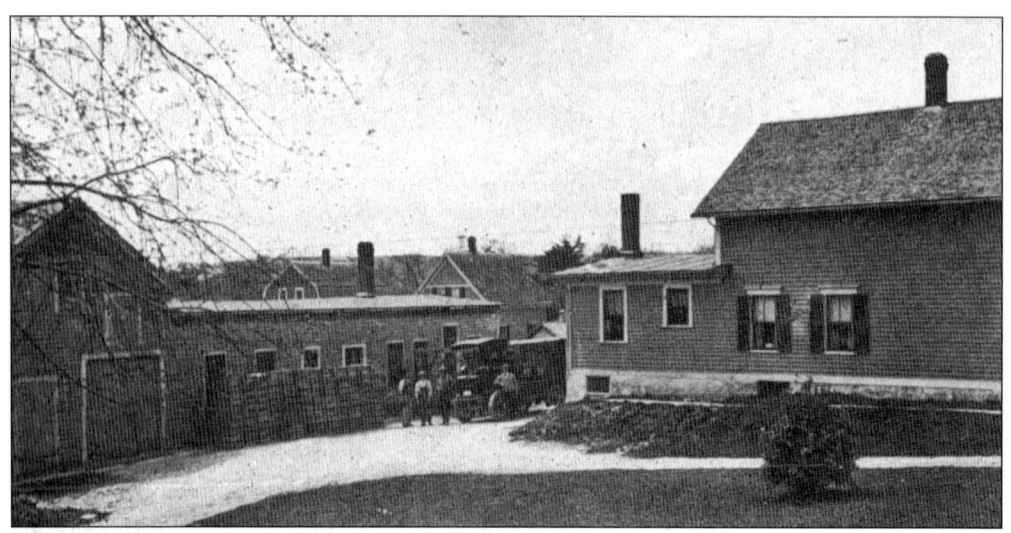

THE WARWICK BOTTLING WORKS ON POND STREET, ARCTIC, 1913.

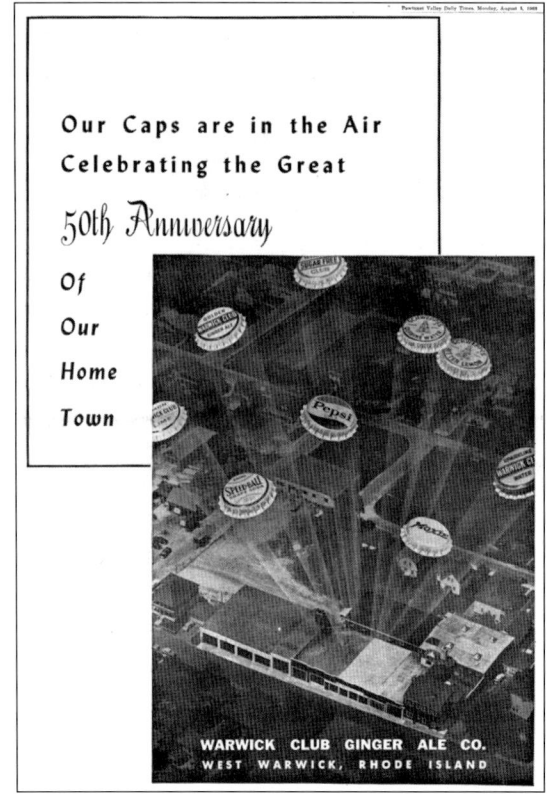

A WARWICK BOTTLING WORKS ADVERTISEMENT, 1963. Warwick Bottling Works produced Pepsi, Moxie, and other favorites until the 1970s.

THE ST. ONGE STORE, 1913. The St. Onge Store continued to provide quality men's and boys' clothing into the 1970s.

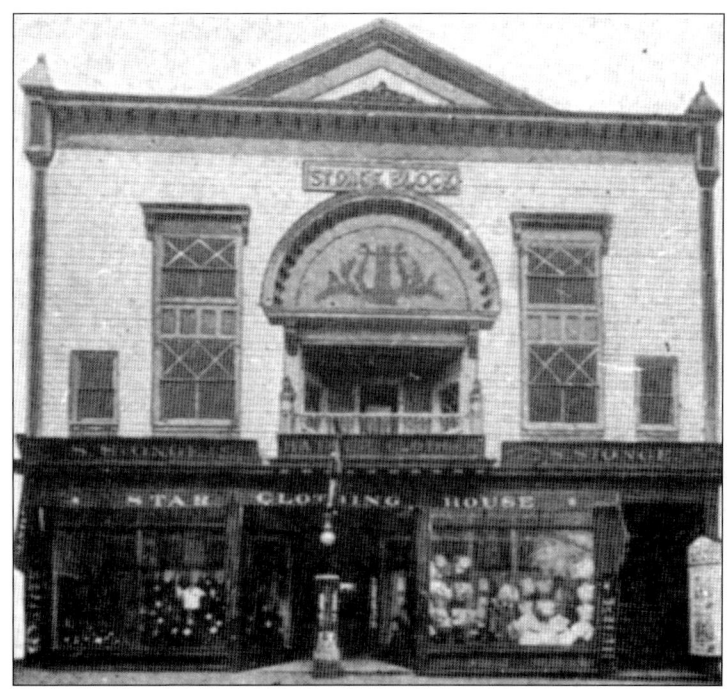

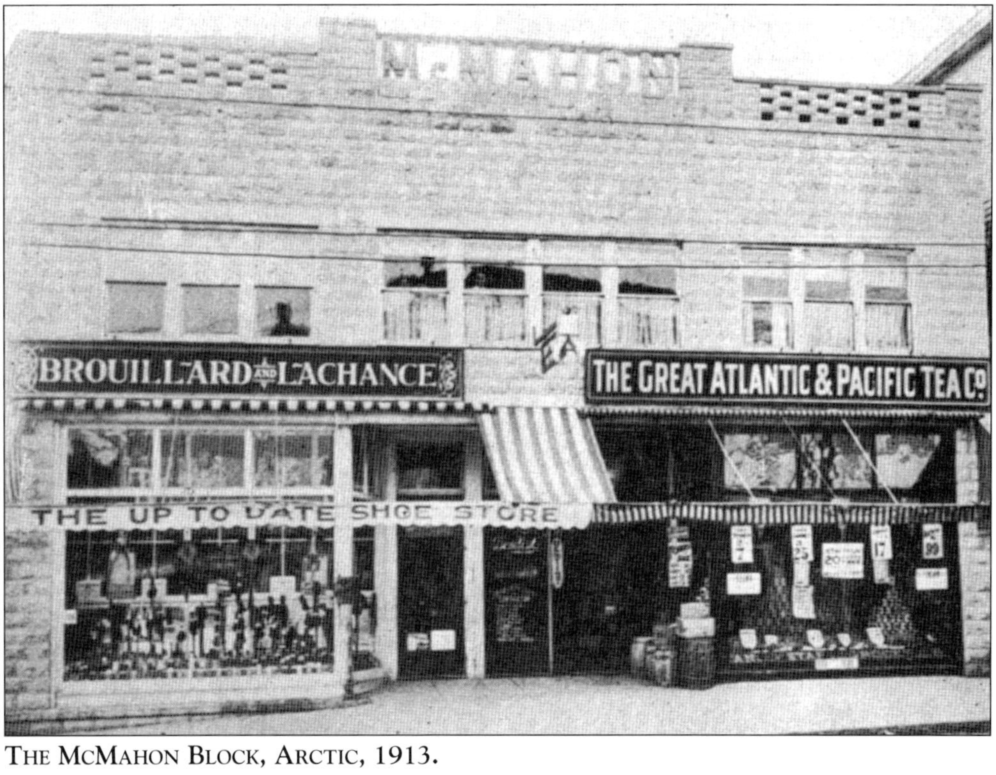

THE MCMAHON BLOCK, ARCTIC, 1913.

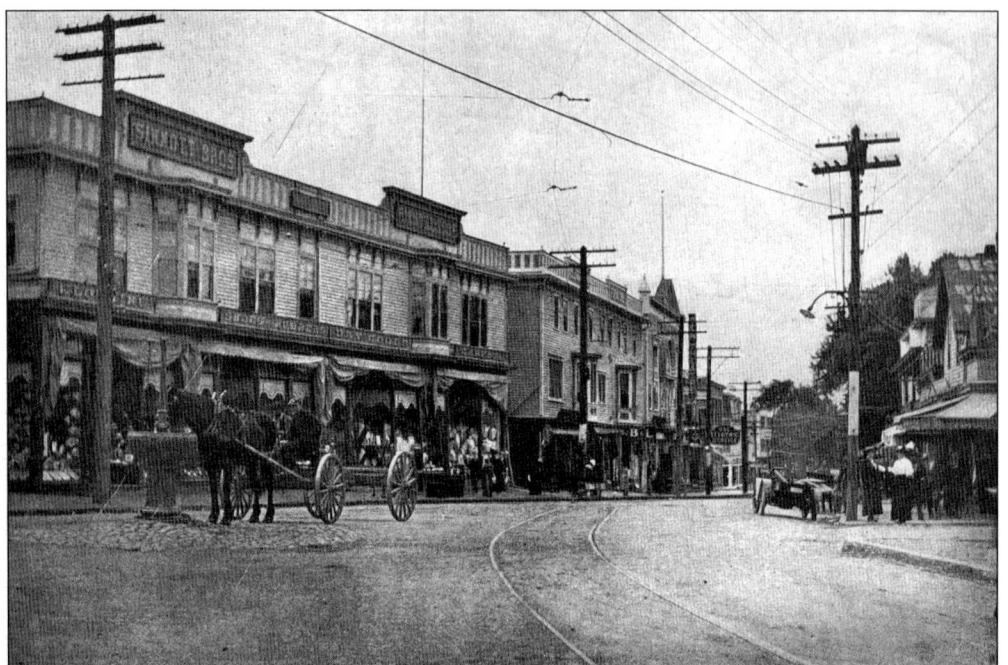

THE ARCTIC SQUARE, 1910. The Sinnott Brothers Department Store is on the left in this view looking up Main Street.

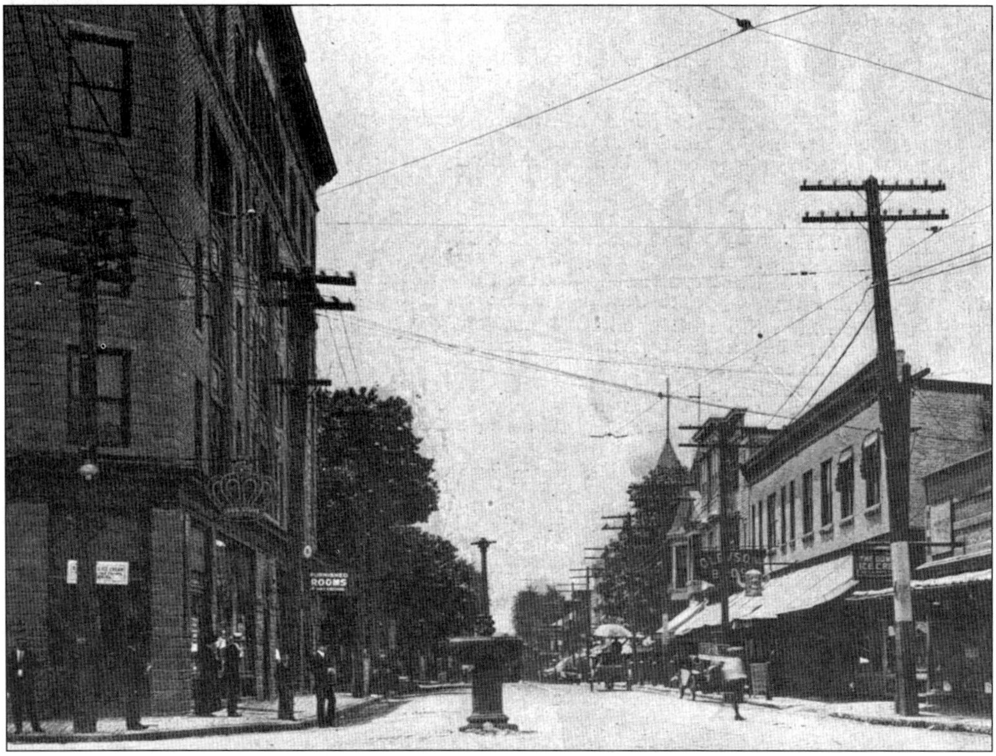

QUIDNICK, NOW WASHINGTON STREET, ARCTIC. The Majestic Building is visible on the left. This impressive structure housed shops, a theater, a hotel, offices, and a bowling alley.

THE CENTREVILLE NEWS DEPOT AND POST OFFICE, c. 1910. This building was the original home of the Centreville Bank. The Centreville Bank is one of a dwindling number of local banks in the region today. It continues to serve the region from its main branch in Arctic.

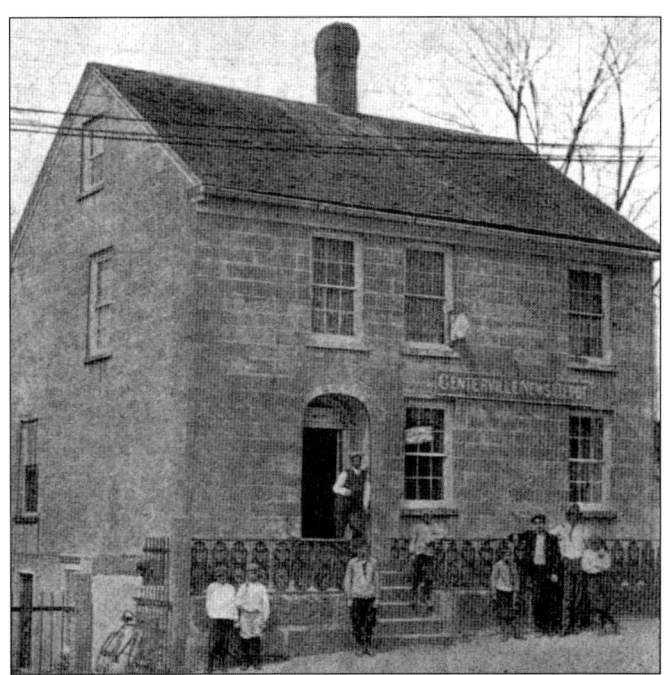

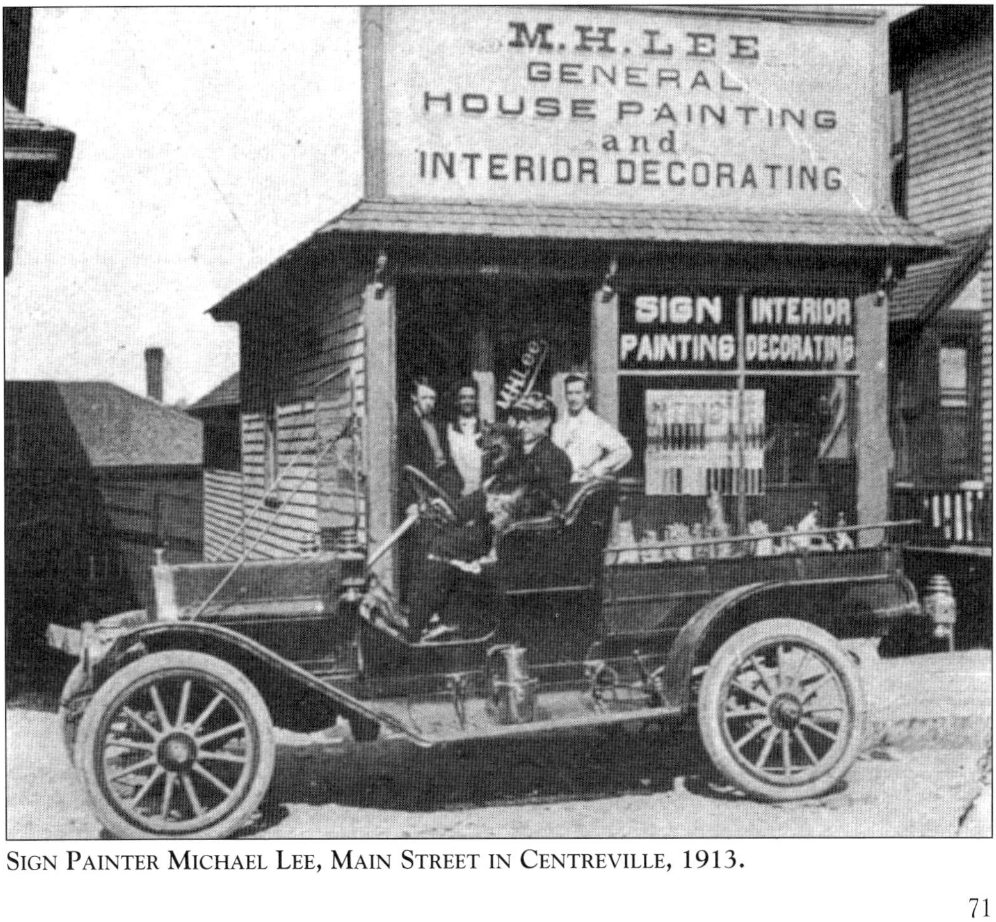

SIGN PAINTER MICHAEL LEE, MAIN STREET IN CENTREVILLE, 1913.

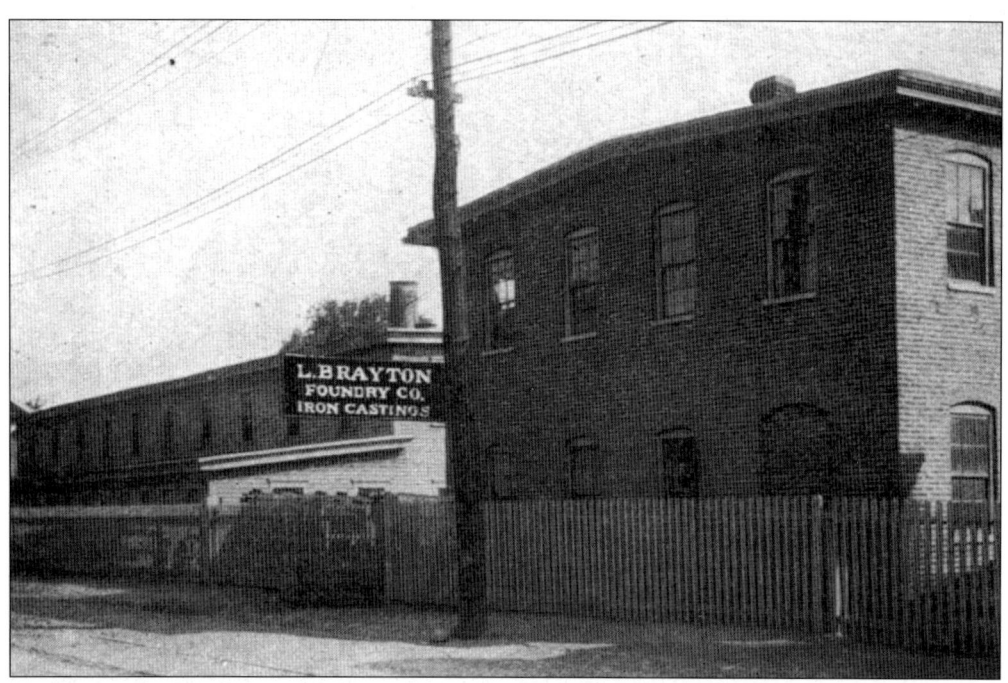

THE BRAYTON FOUNDRY, RIVERPOINT, 1913. The Brayton Foundry continued in operation until the 1970s.

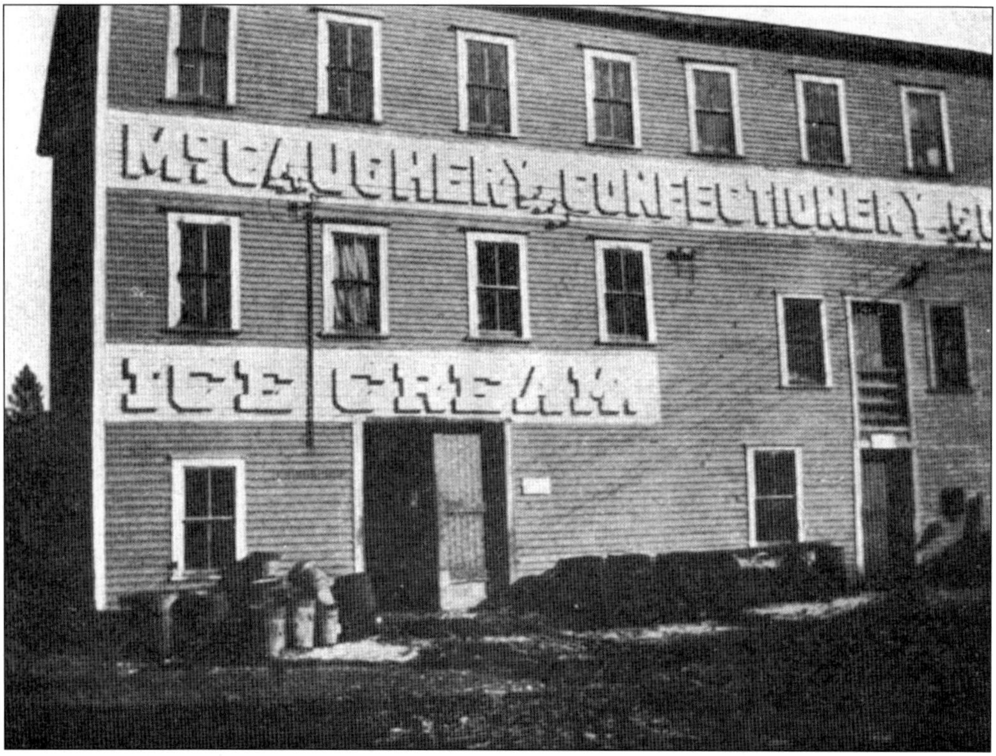

THE MCCAUGHERY CONFECTION AND ICE CREAM COMPANY, ALLEN STREET IN RIVERPOINT, 1913.

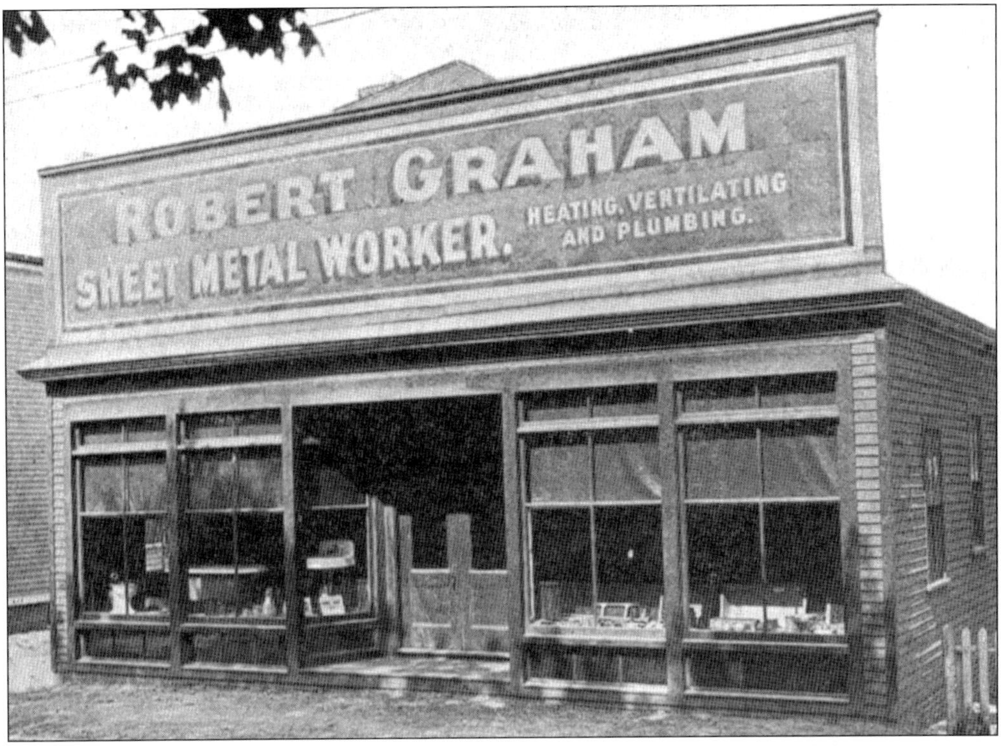

Robert Graham Sheet Metal and Plumbing on Main Street, West Warwick, 1913.

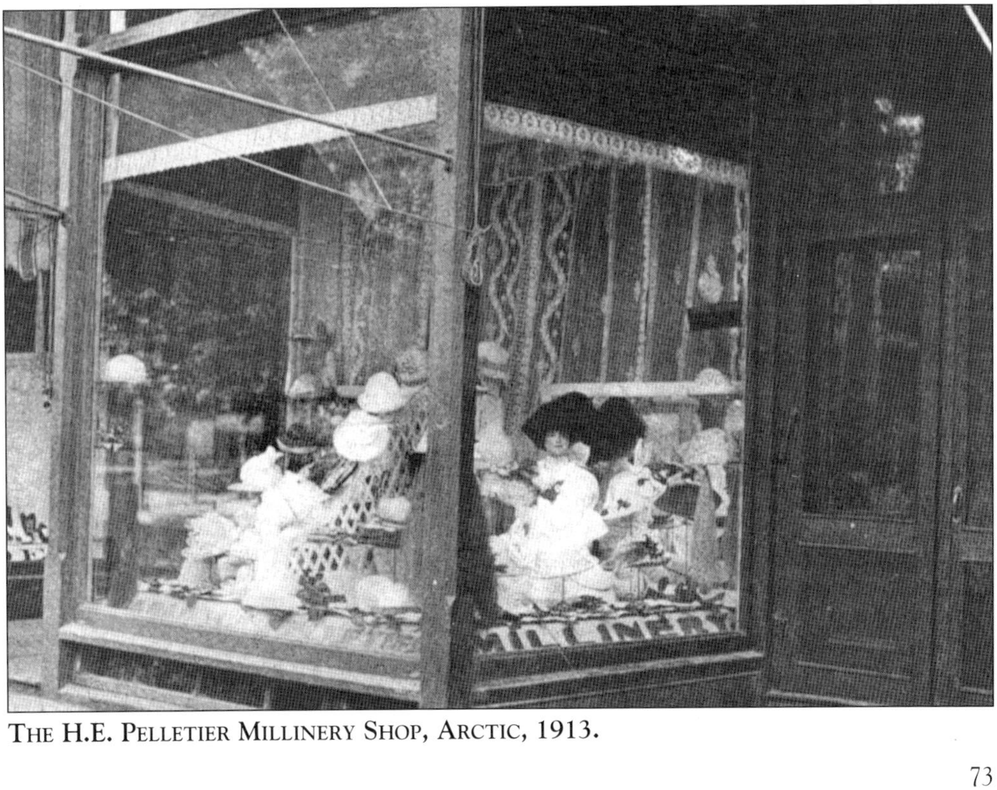

The H.E. Pelletier Millinery Shop, Arctic, 1913.

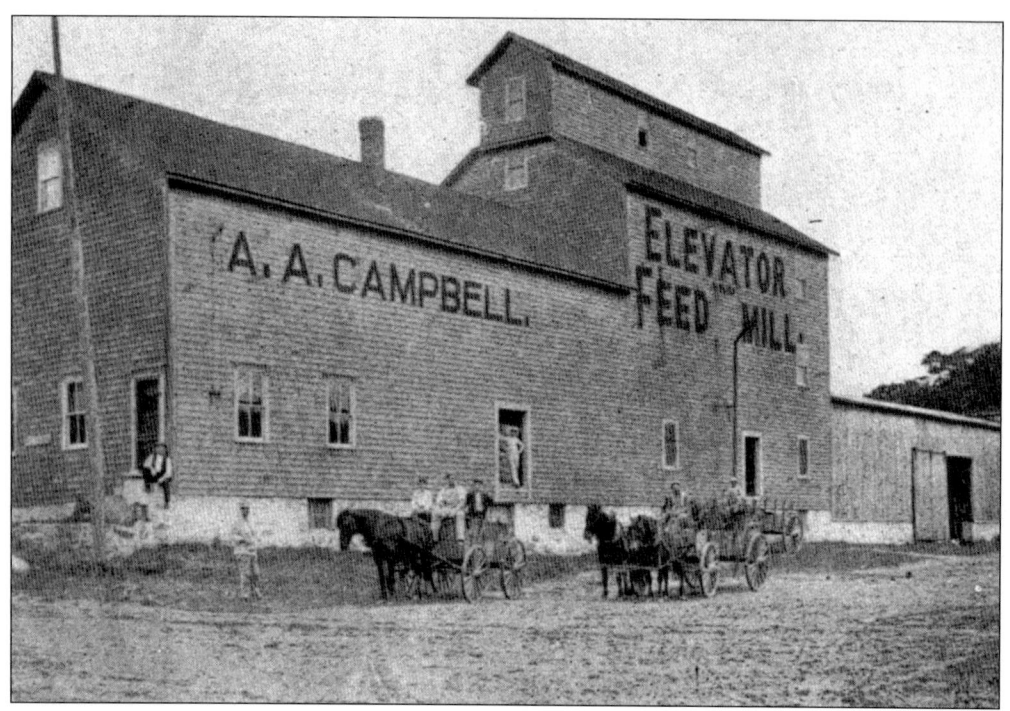

The Allan A. Campbell Coal, Wood, Hay, Grain and Feed Company, Phenix, 1913.

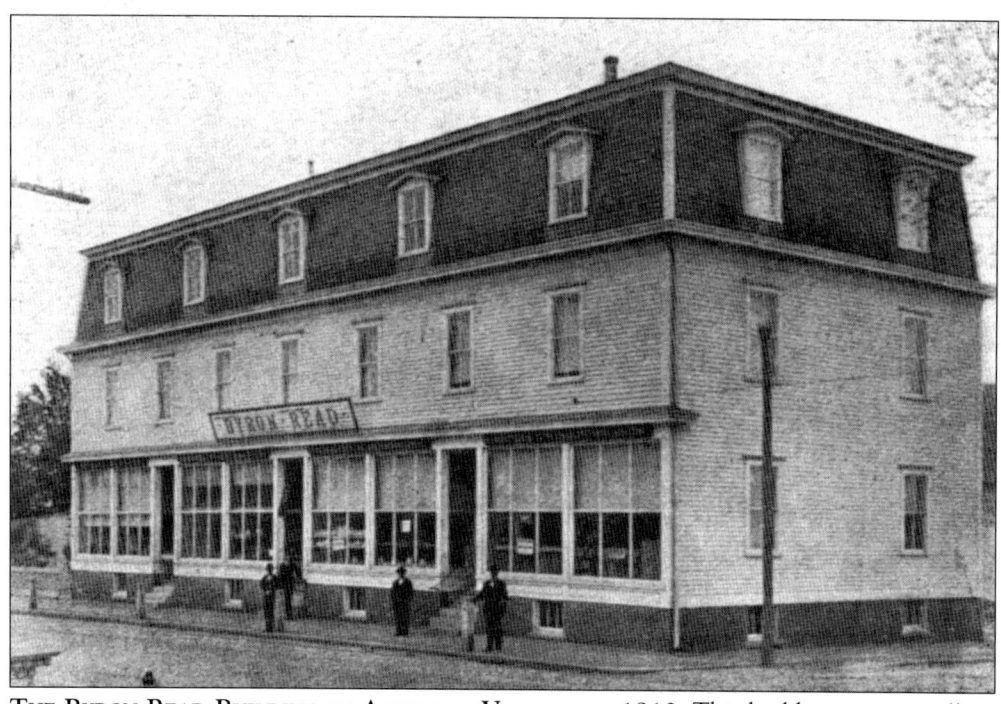

The Byron Read Building in Anthony Village, c. 1910. This building is an excellent specimen of mid-19th-century business construction and is still standing virtually unchanged.

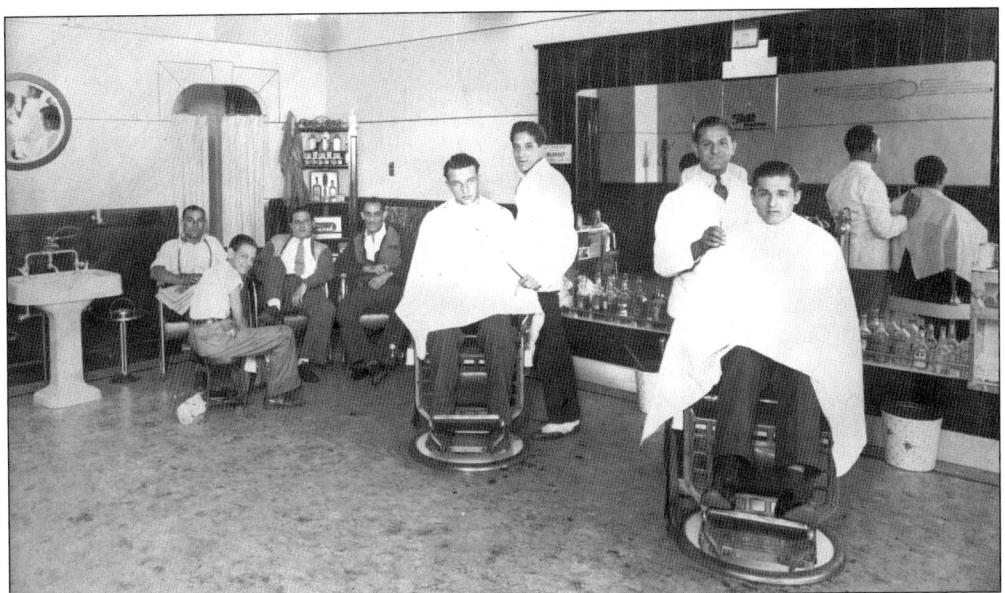

"AL THE BARBER" MUSCHIANO AT WORK IN HIS SHOP ON PROVIDENCE STREET IN NATICK, 1941. From left to right are Art Garrisa, Victor DiCaprio (with his back to the camera), Roy ?, Ugo Muschiano, Dr. Paul Barber, Olindo (Bill) Muschiano, Al Muschiano, and James Imbriglio.

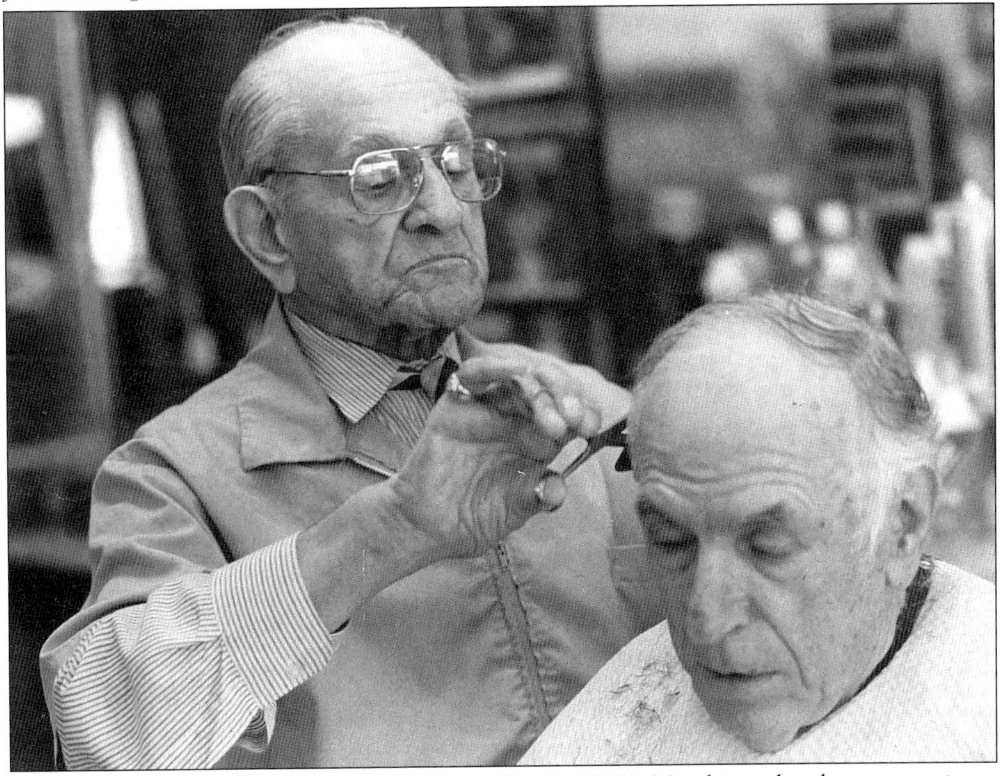

"AL THE BARBER" AT WORK IN THE SAME SHOP, 1995. Muschiano has been operating a barbershop in Natick since 1933.

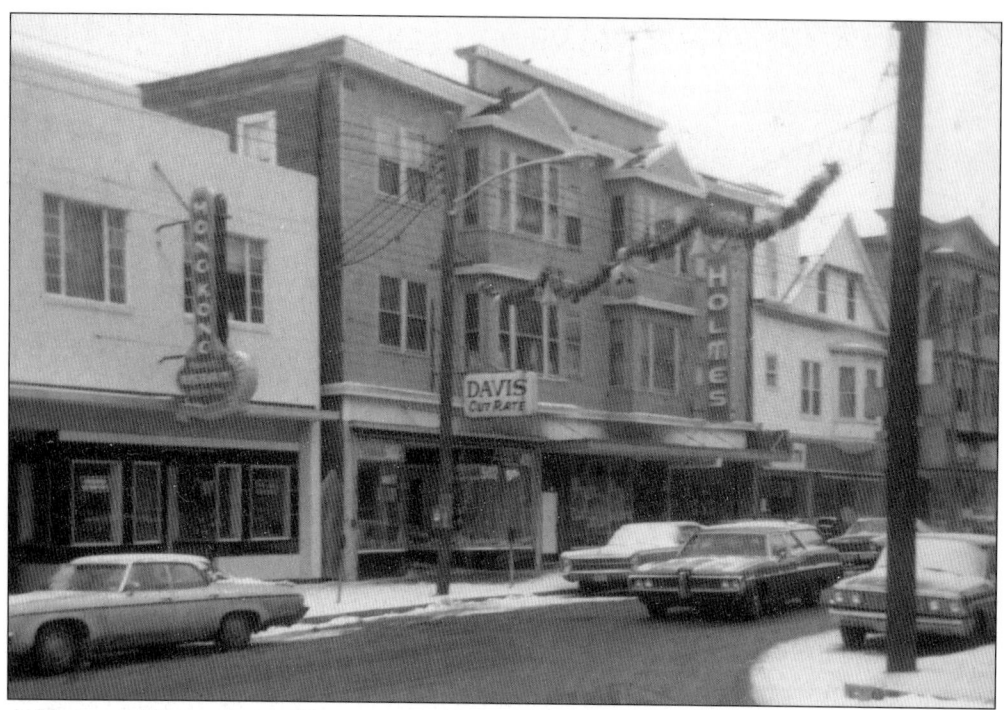

A View of Washington Street and Brookside Avenue, 1976. From the 1870s to the 1970s, Arctic Center was the retail hub of central Rhode Island. This photograph shows Washington Street and Brookside Avenue with longtime stores Holmes Jewelers, Davis Cut Rate, and the Hong Kong Restaurant visible.

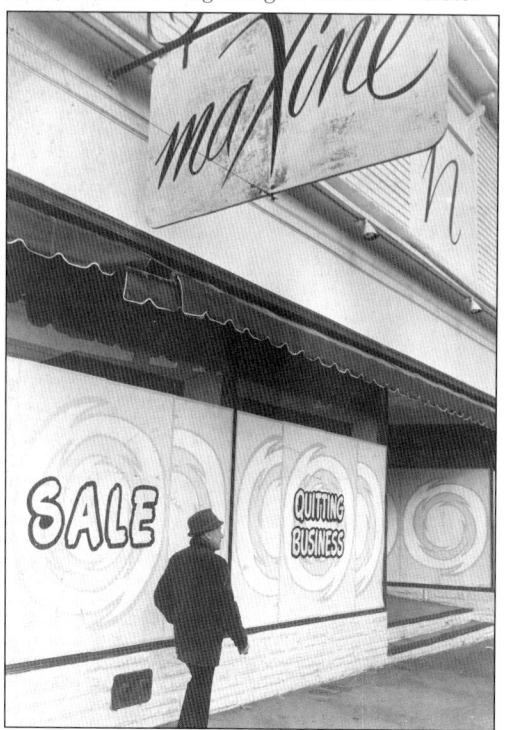

Maxine's Store. Maxine's, in Arctic Square, was a retail outlet for women's clothing. It went out of business in 1977. The building was once Sinnott's Department Store and is now Mastro Electric.

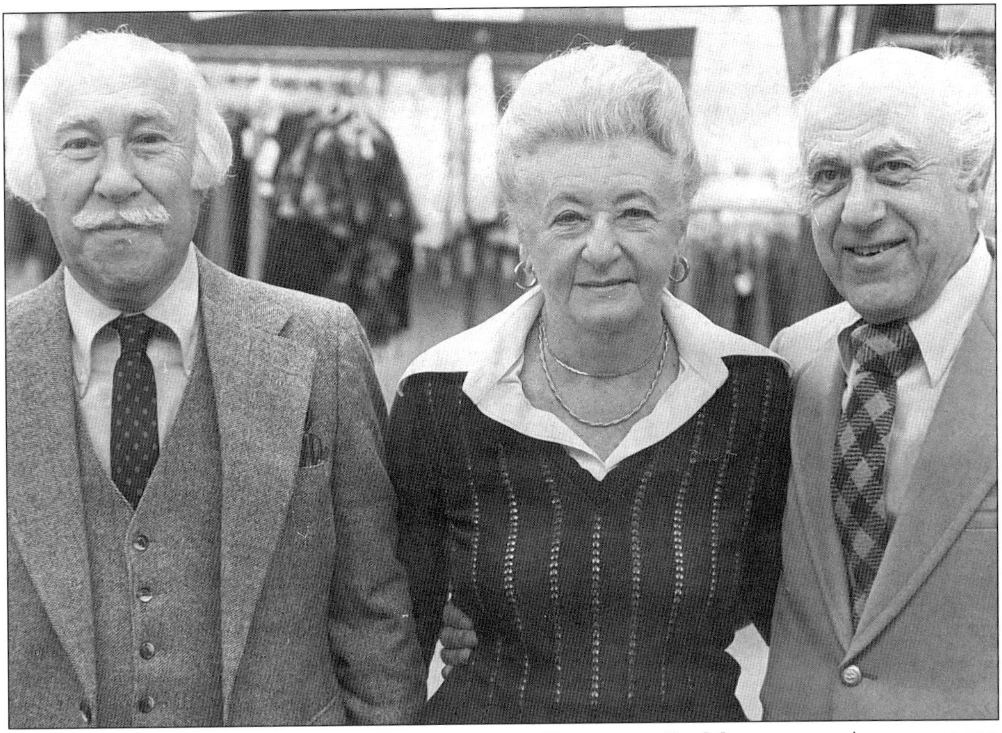

OWNERS OF MAXINE'S—MAX, SEENA, AND BERNARD J. MARGOLIS—ANNOUNCING RETIREMENT, 1977.

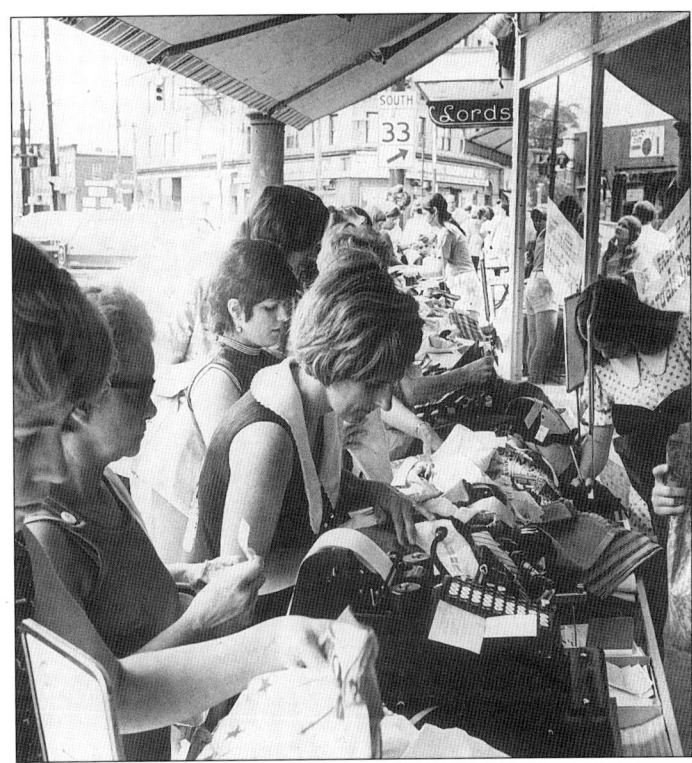

A SIDEWALK SALE AT SEENA'S, ARCTIC SQUARE, 1972. Nearby shopping malls spelled the end for major retail in Arctic by the mid-1970s.

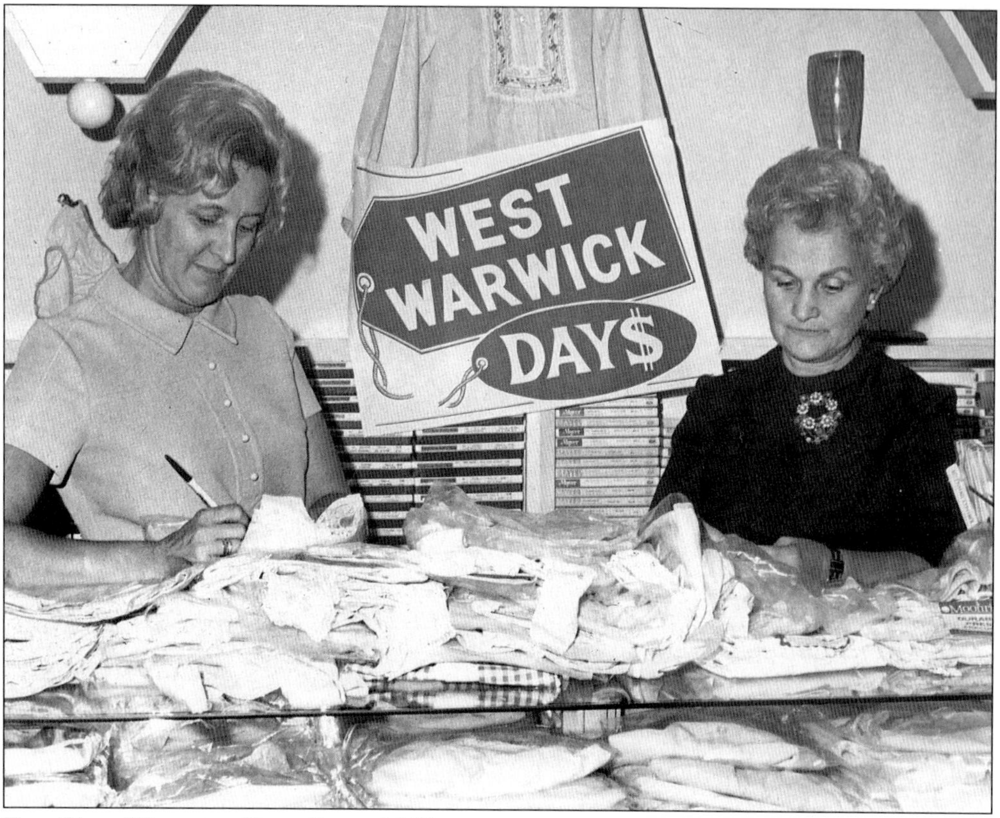

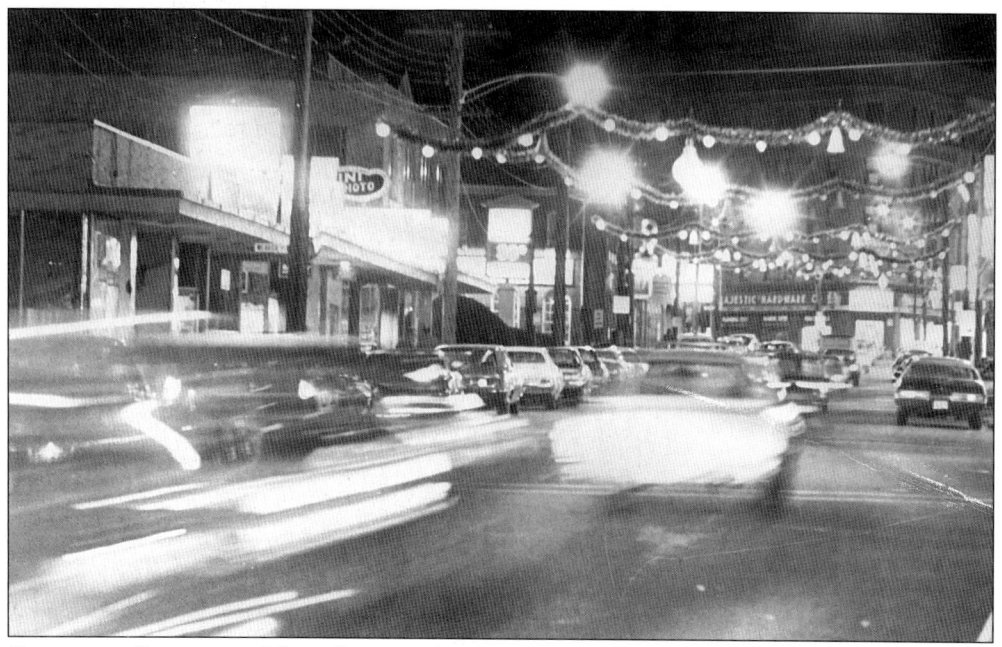

THE WEST WARWICK DAYS SALE, 1969.

CHRISTMAS LIGHTS ON MAIN STREET, ARCTIC, 1972.

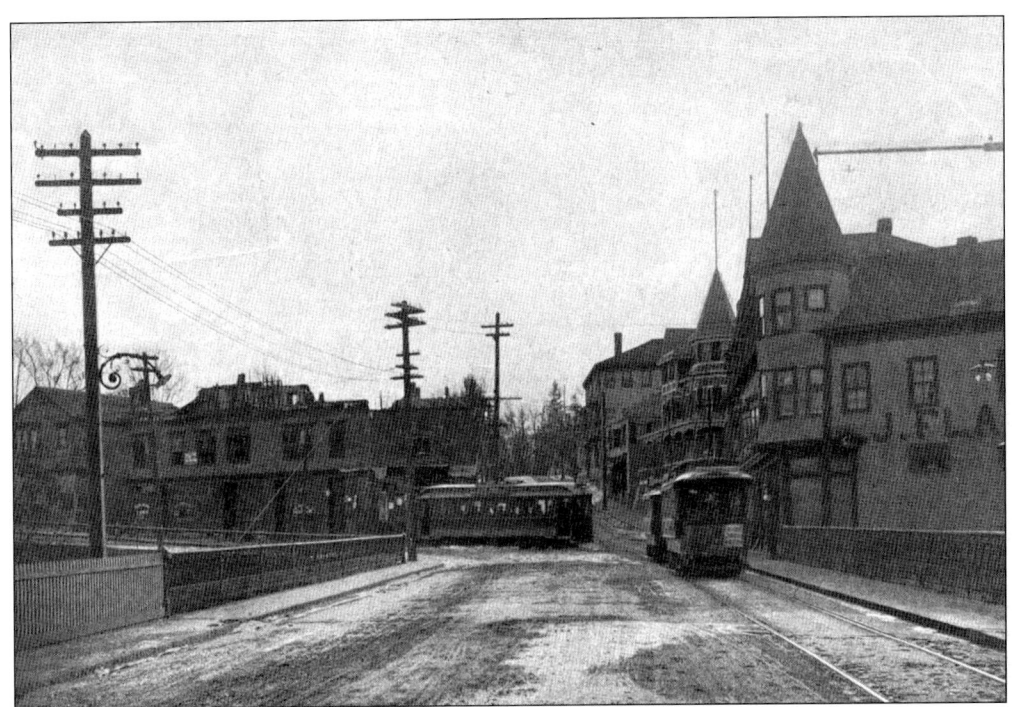

CLYDE SQUARE WITH TROLLEYS, 1910.

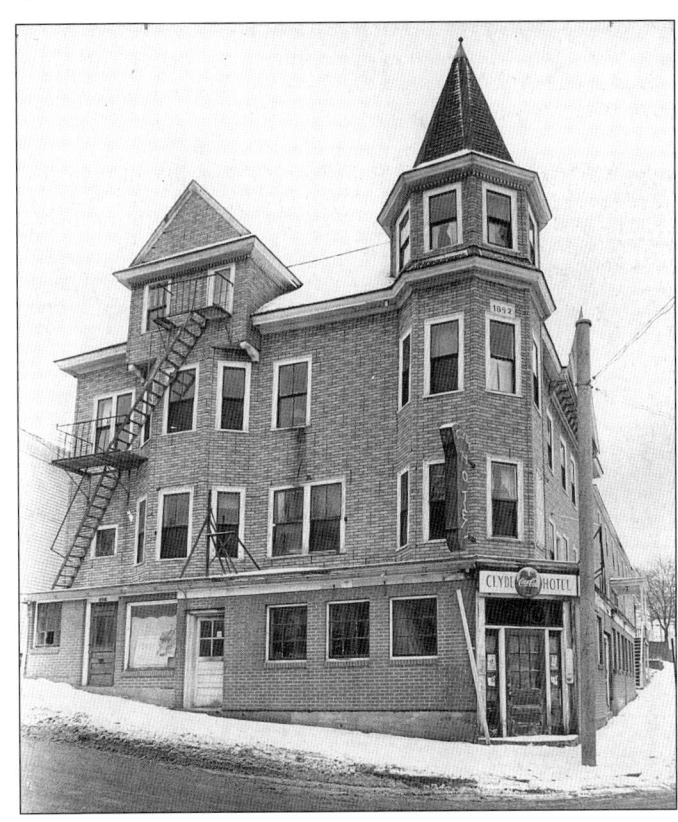

THE CLYDE HOTEL, 1971.

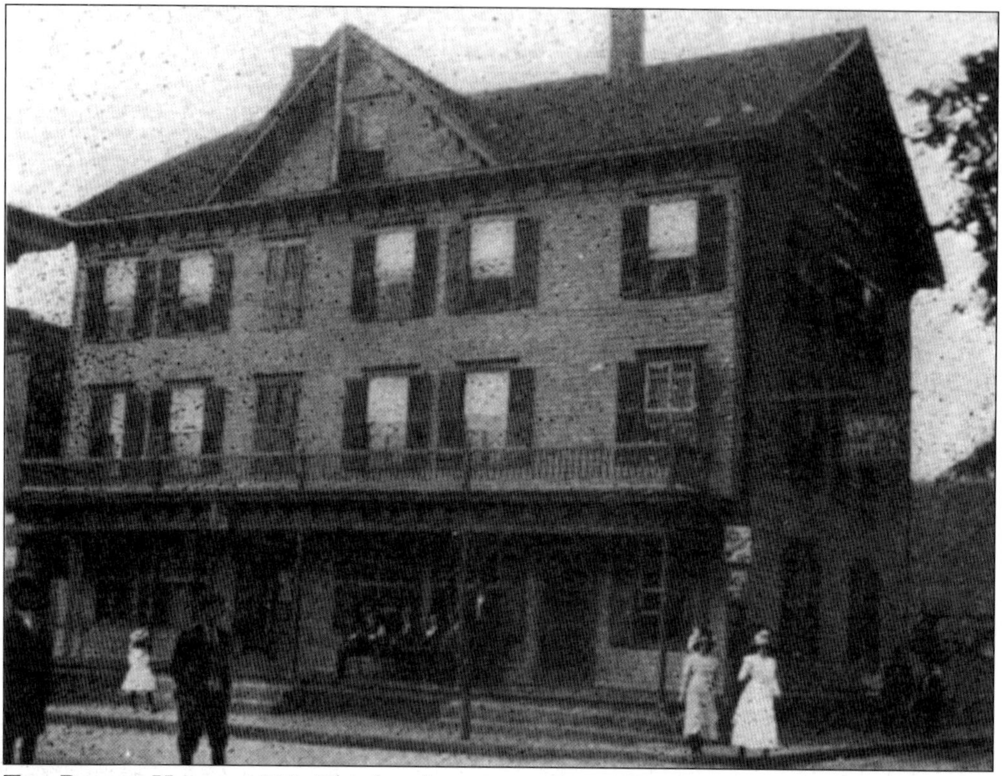

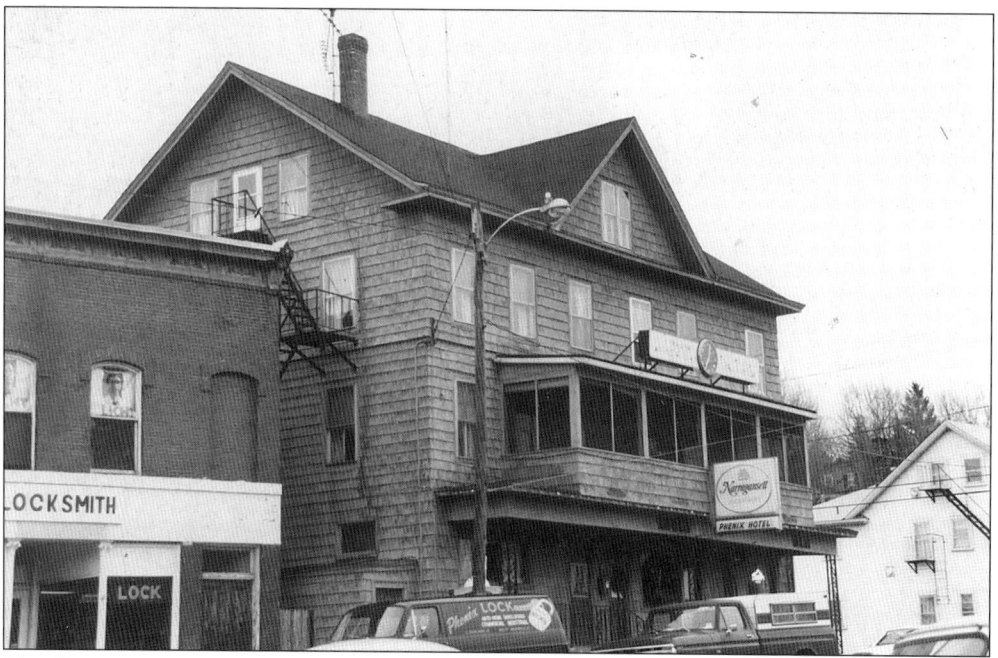

THE PHENIX HOTEL, 1913. This hotel was opened in 1871 to cater to business and other travelers arriving at Phenix Square. It was one of many such establishments built in the valley, but it is the only one remaining today.

THE PHENIX HOTEL, 1970s.

Five
SPORTS, RECREATION, AND GETTING AROUND

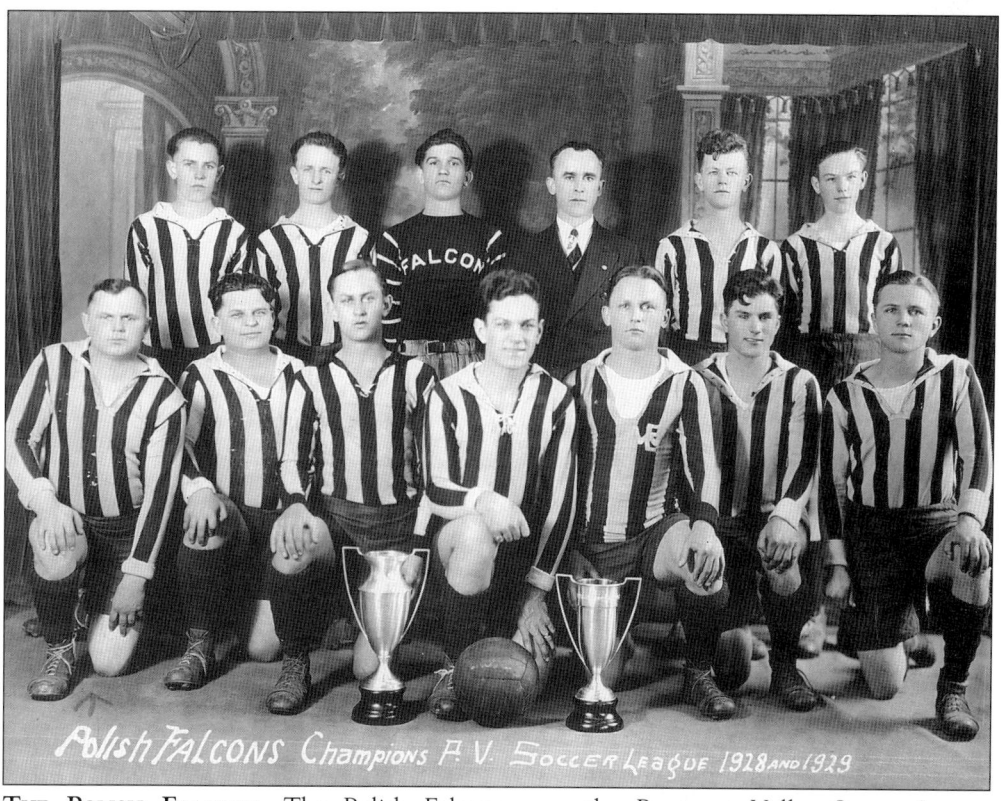

THE POLISH FALCONS. The Polish Falcons were the Pawtuxet Valley Soccer League Champions in 1928–1929. They are seen here at the Polish Social and Benevolent Club.

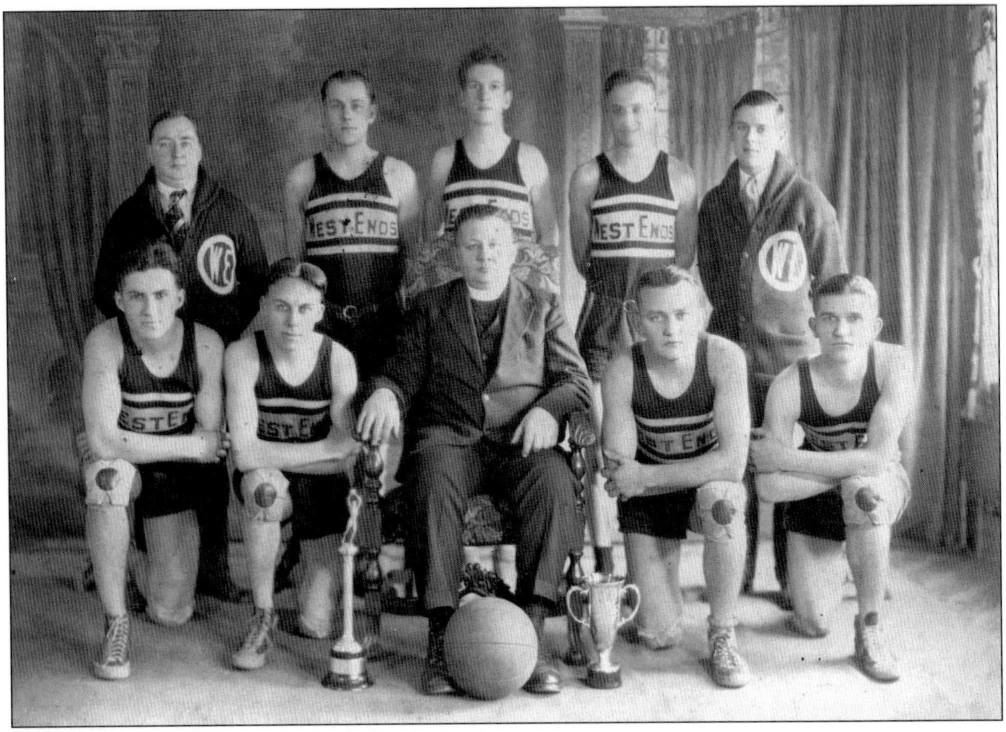

The West Ends Basketball Team, 1930–1931 Champions.

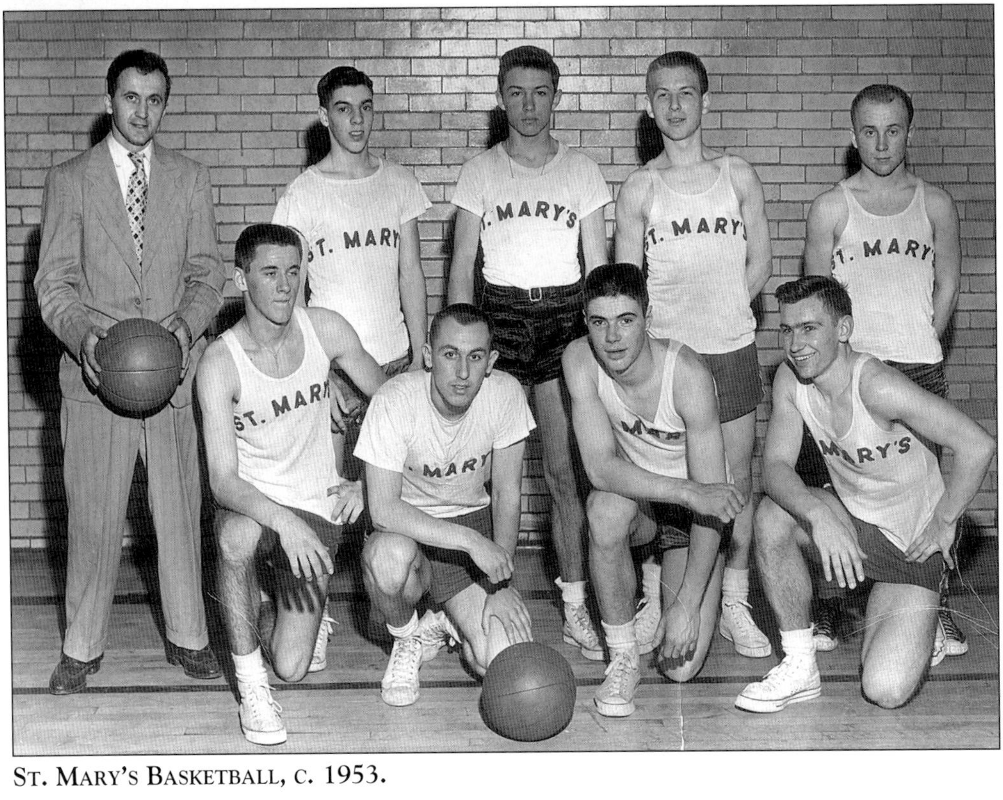

St. Mary's Basketball, c. 1953.

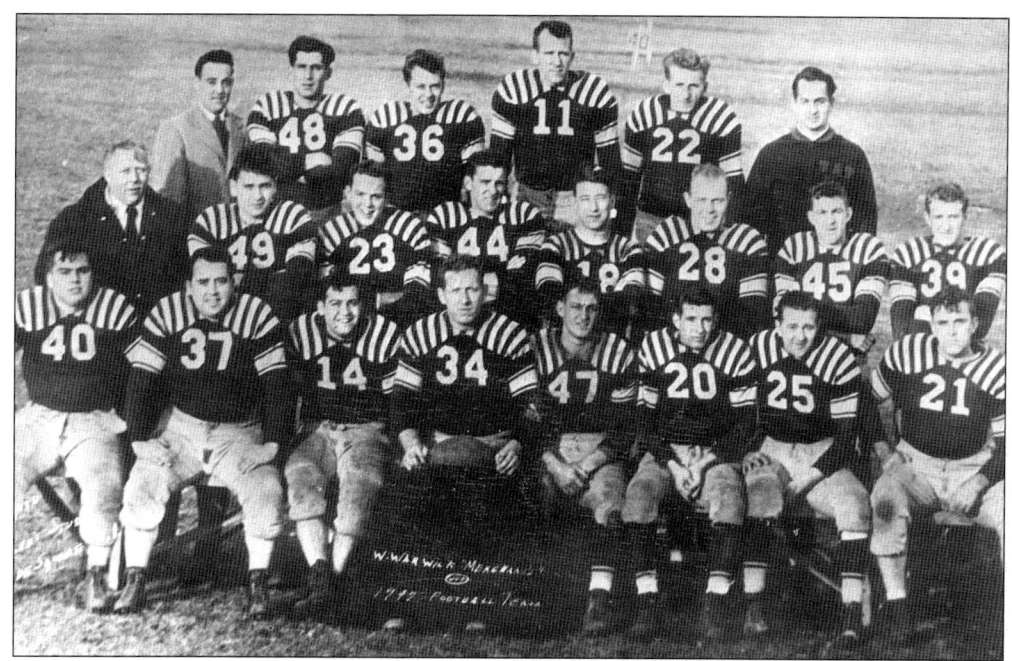

THE WEST WARWICK MERCHANT'S FOOTBALL TEAM, 1947.

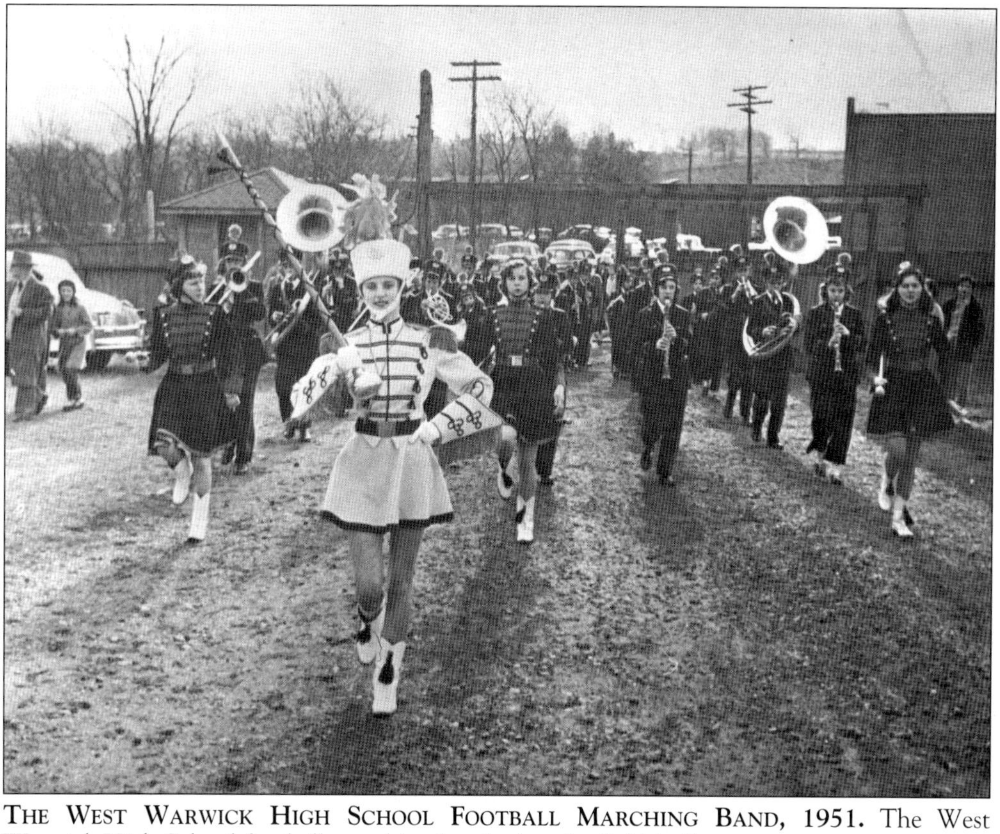

THE WEST WARWICK HIGH SCHOOL FOOTBALL MARCHING BAND, 1951. The West Warwick High School football marching band takes the field in Riverpoint.

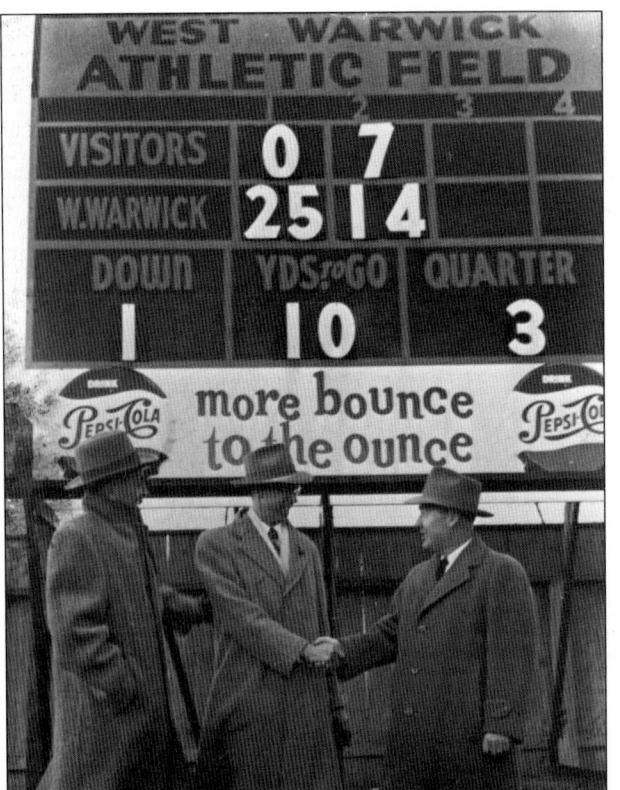

FANS OF THE WEST WARWICK FOOTBALL TEAM, C. 1951. The West Warwick football team racks up points at the West Warwick Athletic Field in Riverpoint. Success in high school football was an important part of the valley experience. It still is.

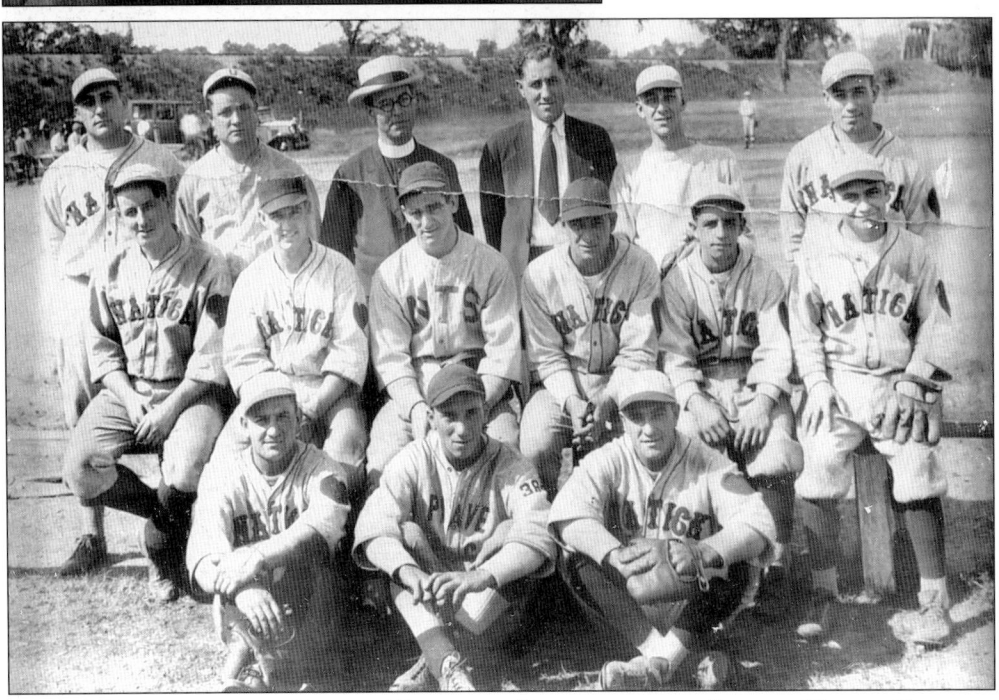

NATICK BASEBALL WITH FATHER TIROCCHI, PASTOR OF THE SACRED HEART CHURCH, C. 1936. This field in East Natick is now named for Tirocchi.

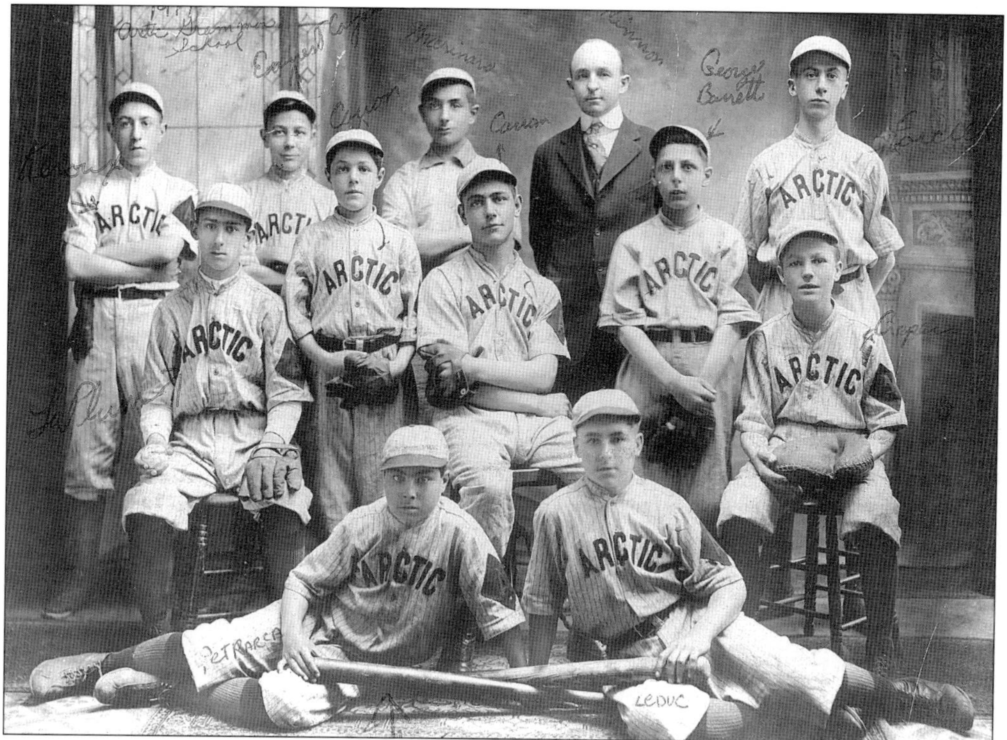

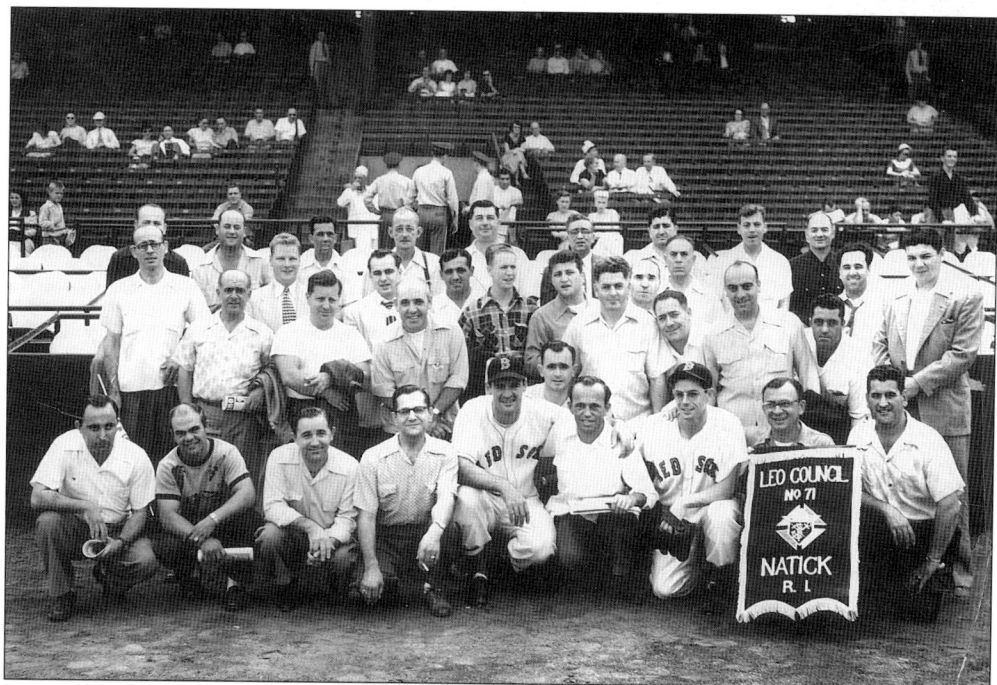

ARCTIC GRAMMAR SCHOOL BASEBALL, 1918.

NATICK LEO COUNCIL, KNIGHTS OF COLUMBUS OUTING AT FENWAY PARK, 1951. This outing included a meeting with Red Sox stars, including Domenic Dimaggio (front row, third from right).

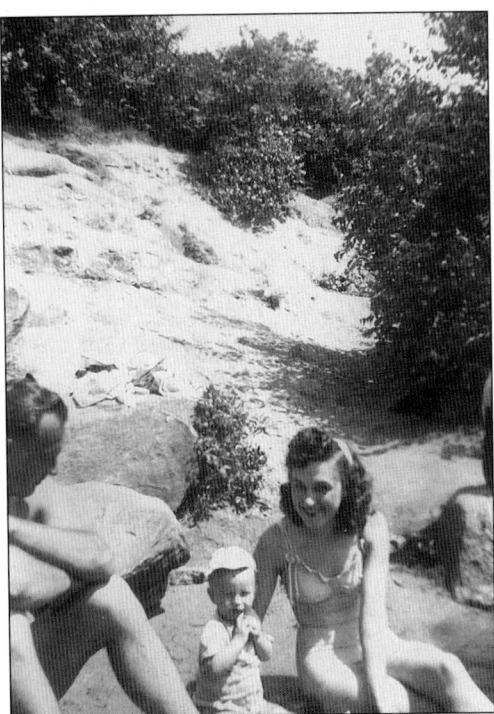 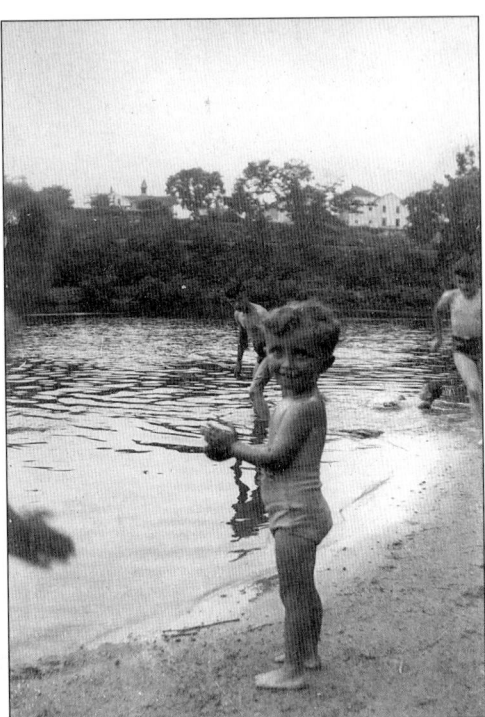

DIVING ROCK ON THE PAWTUXET RIVER, ARCTIC HILL, C. 1945. Diving Rock was one of many swimming areas along the Pawtuxet River. Each village had its own favorite spot for cooling off.

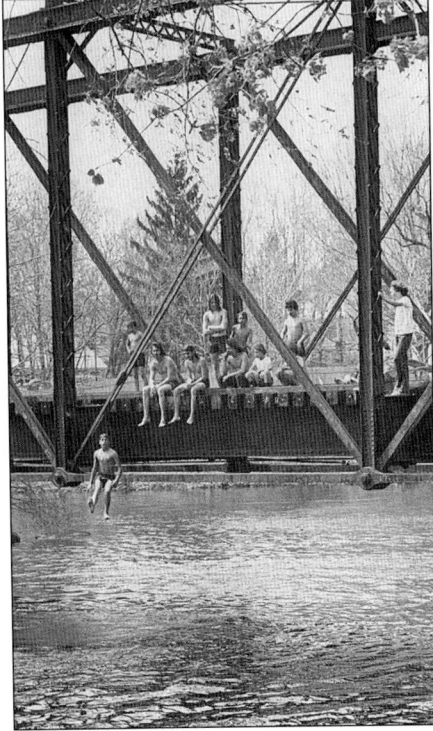

DIVERS AT THE ANTHONY BRIDGE, SUMMER 1976.

Professor Sweet. A native of Phenix, Sweet made a name for himself as a tightrope walker. On September 3, 1859, he made his debut at Phenix by walking a 360-foot-long rope suspended over the Pawtuxet River.

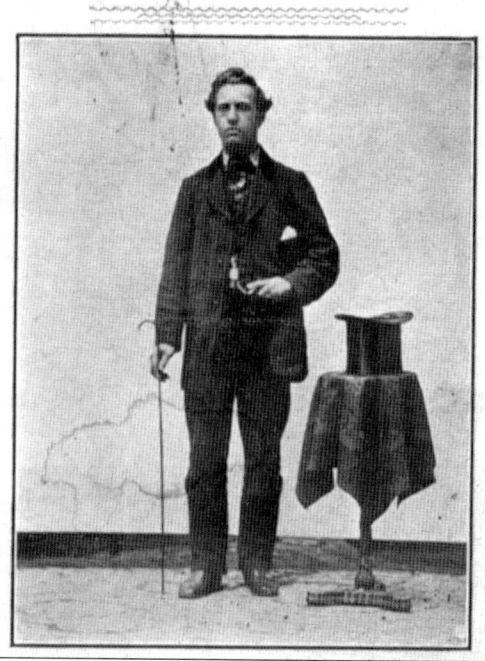

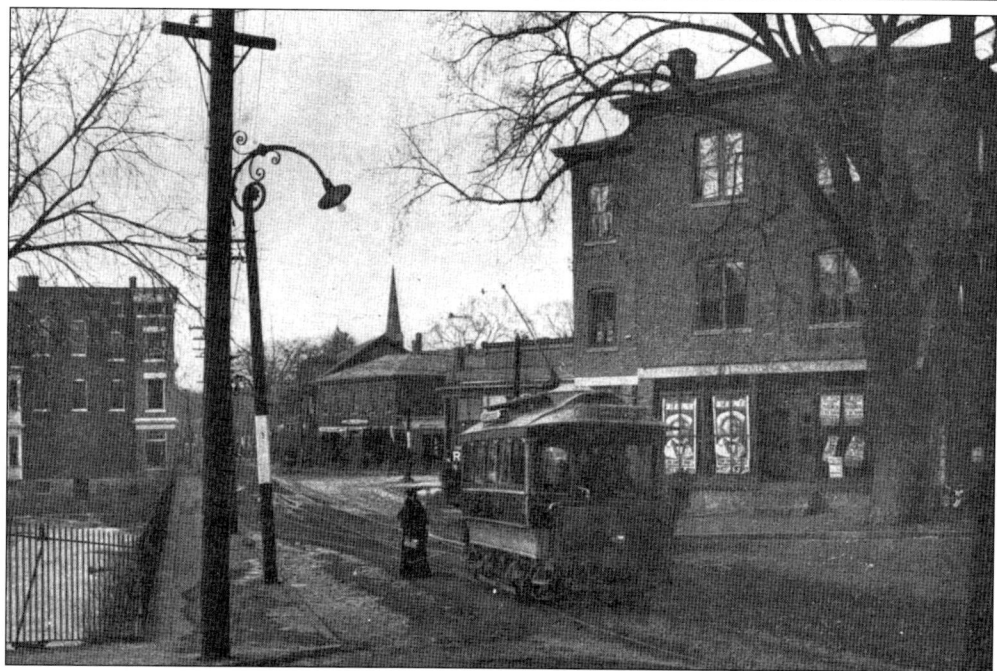

A Trolley in Phenix Square, 1913. From the late 19th through the early 20th centuries, the area was served by streetcar lines, making travel easy and inexpensive between villages and to places like Providence and the shore at Rocky Point.

A Rumble Seat, 1940.

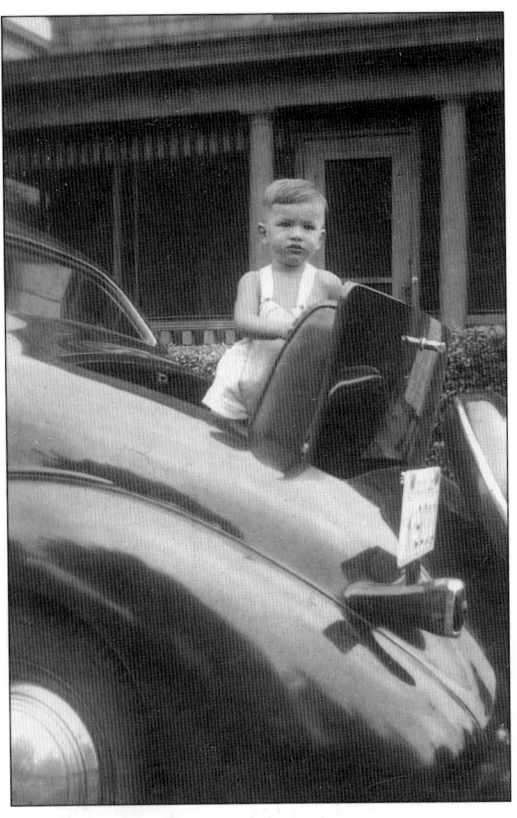

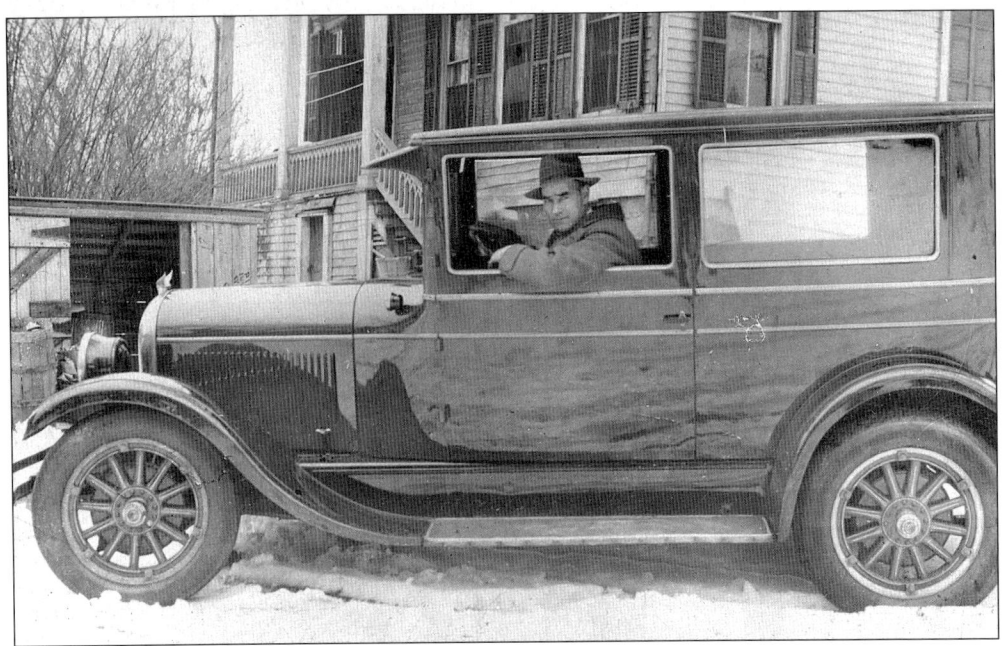

On Business by Car, 1928.

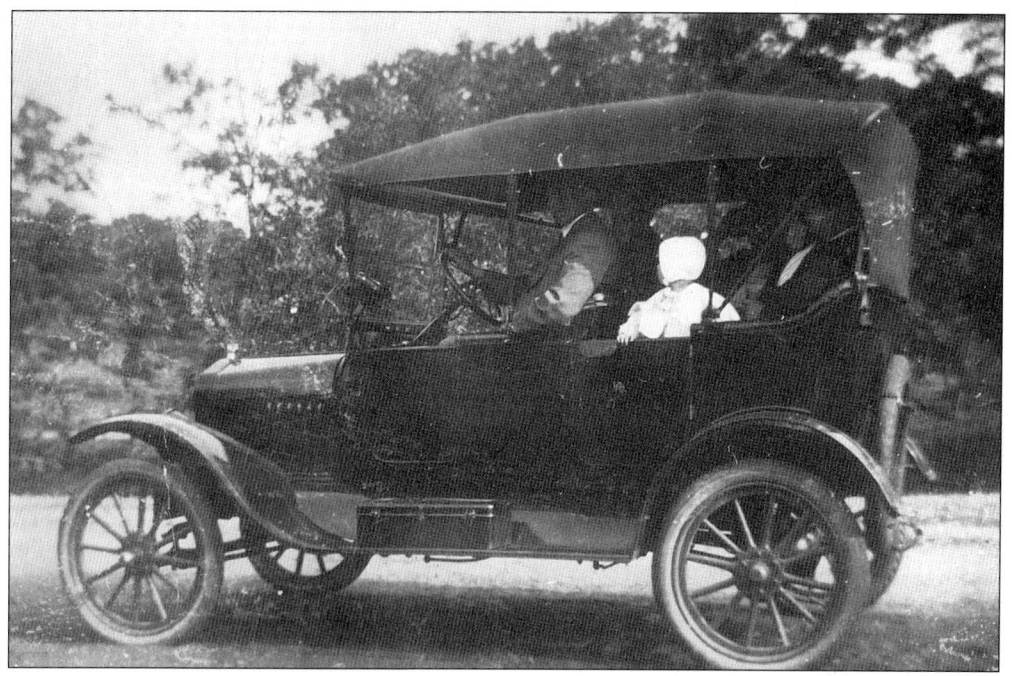

A Drive in the Country, 1924.

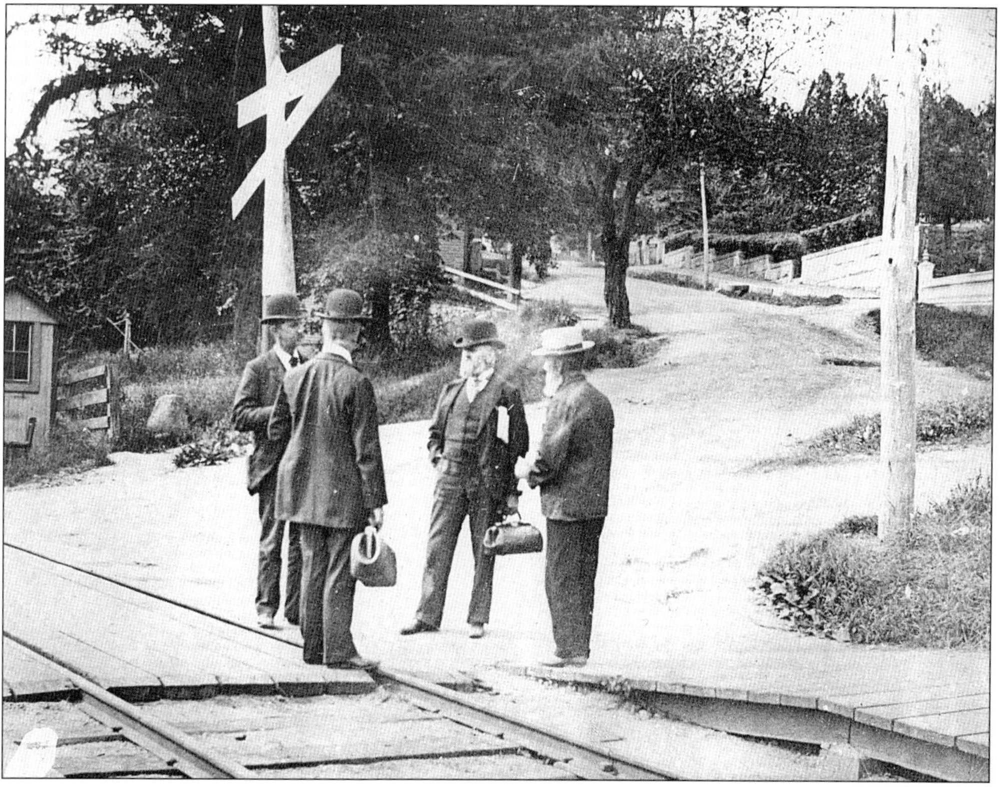

The Phenix Square Station with Passengers Waiting, 1890. Passenger train service was available from the mid-19th century to the early 20th century in the Pawtuxet Valley.

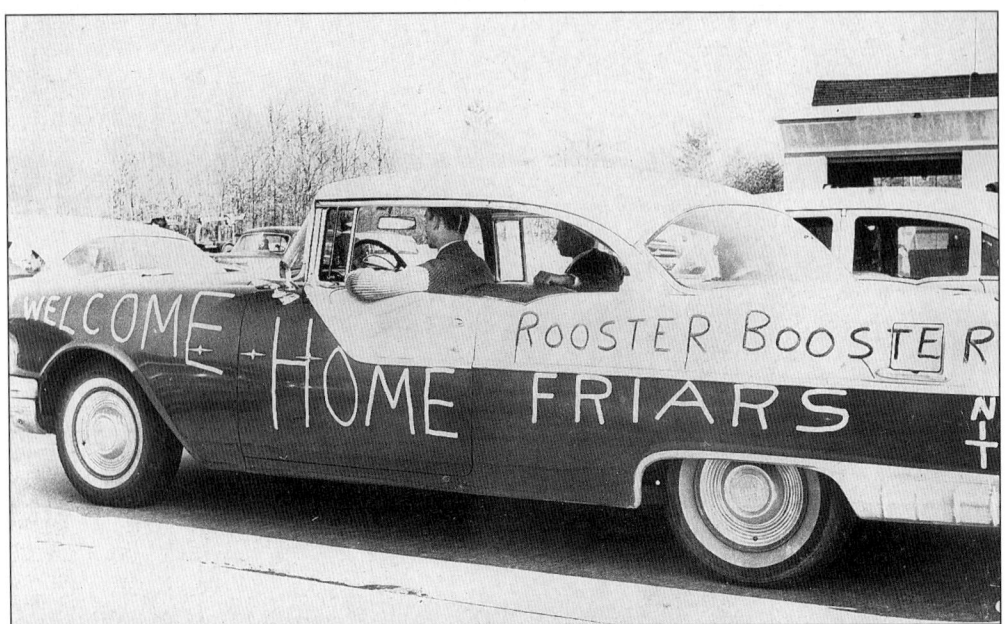

ROOTING FOR THE PROVIDENCE COLLEGE FRIARS BASKETBALL TEAM, C. 1959.

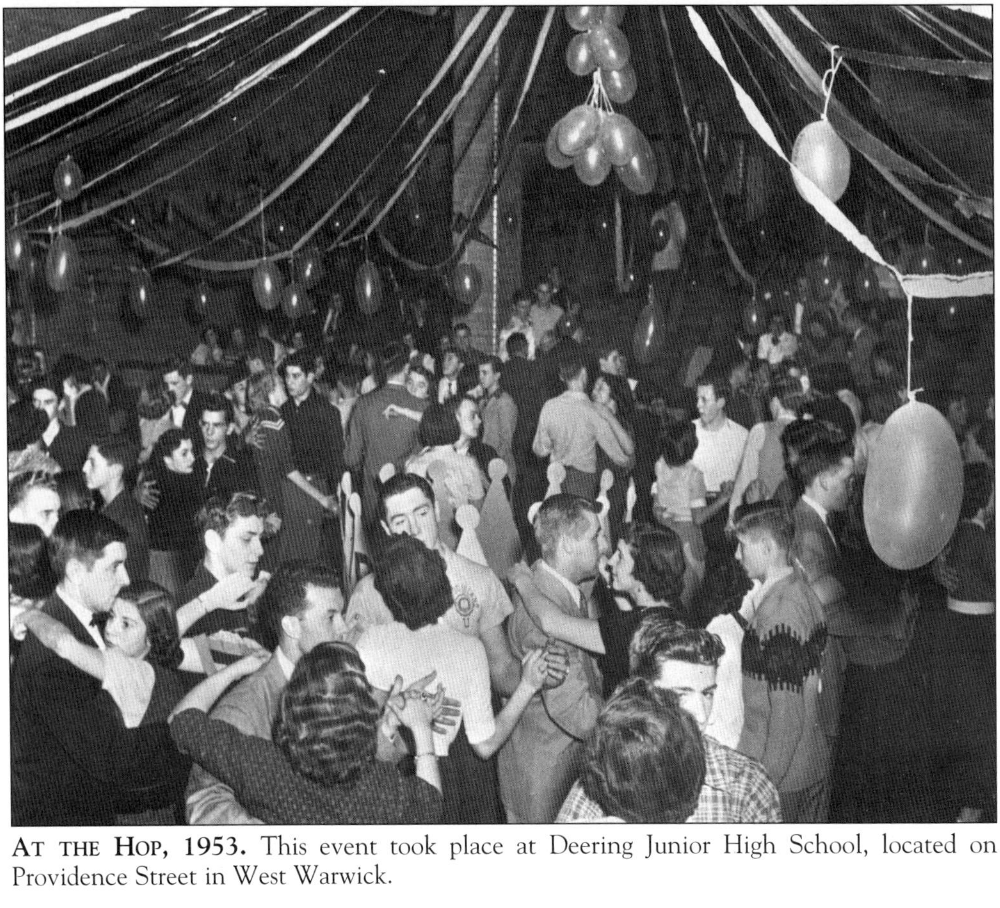

AT THE HOP, 1953. This event took place at Deering Junior High School, located on Providence Street in West Warwick.

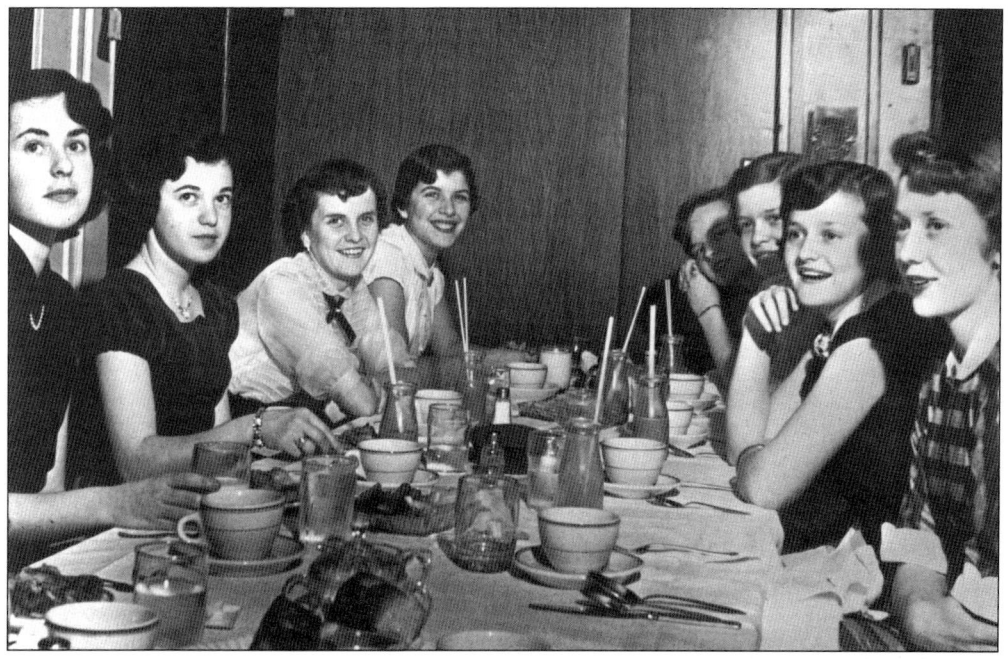

A Girls' Night Out, 1953.

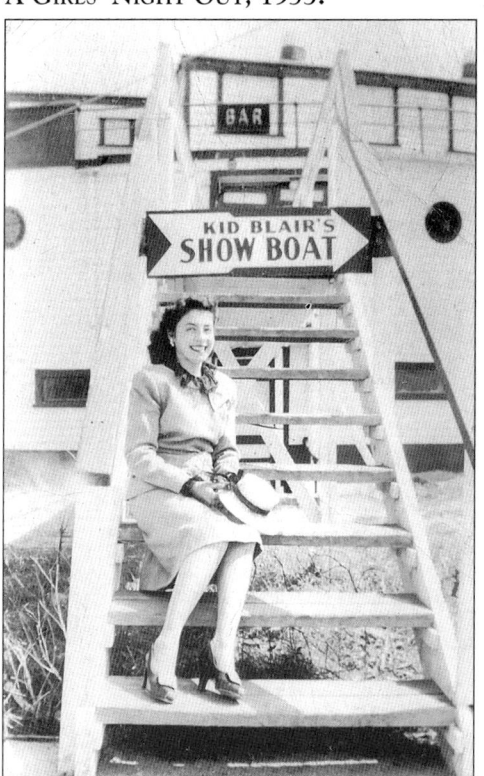

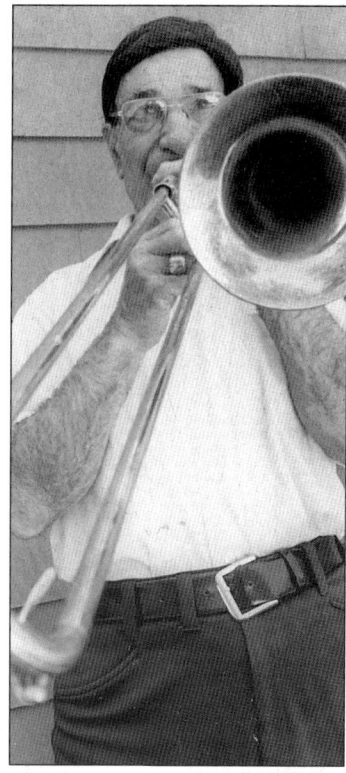

Left: Outside Kid Blair's Showboat Nightclub, 1943. This club was located on Route 3 in Coventry on Lake Tiogue. Right: Pete Salemi, 1977. This longtime jazz trombone favorite is still playing as of this writing at nearly 100 years old.

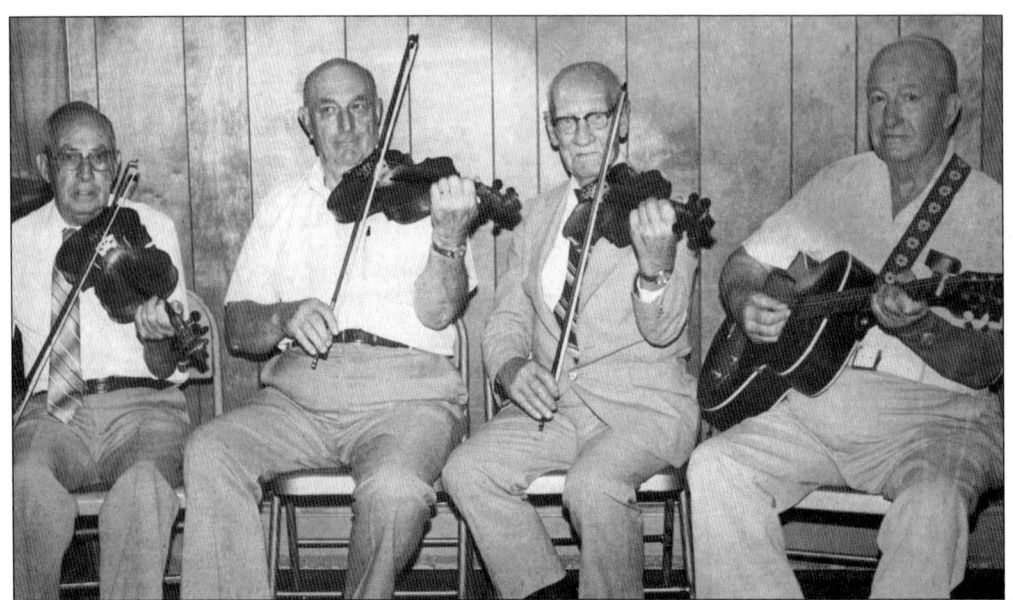

The Pawtuxet Valley Old Time Fiddlers at Club Jogues, Coventry, 1983.

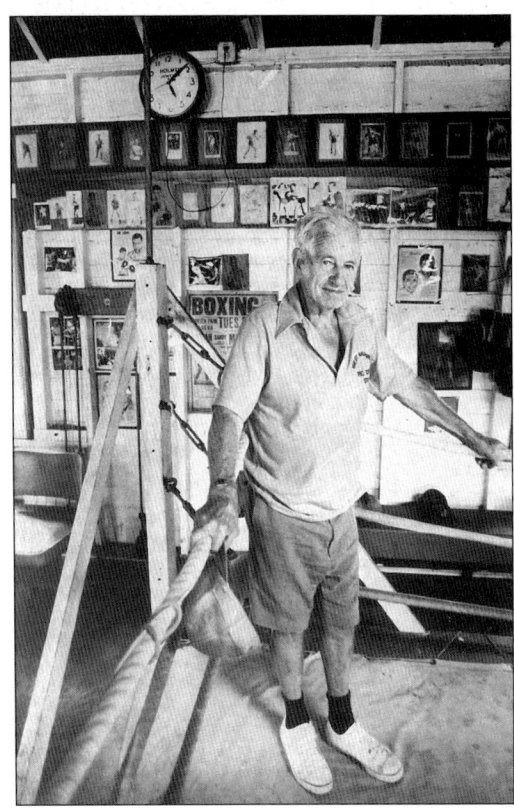

Larry McManus, 1980. Larry McManus, boxer and trainer, poses at Camp Ayoho on Johnson's Pond in Coventry.

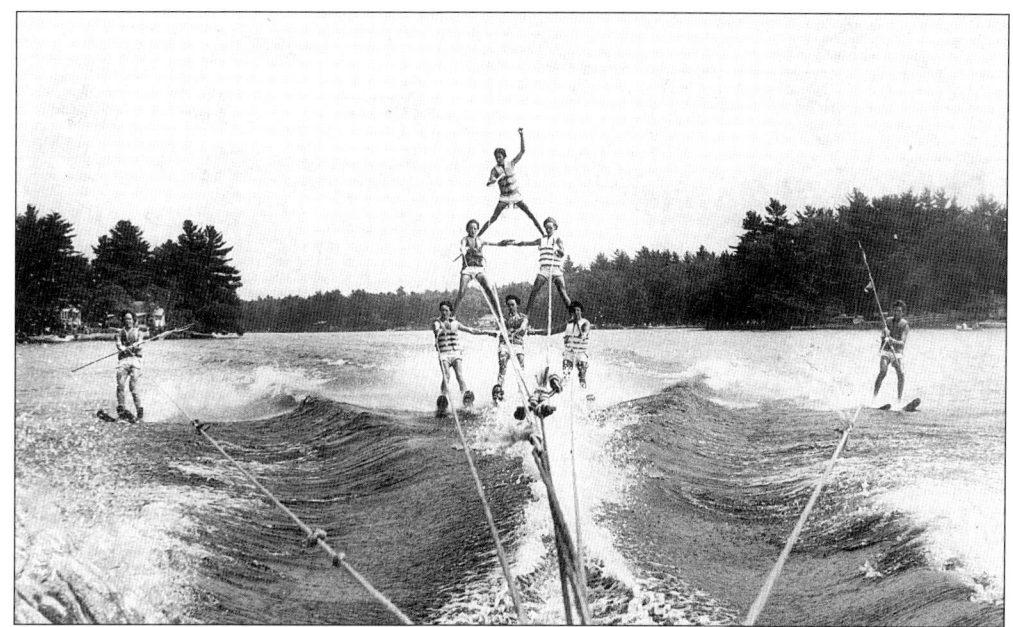

A View of Johnson's Pond, 1980. This view shows Johnson's Pond, the headwaters of the South Branch of the Pawtuxet River, during the annual ski fest.

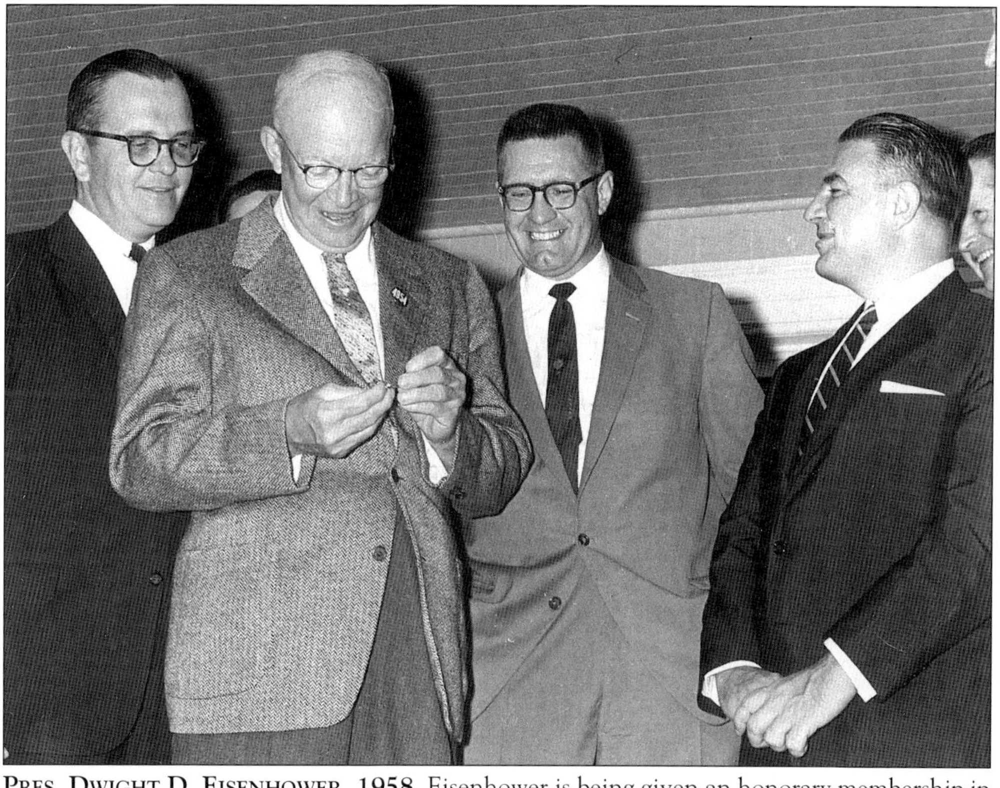

Pres. Dwight D. Eisenhower, 1958. Eisenhower is being given an honorary membership in the Pawtuxet Valley Country Club by Leo Charbonneau, Republican secretary of state candidate, as future governor Delsesto and senate candidate Bayard Ewing look on.

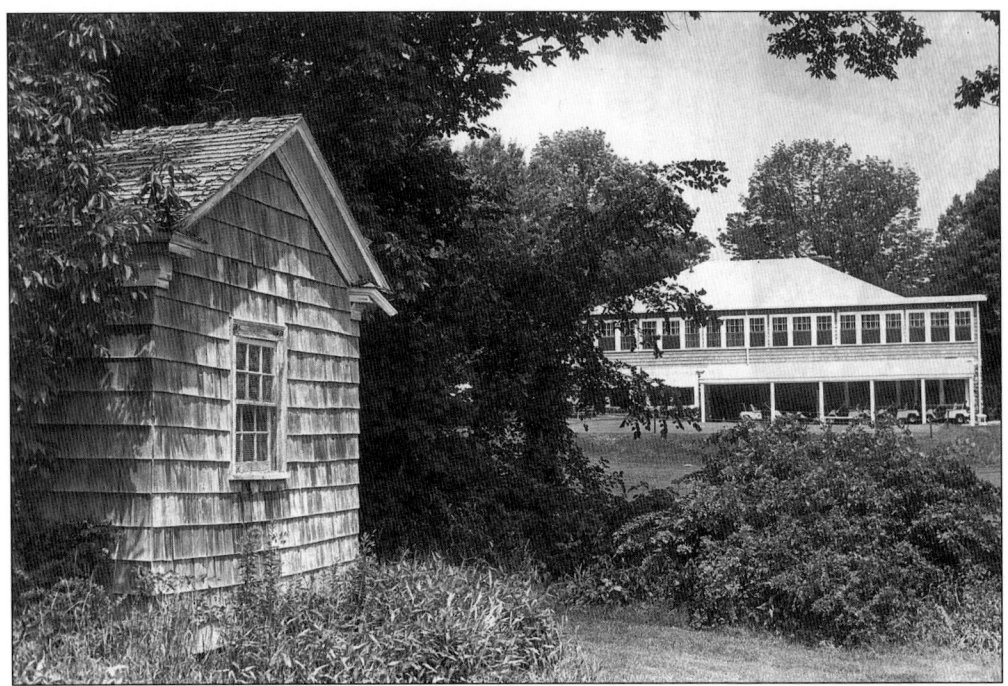

THE WEST WARWICK COUNTRY CLUB ON WAKEFIELD STREET, 1975. Several golf courses were built in the area as the valley became more suburban after World War II.

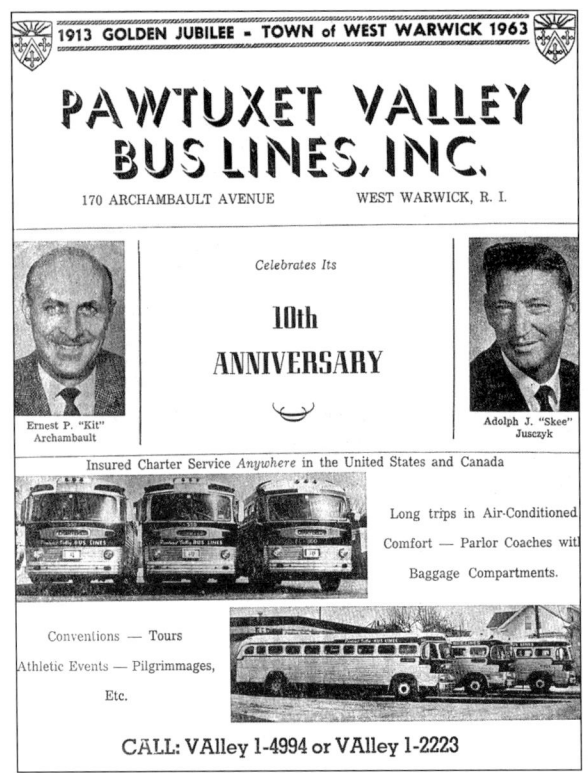

A PAWTUXET VALLEY BUS LINES ADVERTISEMENT, 1963. The company is still in business serving the region's transportation needs.

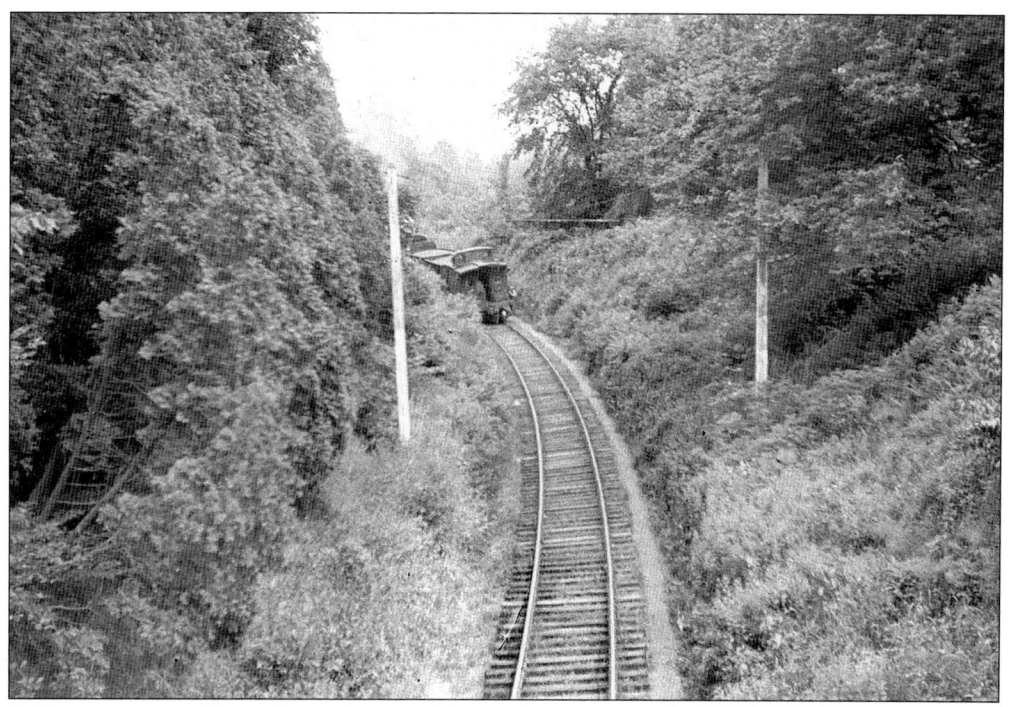

A Train on the Hope Spur Line at Maple Avenue, 1920.

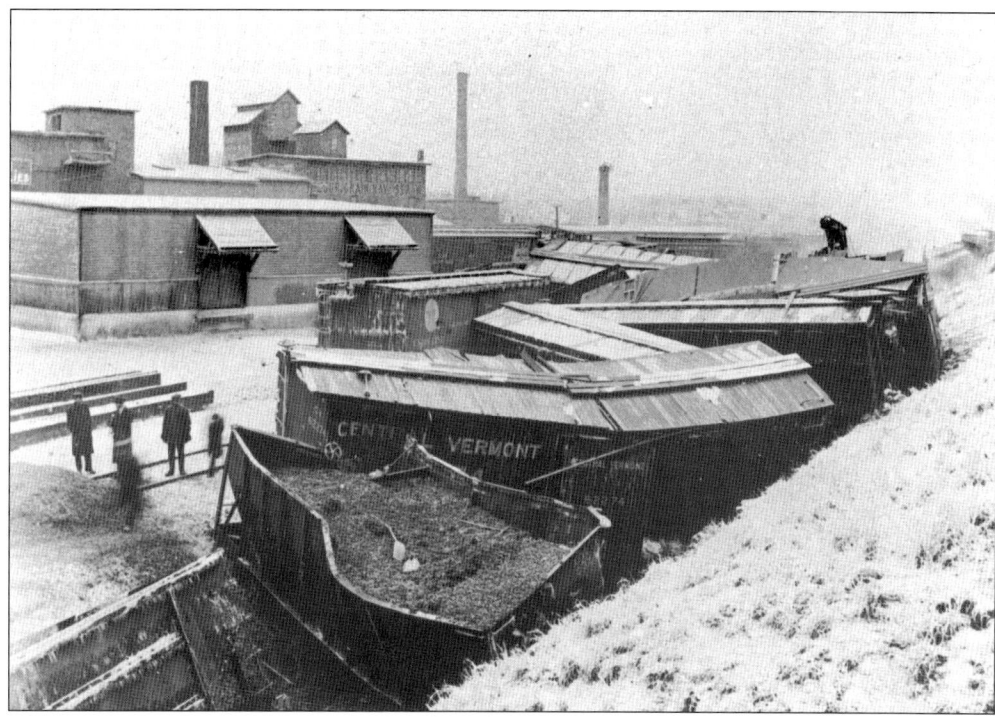

A Train Wreck at the Arctic Depot, January 1918. Freight service continued on the Washington Secondary Line until the 1980s. Train wrecks like this were infrequent and, in this case, the train wreck was probably brought about by heavy volume due to war demands.

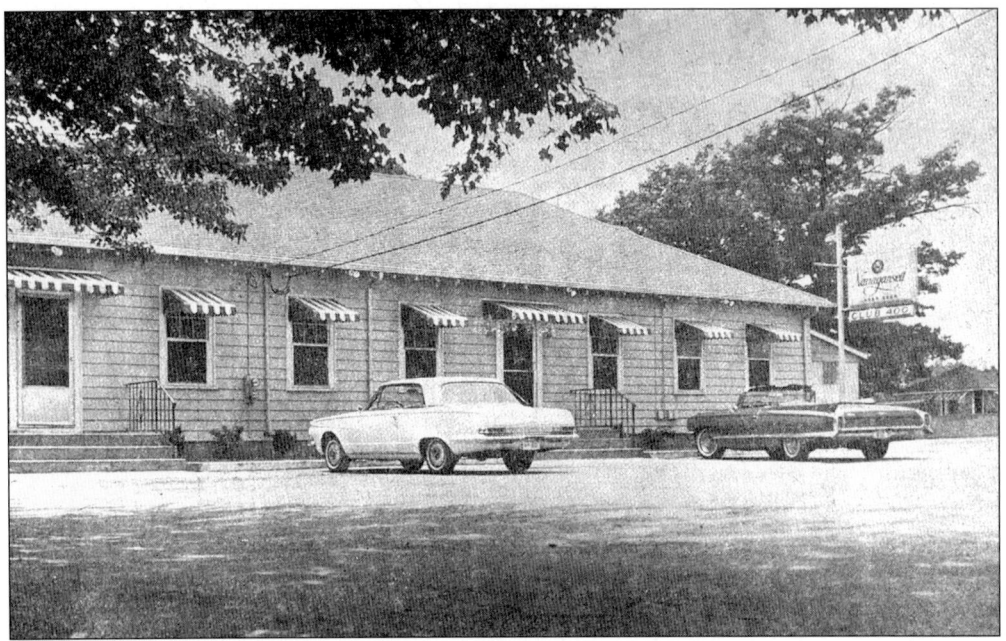

THE CLUB 400, 1963. The Club 400 was the scene of many events over the decades. Long connected to the Giorgio family, it is now the West Valley Inn off Providence Street in Natick.

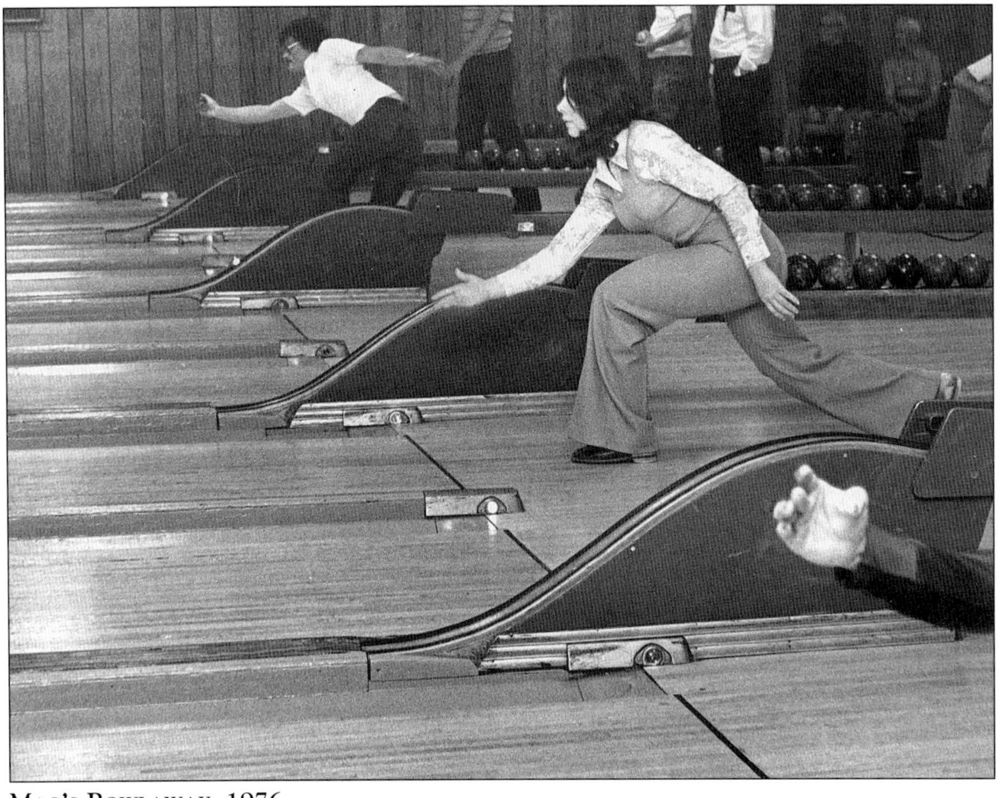

MAC'S BOWLAWAY, 1976.

Six
Familiar Faces, Change, and Continuity

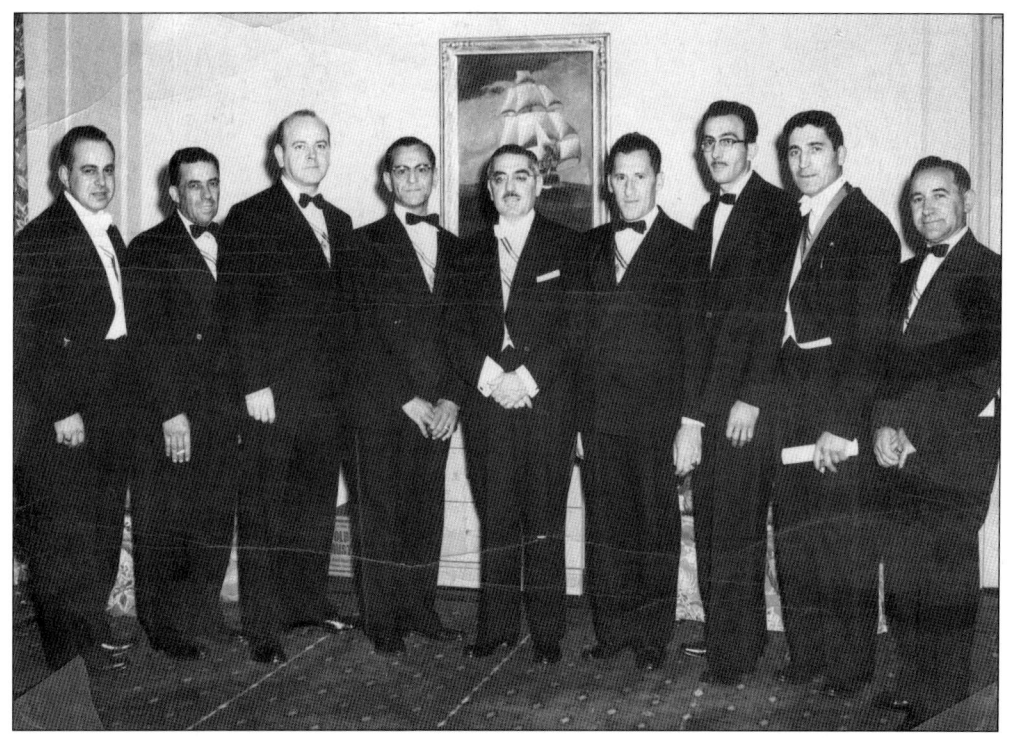

Sen. John O. Pastore Addressing the Knights of Columbus, 1955.

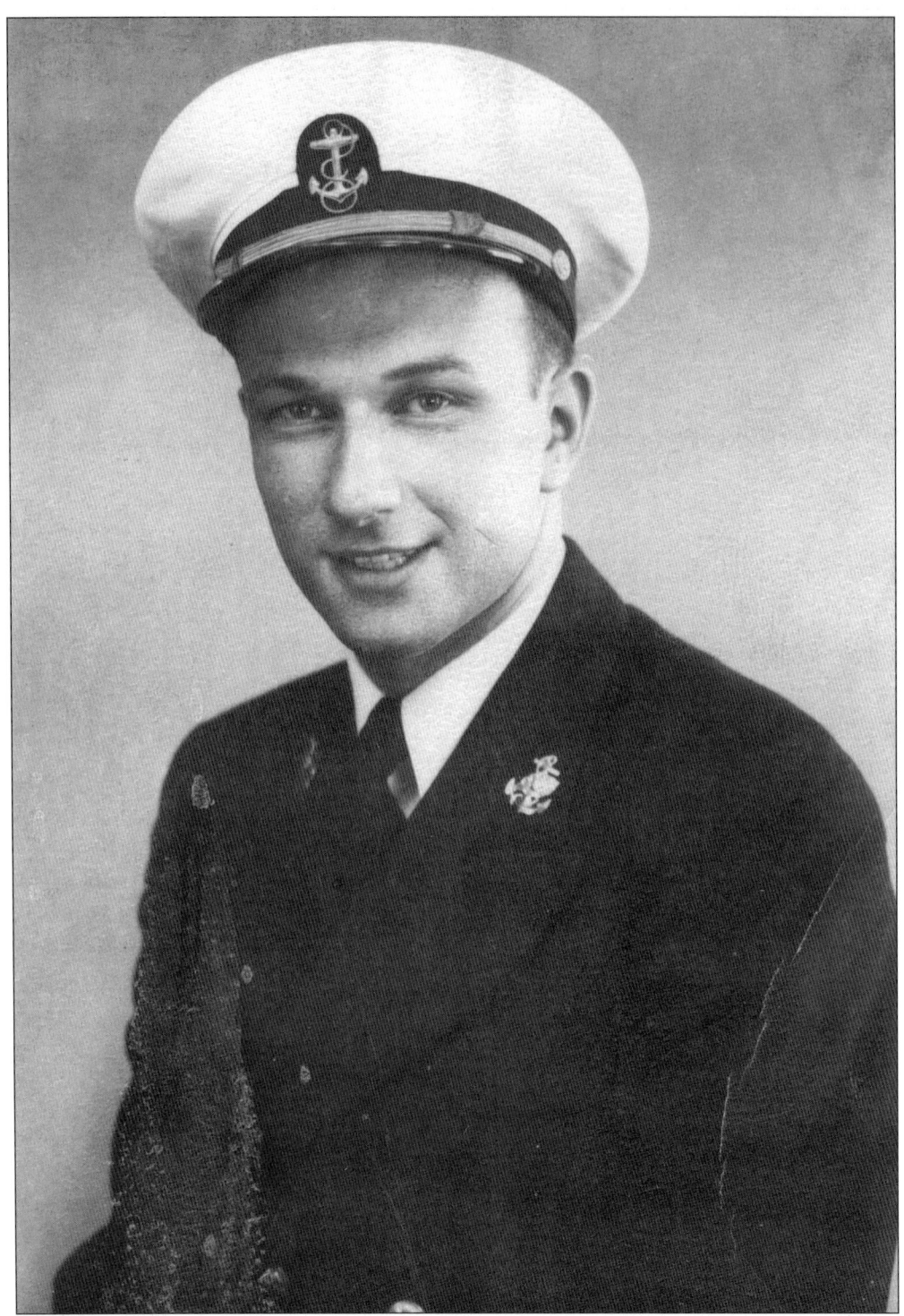

LT. PAUL BARBER, U.S. NAVY MEDICAL OFFICER, 1945. In February 1950, after his service, Dr. Barber opened a practice in the Pawtuxet Valley as a general practitioner. He continues to serve the valley today.

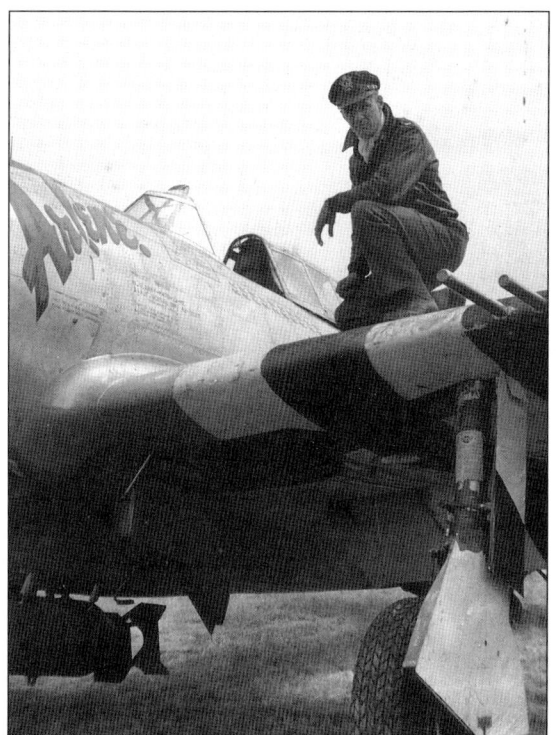 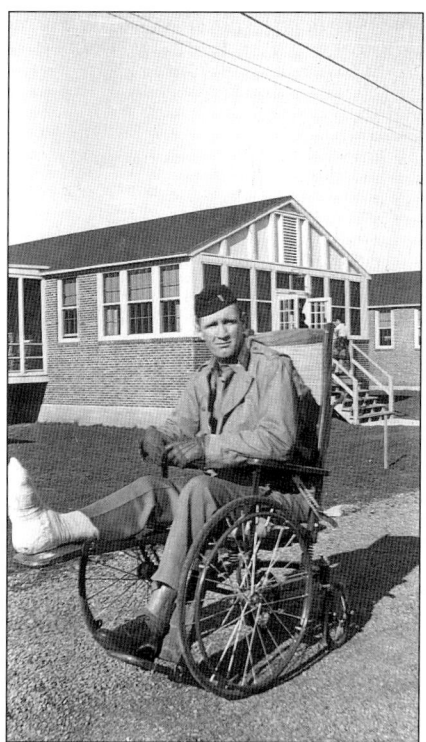

LEO CHARBONNEAU. *Left:* Charbonneau is shown with his Thunderbolt Fighter in England in 1944. Soon after this photograph was taken, he was shot down behind enemy lines. *Right:* Successfully evading capture, Charbonneau was smuggled through France by the Resistance. He is shown here recuperating at the Framingham Hospital in Massachusetts in 1945. He went on to become a lawyer and politician.

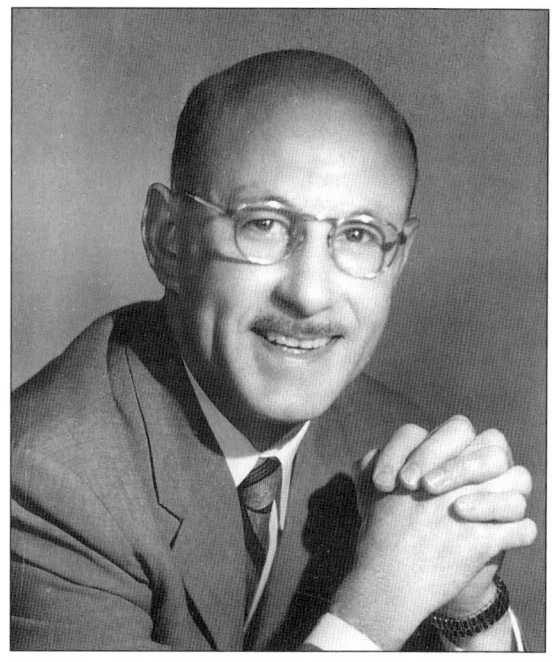

DR. JAMES KERSHAW, D.D.S., 1964. Dr. Kershaw has served as president of the Rhode Island Dental Association and has maintained an office in the valley since the 1930s.

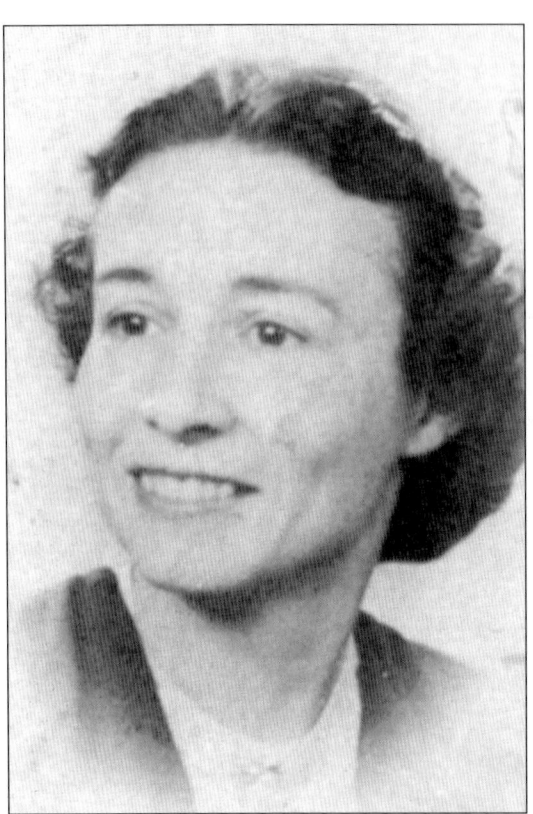

ALICE MORTON, 1933. Art teacher for over 40 years in the West Warwick school system, she is also the founder and first president of the Pawtuxet Valley Historical and Preservation Society.

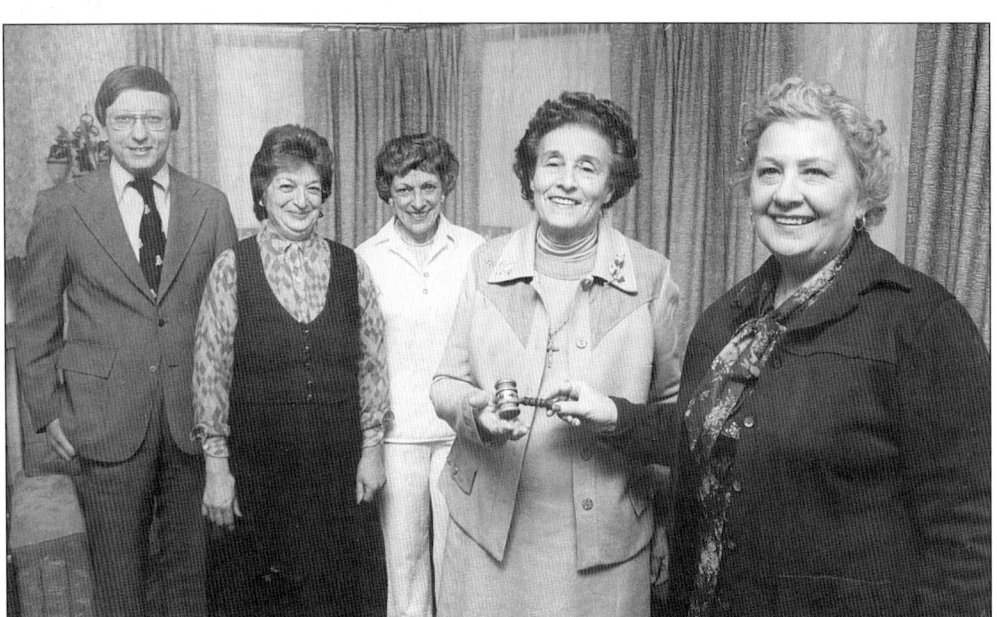

THE PAWTUXET VALLEY HISTORICAL AND PRESERVATION SOCIETY OFFICERS, 1982. The Pawtuxet Valley Historical and Preservation Society officers are shown in this view with Alice Morton, president.

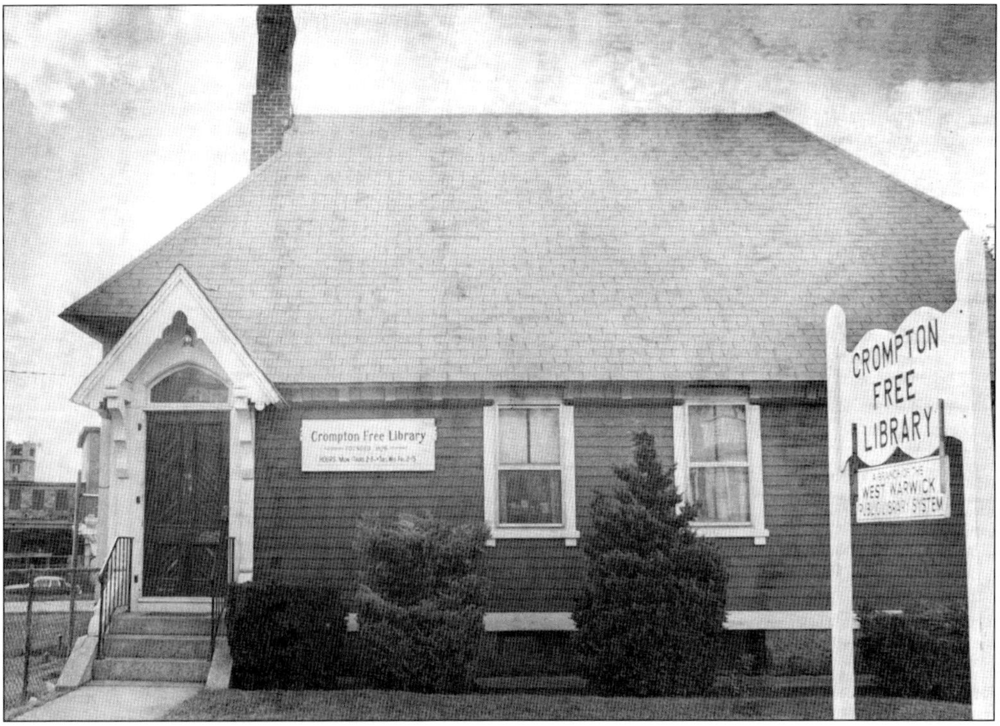

THE CROMPTON LIBRARY, C. 1985. This Queen Anne–style library was built in 1876 by the Crompton Company for the use of its employees and families. It was taken over by the town of West Warwick as a branch library after the end of the company village in the late 1940s.

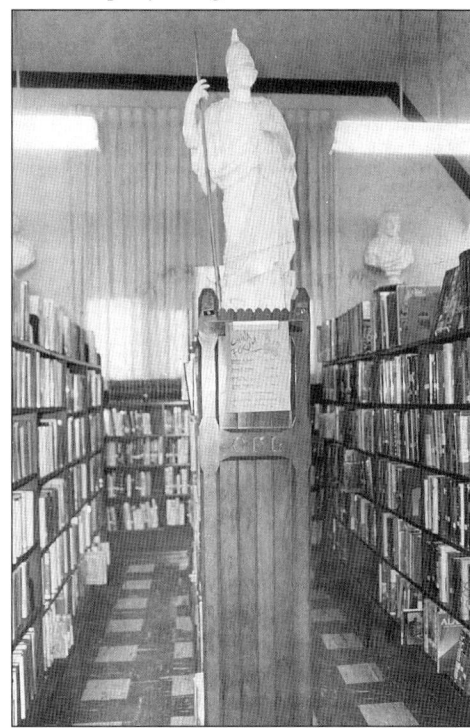

THE INTERIOR OF THE CROMPTON LIBRARY, C. 1985. The town of West Warwick closed the branch library and gave it to the Pawtuxet Valley Historical and Preservation Society as a museum and archive.

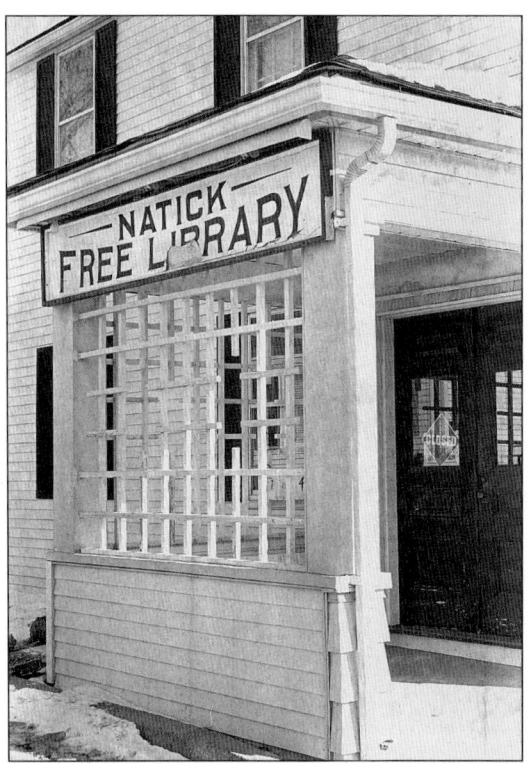

THE NATICK LIBRARY, 1982.

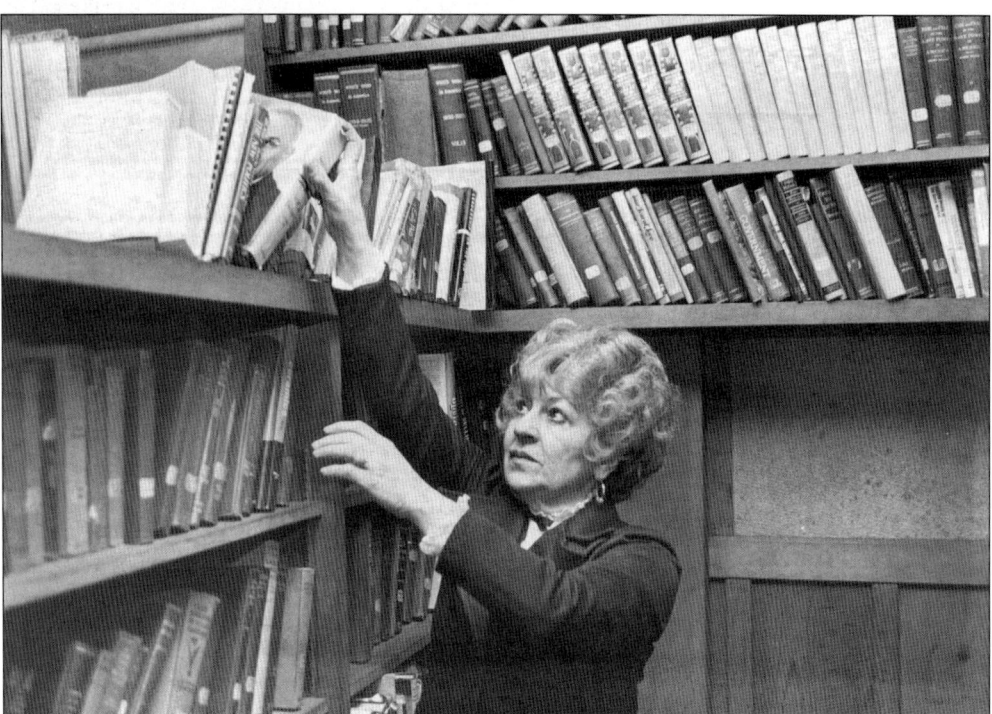

LIBRARIAN MARY MANNI, NATICK LIBRARY, JUST BEFORE CLOSURE, 1982. The Natick Library was another village library but was not acquired by the town.

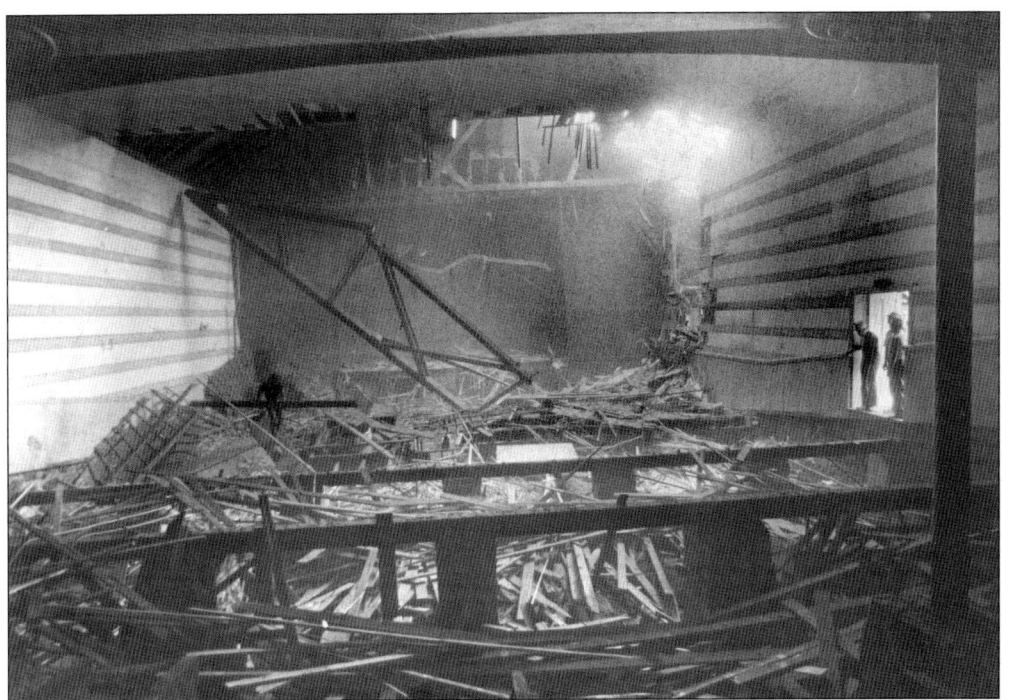

THORNTON'S THEATRE DEMOLITION, CLYDE, 1968.

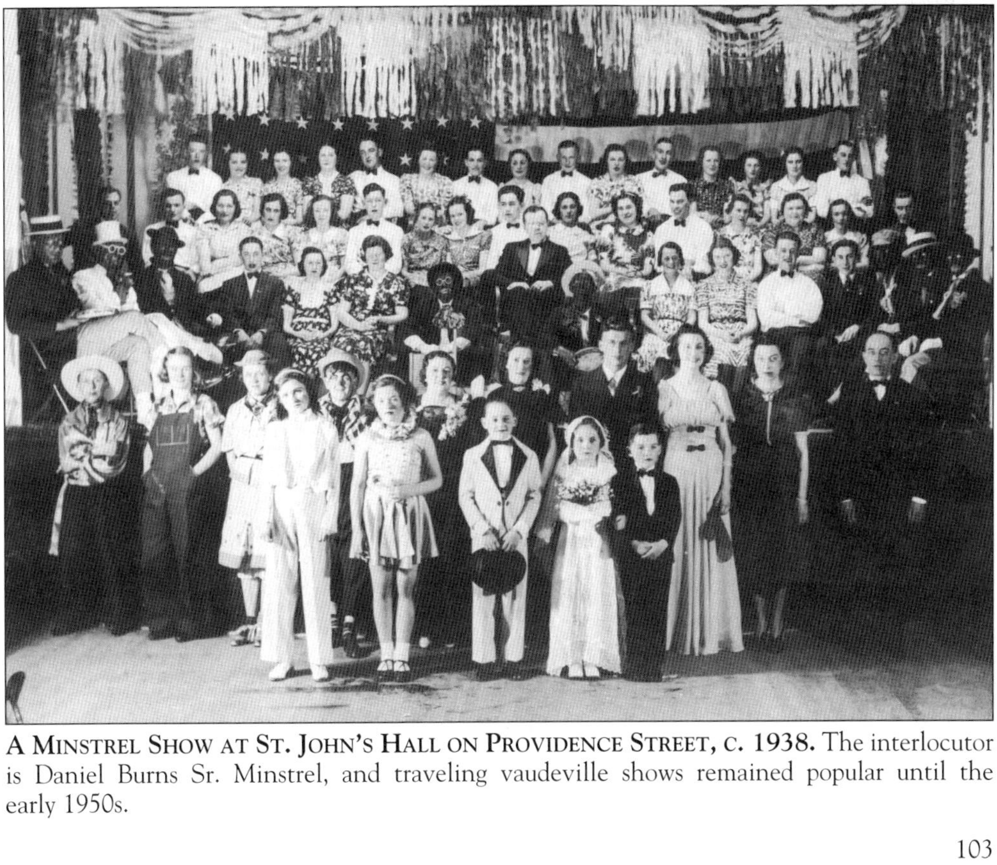

A MINSTREL SHOW AT ST. JOHN'S HALL ON PROVIDENCE STREET, C. 1938. The interlocutor is Daniel Burns Sr. Minstrel, and traveling vaudeville shows remained popular until the early 1950s.

AMBY SMITH, C. 1965. Amby Smith has been a beloved writer on sports, senior citizens, and other matters for the Pawtuxet Valley and now *Kent County Daily Times* newspaper. Smith has been covering Pawtuxet Valley events since the 1930s. He is shown at his desk at the Kent County Daily Times.

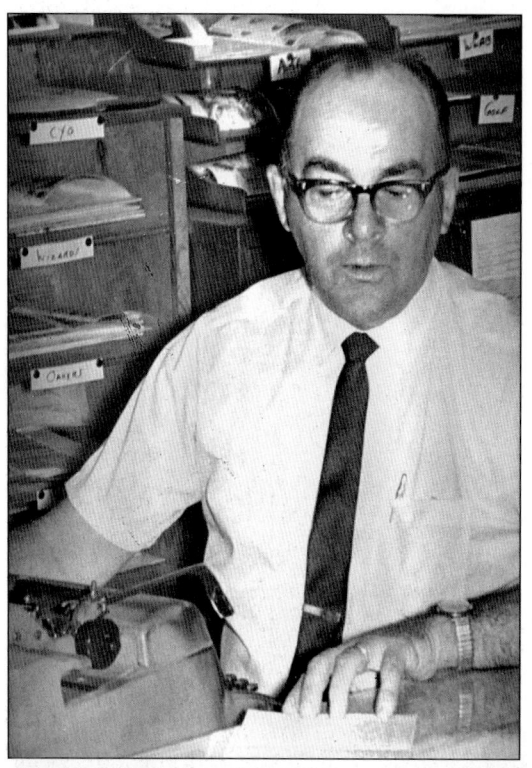

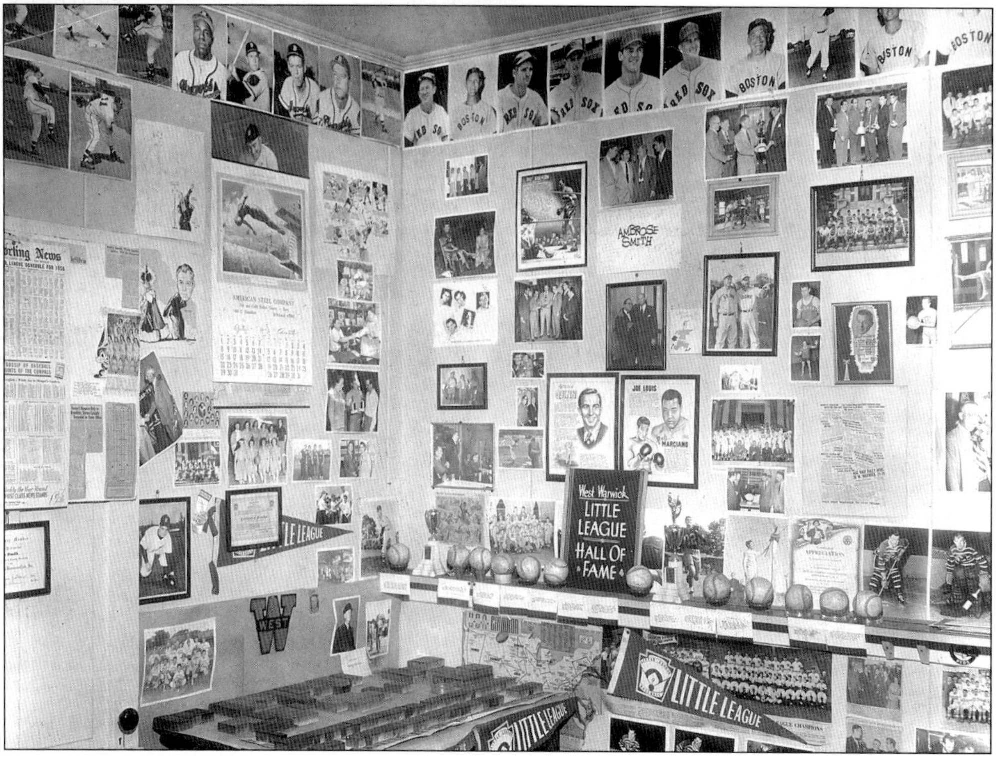

AMBY SMITH'S CORNER OFFICE, C. 1965.

THE PAWTUXET VALLEY DAILY TIMES, 1971. Old hot metal linotype machines are being replaced in this view. The newspaper was begun in 1892 and continues to report on valley events as the *Kent County Daily Times* today.

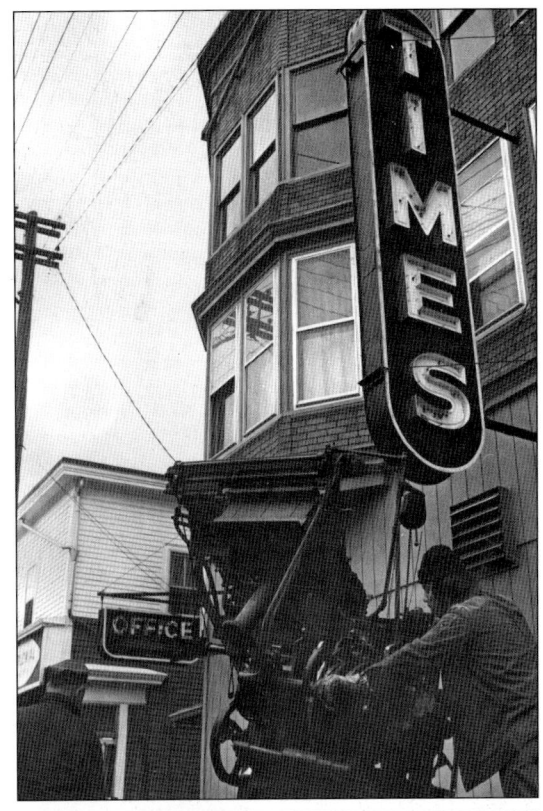

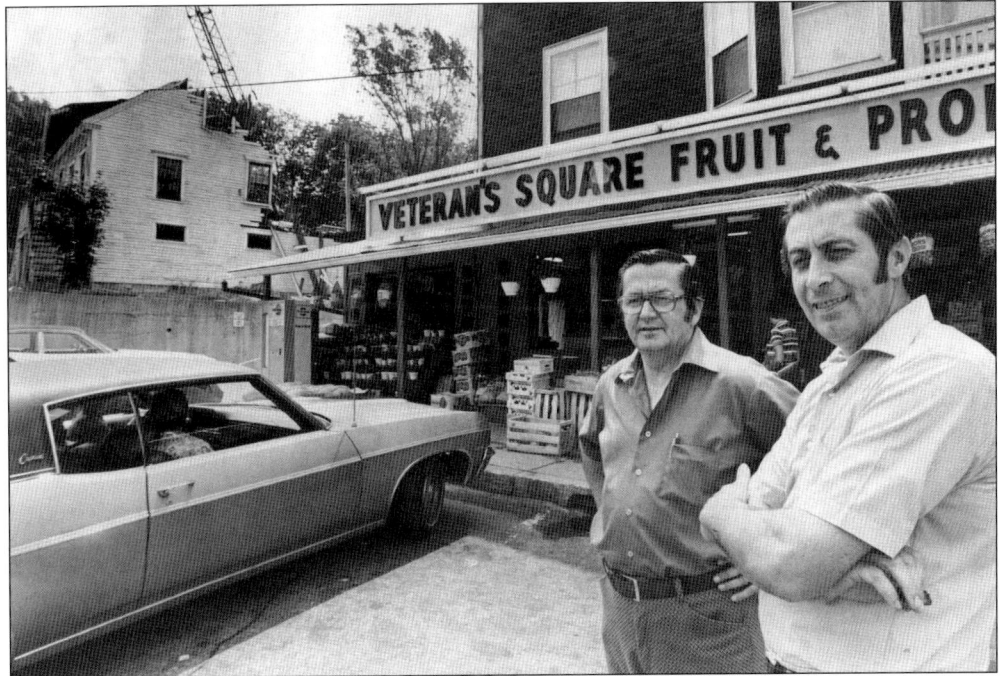

THE ROCH BROTHERS PLAN A NEW MARKET AT CENTREVILLE, 1976. Pictured are Gerry and brother "Legs" Roch at the busy corner of Main Street and Route 117.

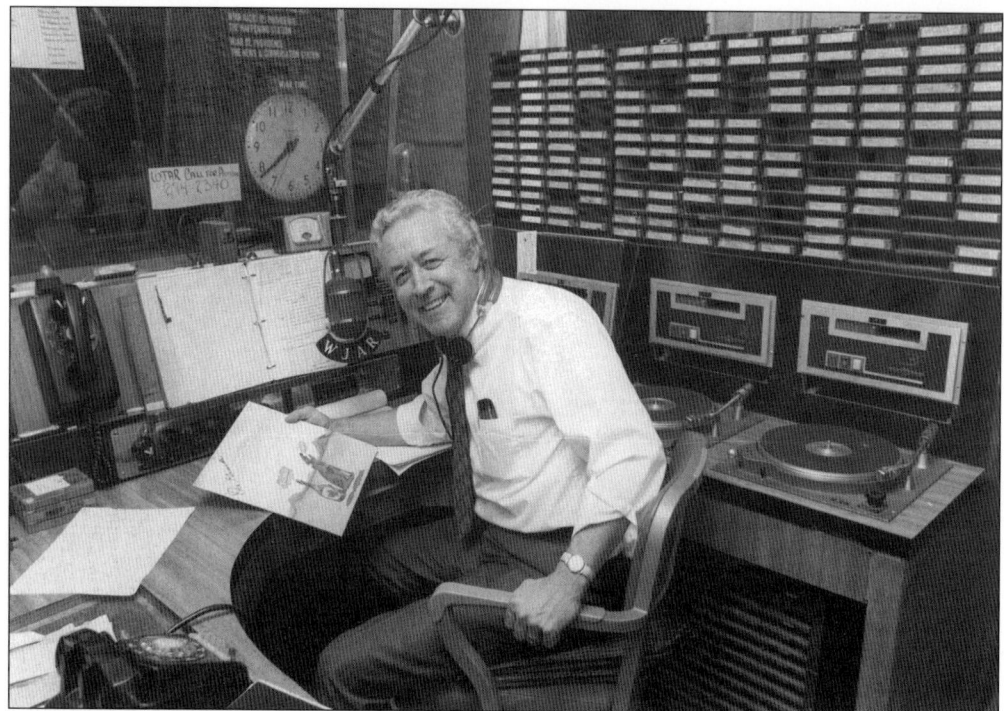

VOICE OF THE VALLEY GENE DEGRAIDE. A familiar sound to everyone in the area, DeGraide was at the local radio station WWRI for many years and is pictured here on moving to WJAR in the early 1970s.

 1913 GOLDEN JUBILEE – TOWN of WEST WARWICK 1963

WWRI

KENT COUNTY'S MOST EFFECTIVE ADVERTISING MEDIUM

1450 On Every Dial

AN ADVERTISEMENT FROM THE RADIO STATION WWRI, 1963. The Pawtuxet Valley was served by a local radio station until the early 1990s.

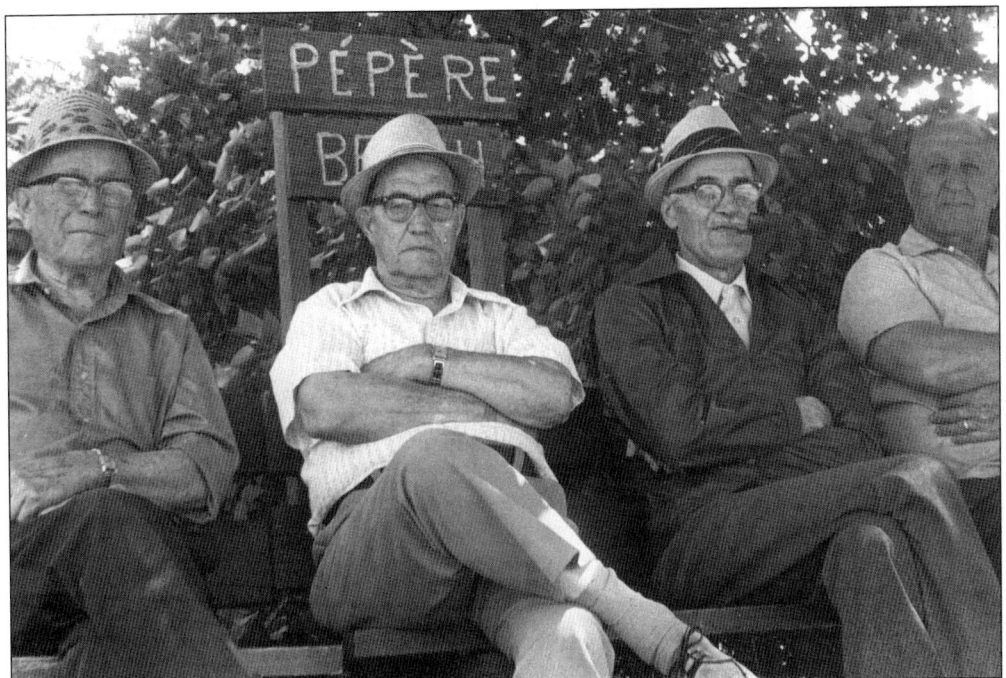

Pepere Bench at Legion Way, Arctic, 1975. This was a choice spot to watch the world go by.

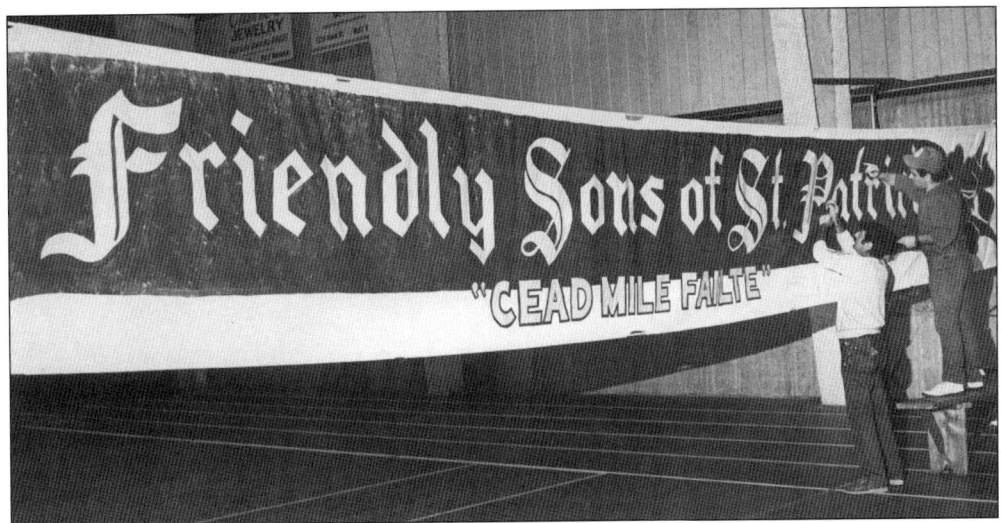

St. Patrick's Day Parade Banner from the Friendly Sons of St. Patrick, 1984. This group continues the tradition of a St. Patrick's Day parade in West Warwick, marching through Arctic Center every year.

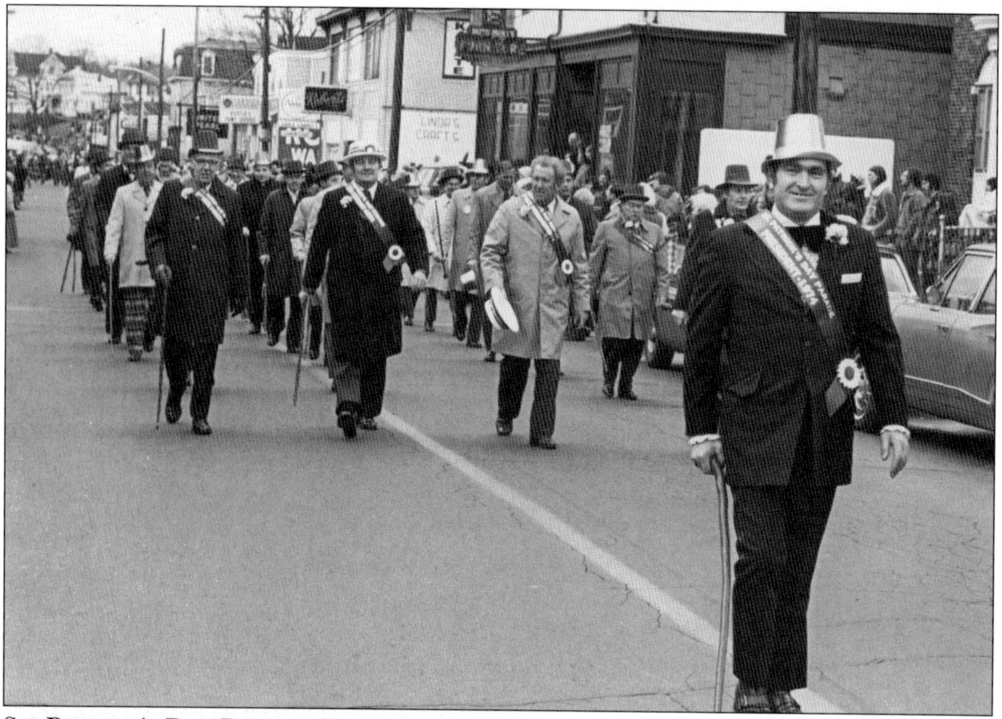

St. Patrick's Day Parade Officials on Washington Street in Arctic, 1974.

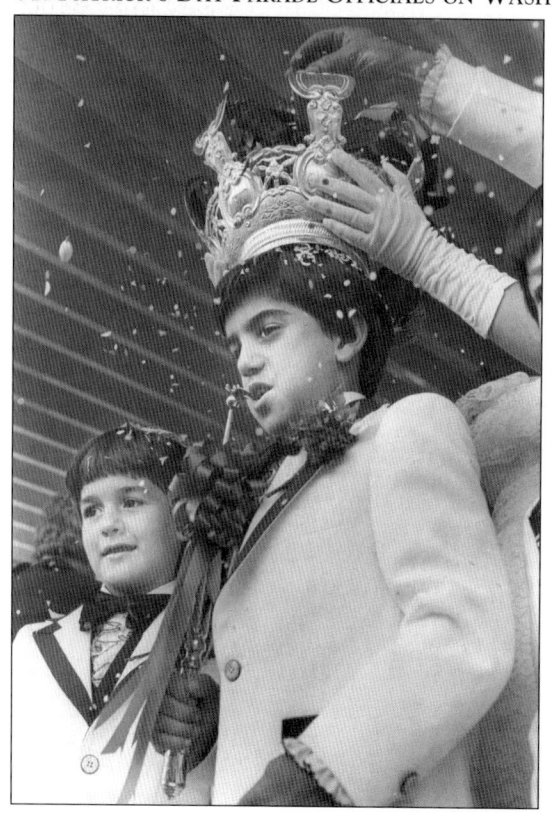

The King and Queen of the Festa in Clyde, 1989.

THE HOLY GHOST HALL IN LIPPITT. This is the destination of parades and processions during the Labor Day Portuguese Festival. It is shown here being readied for the 1989 festa.

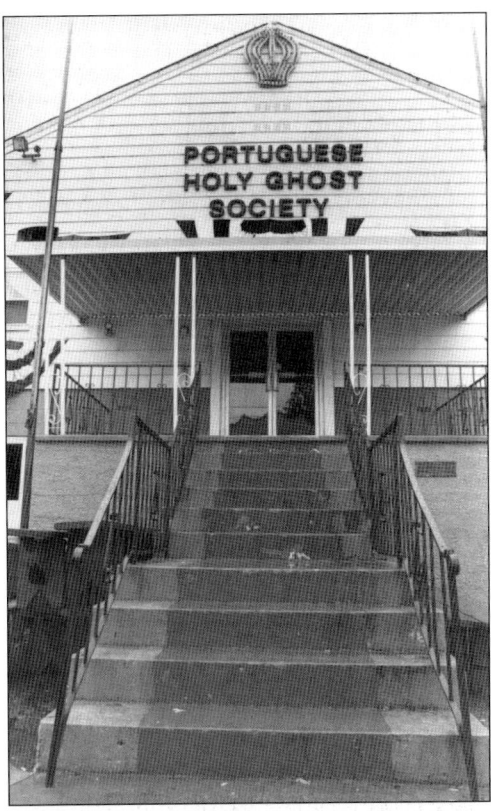

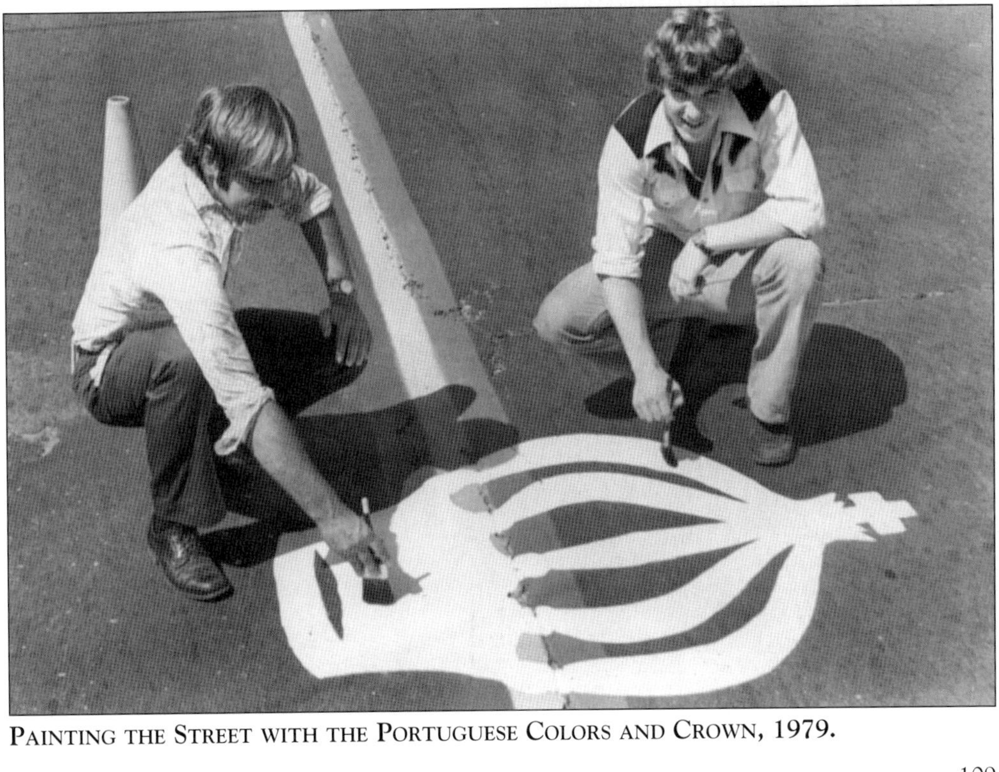

PAINTING THE STREET WITH THE PORTUGUESE COLORS AND CROWN, 1979.

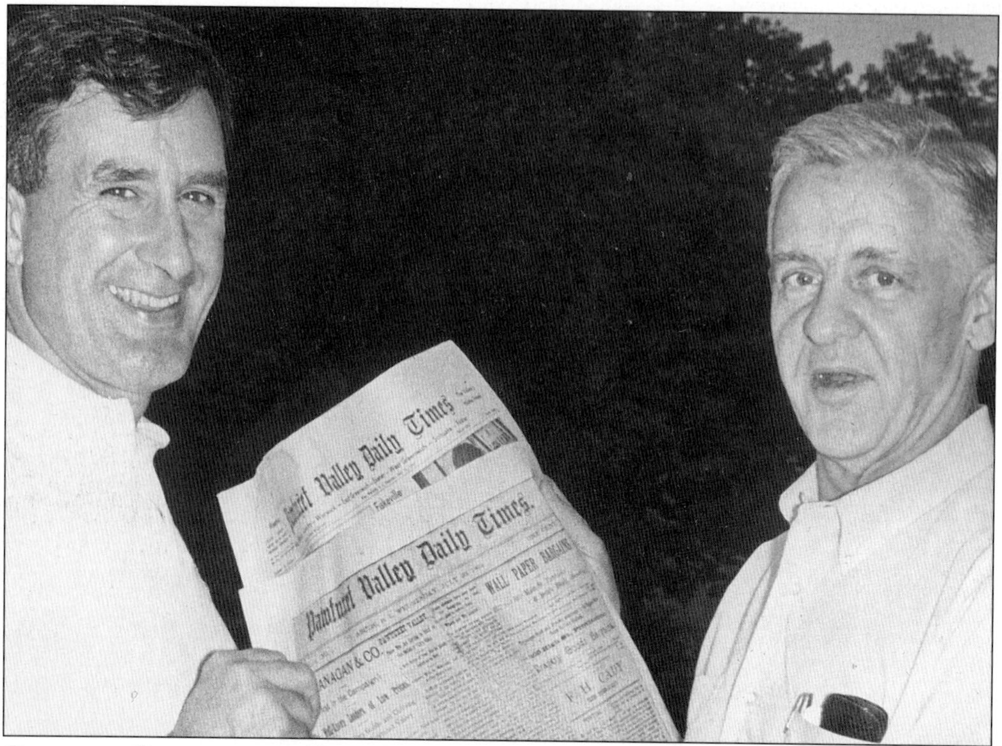

GOVERNOR CHAFEE AT THE KENT COUNTY DAILY TIMES OFFICE, 1967.

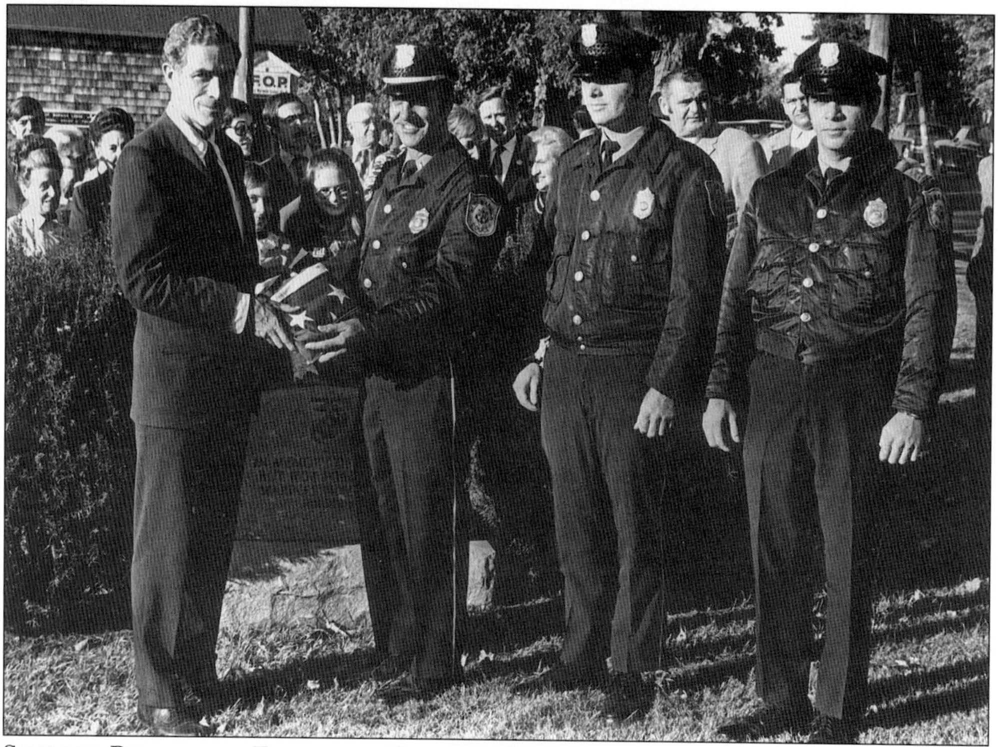

SENATOR PELL AT THE FRATERNAL ORDER OF POLICE IN CENTREVILLE, 1971.

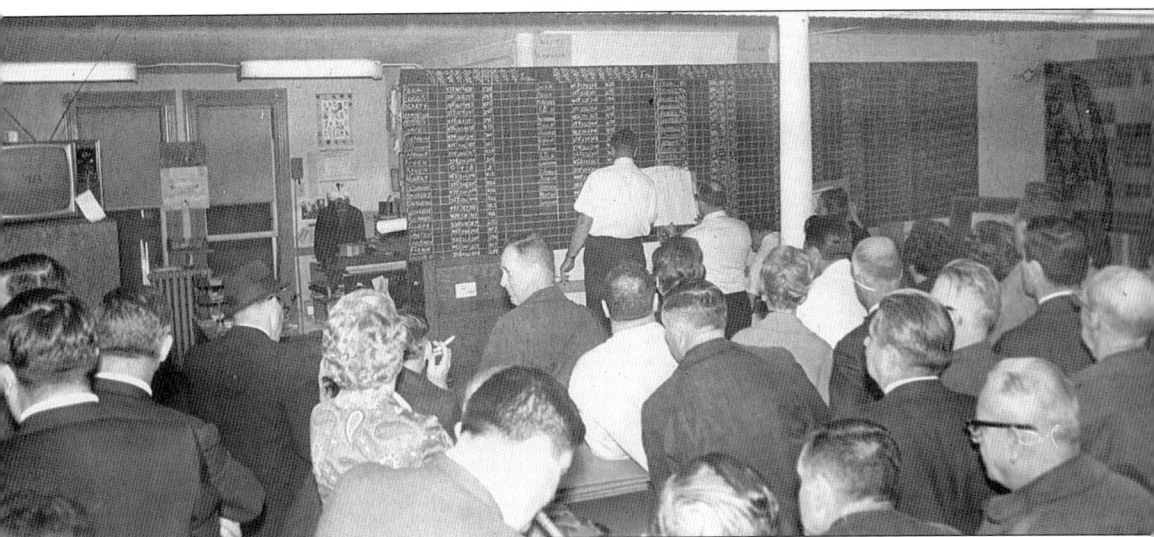

ELECTION NIGHT, 1966. Votes are tallied at the Kent County Daily Times office. Politics in the Pawtuxet Valley was often a raucous and colorful affair.

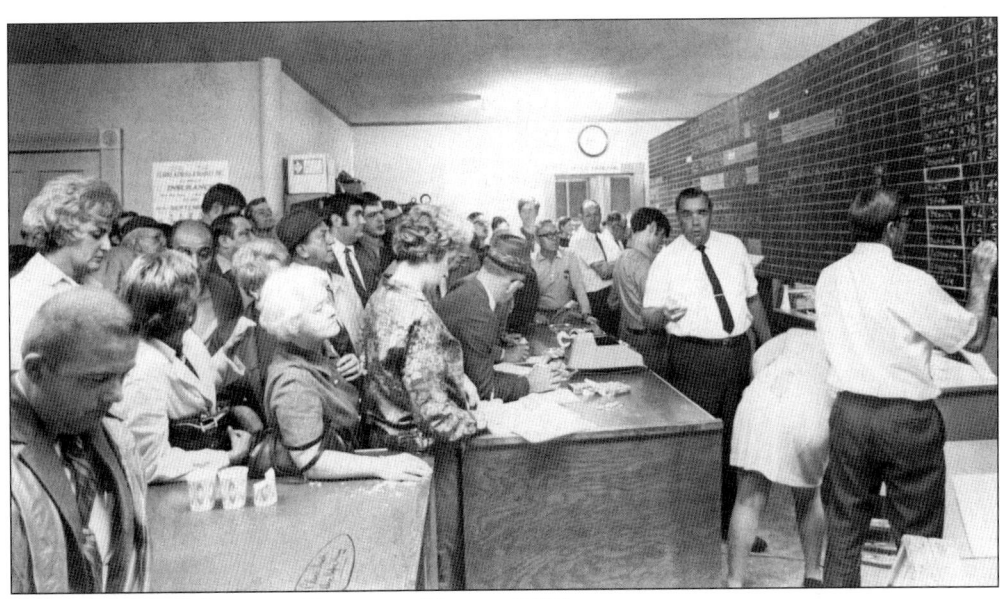

COUNTING THE VOTES ON ELECTION NIGHT, 1970.

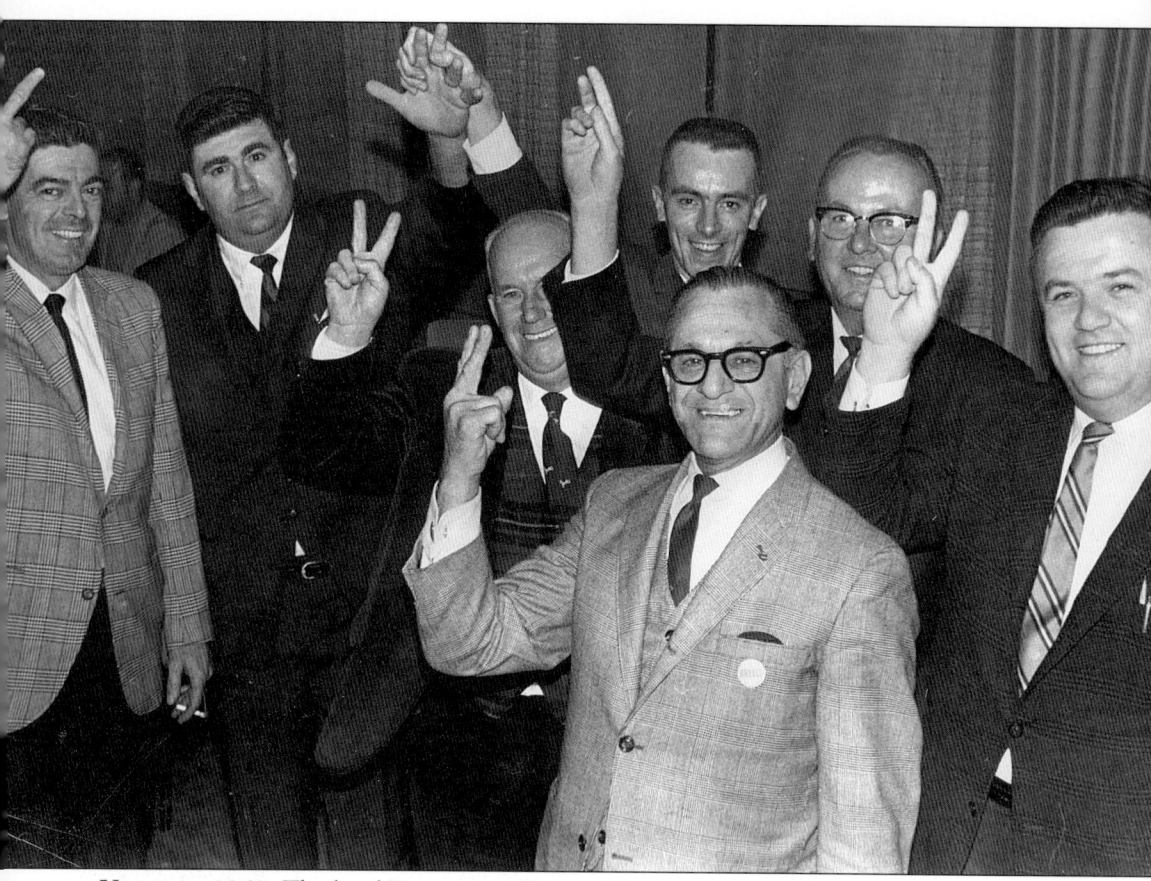

VICTORY, 1968. The local Democratic Party celebrates success at the polls. From left to right are Ray Silva, Anthony Santilli, Senator LaChapelle (partially hidden), Al Muschiano (in front), Dave Brindamour (behind Muschiano), Fulda Geoffroy, and Bob Carley.

Seven
Serving the Public

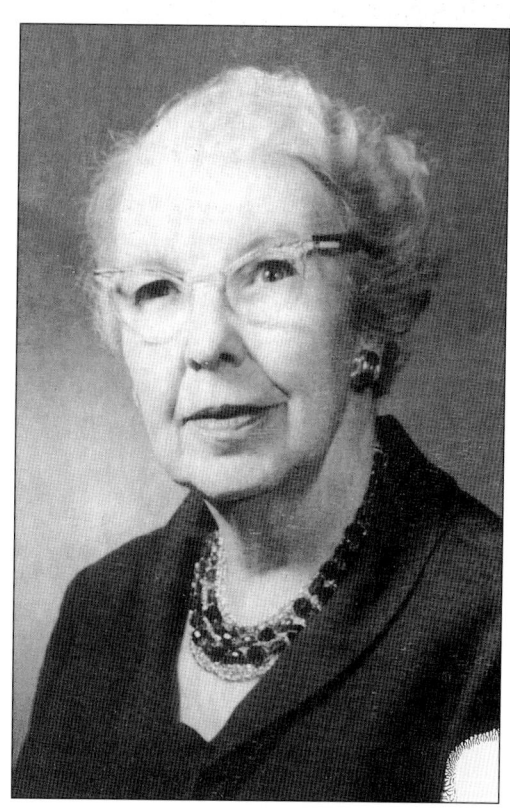

Maisie Quinn, Longtime Superintendent of Schools in West Warwick. The Quinn family figured prominently in the creation of West Warwick in 1913. They have continued to serve the public to the present.

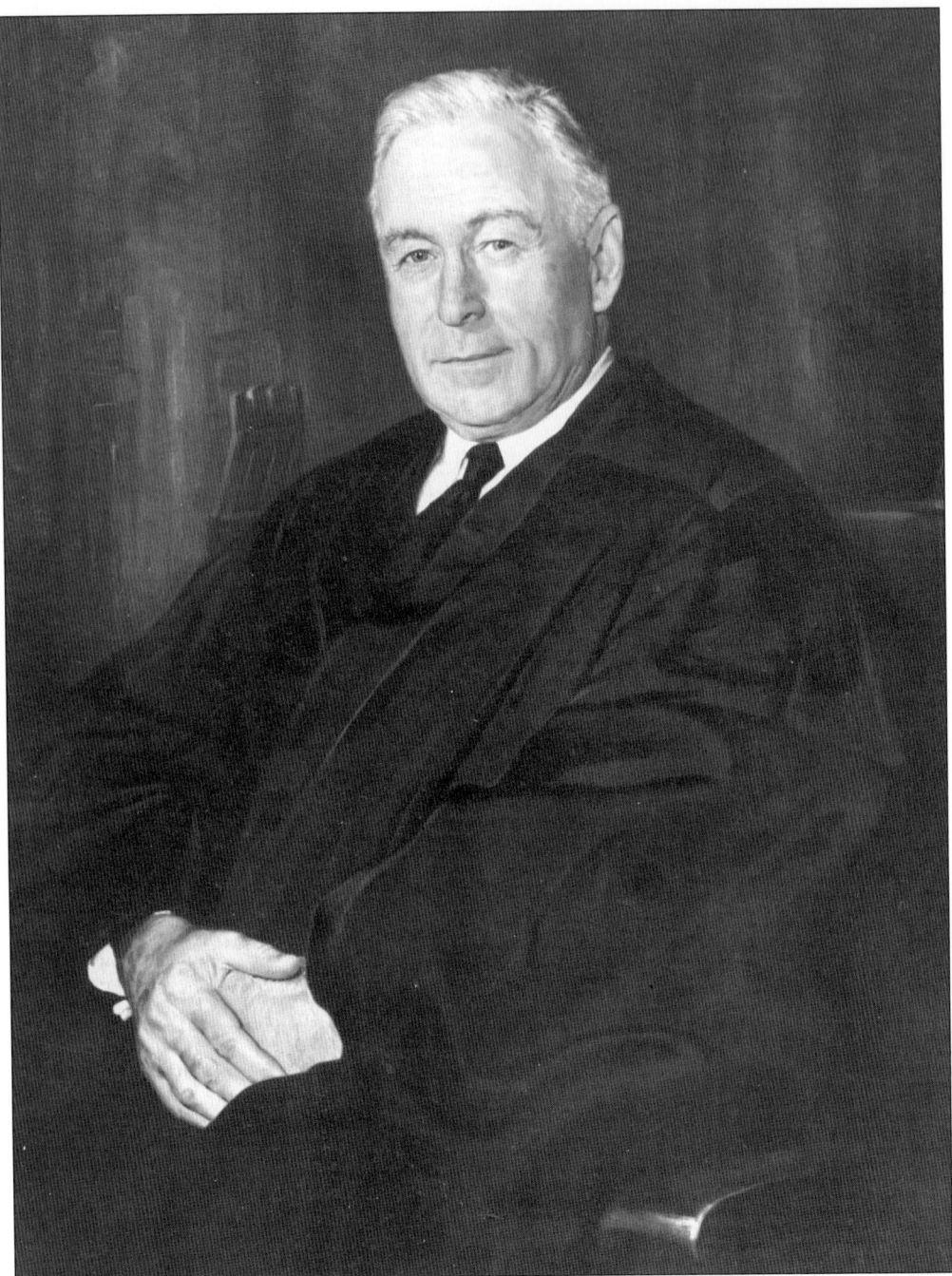

GOVERNOR QUINN, C. 1950. Residing on Wakefield Street in West Warwick, Governor Quinn (and later, Judge Quinn) was the last of a long line of Pawtuxet Valley residents to serve as Rhode Island's governor. As the textile industry waned, the political power of the area declined with it.

THE MAISIE QUINN SCHOOL CHOIR, CHRISTMAS 1974. Students from grades one through five are shown under the direction of music teacher Janice McClintock.

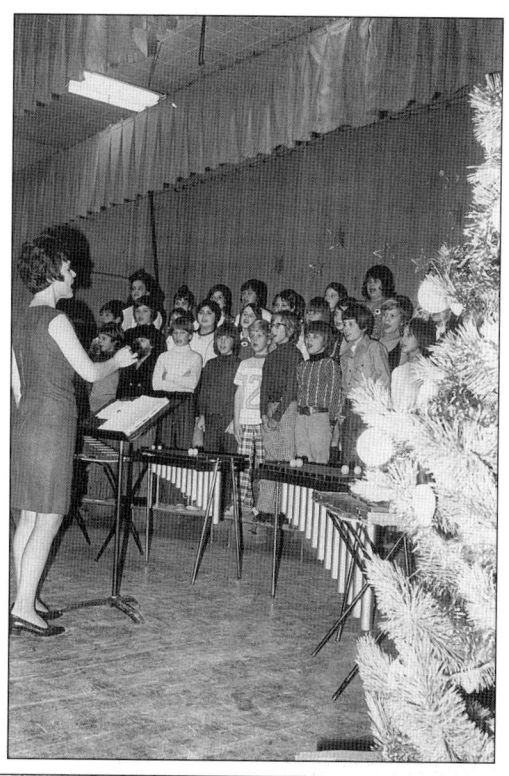

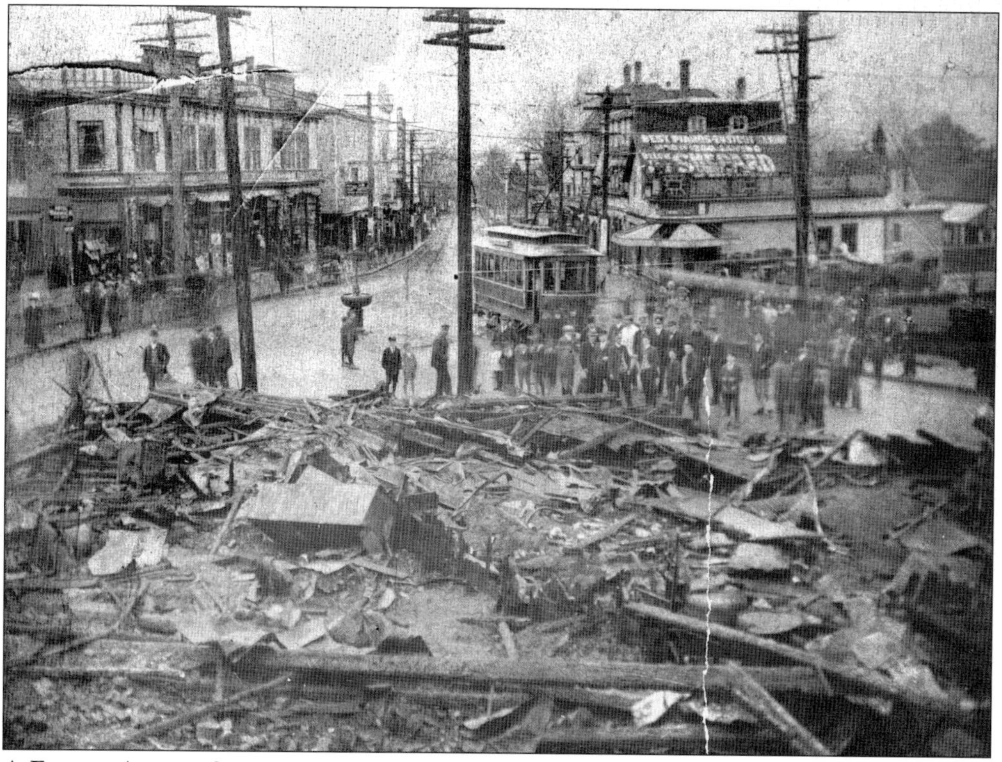

A FIRE IN ARCTIC SQUARE, NOVEMBER 1909.

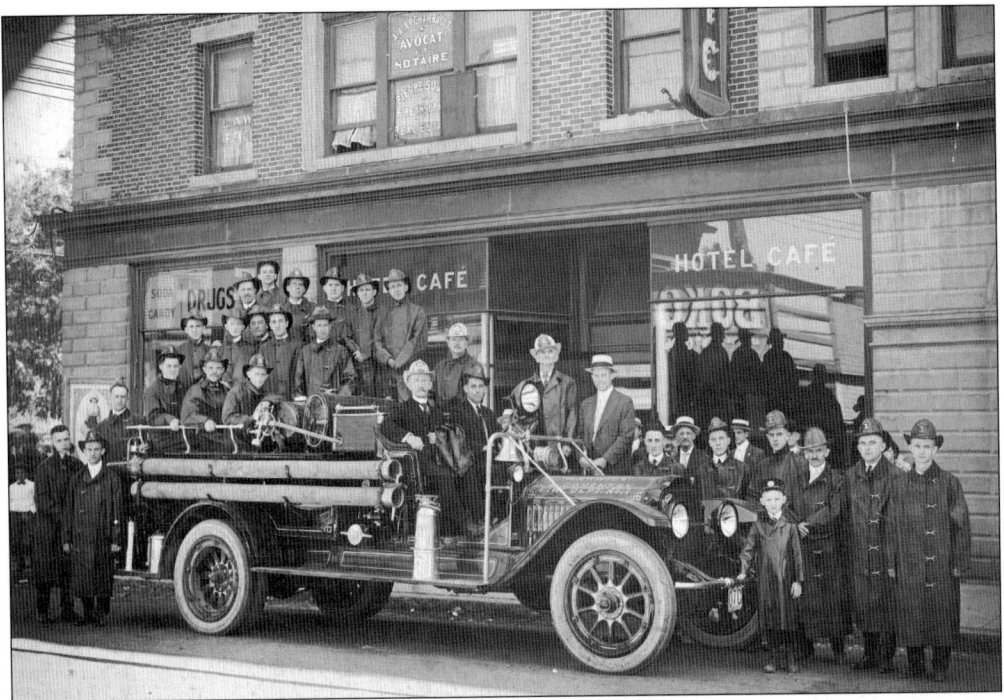

THE WARWICK AND COVENTRY FIRE DEPARTMENT TAKES DELIVERY OF A NEW ENGINE, SEPTEMBER 1918. This is a scene in front of the Majestic Building on Washington Street in Arctic Center.

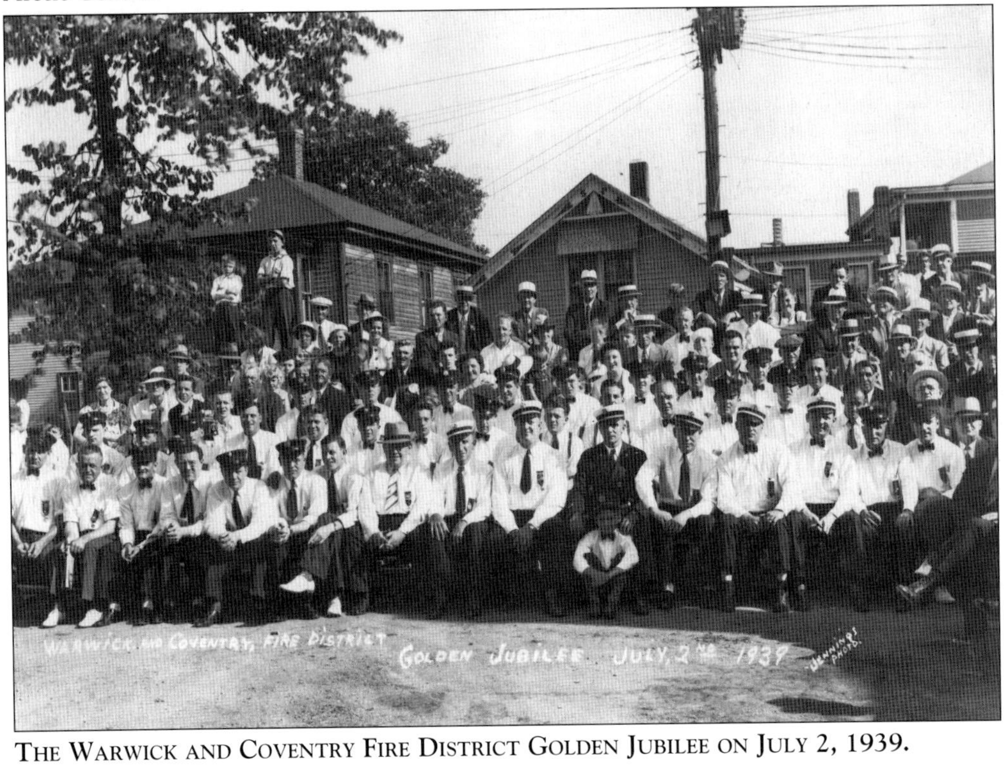

THE WARWICK AND COVENTRY FIRE DISTRICT GOLDEN JUBILEE ON JULY 2, 1939.

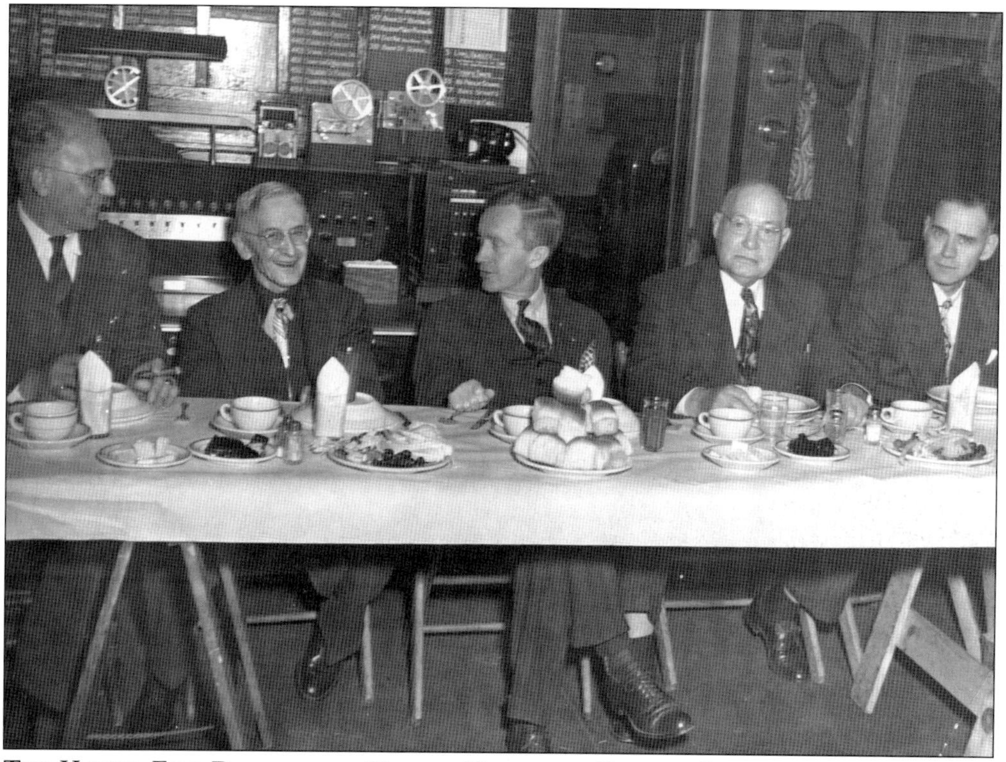

THE HARRIS FIRE DEPARTMENT DINNER HONORING FORMER CHIEF WALTER J. BERARD.
Most fire services were volunteer in the area until the mid-20th century. The last volunteer fire companies in the Pawtuxet Valley were phased out by the city of Cranston in the village of Fiskeville in the 1990s.

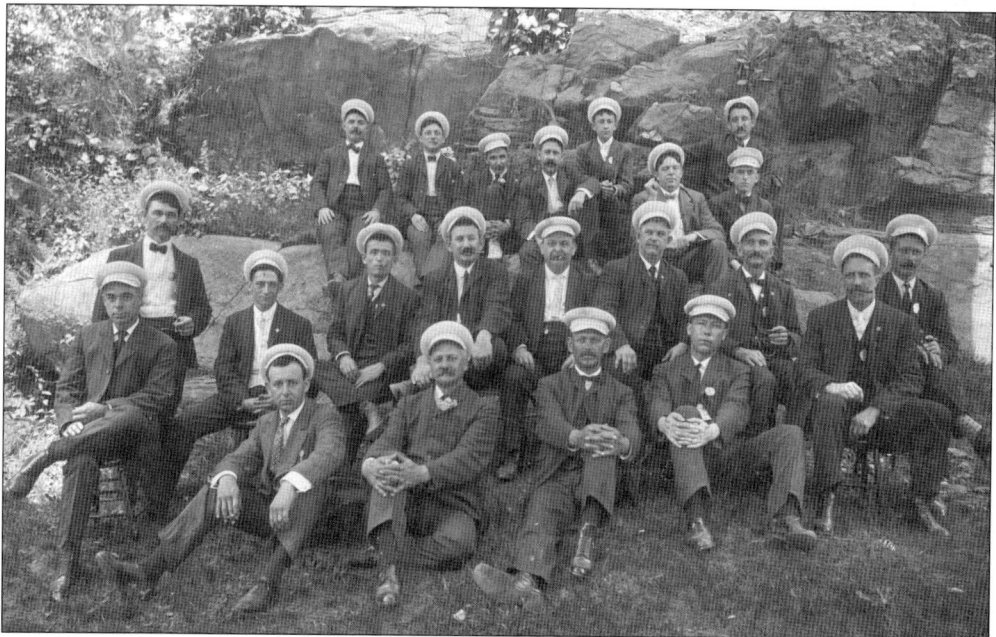

HARRIS FIRE DEPARTMENT OUTING, ROCKY POINT, JULY 1905.

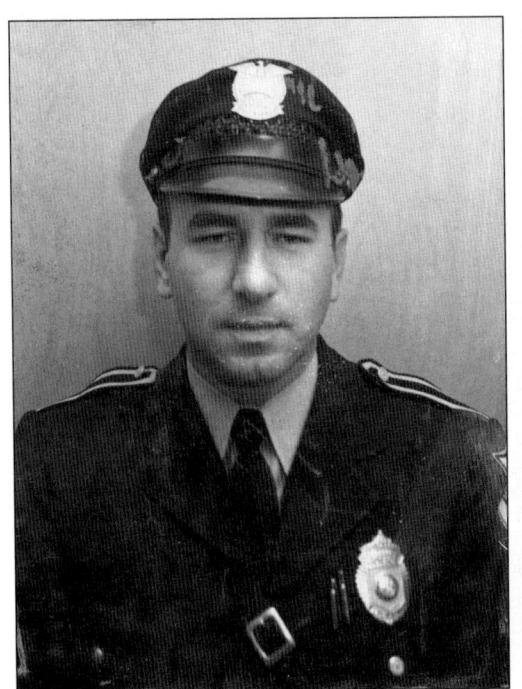 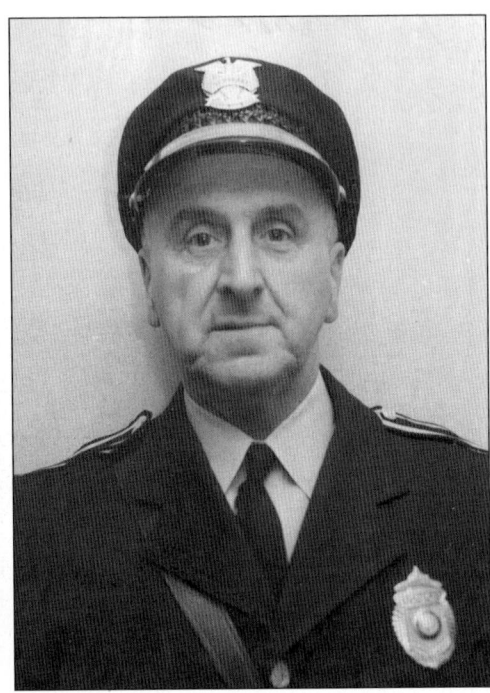

MEMBERS OF THE WEST WARWICK POLICE DEPARTMENT, 1961. Shown here are Sgt. Manuel Simas Jr. (left) and Lt. Leo Ritchotte.

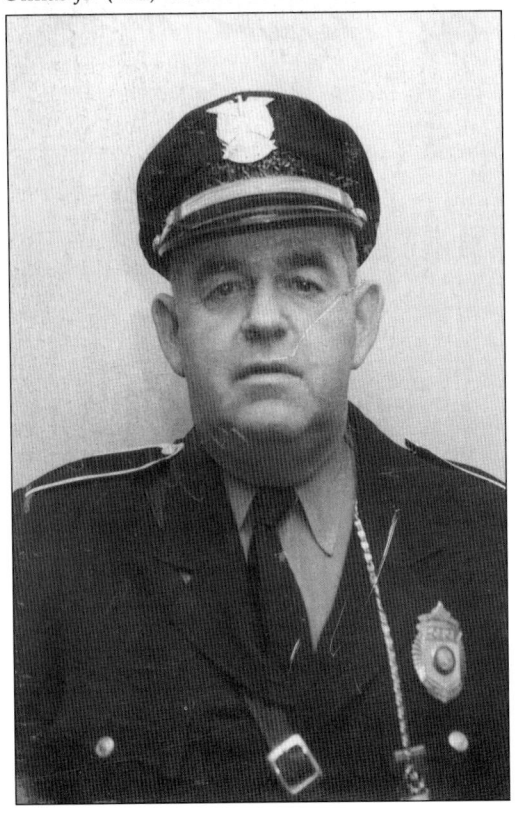

SGT. RAYMOND MILLER OF THE WEST WARWICK POLICE DEPARTMENT, 1961.

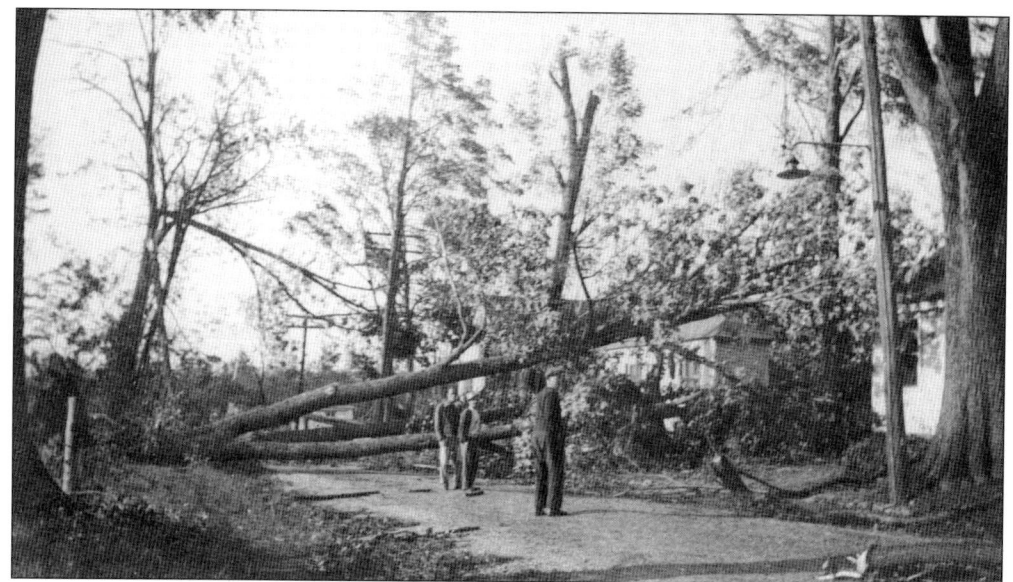

TREES DOWN FROM THE HURRICANE OF 1938 IN THE VILLAGE OF HOPE.

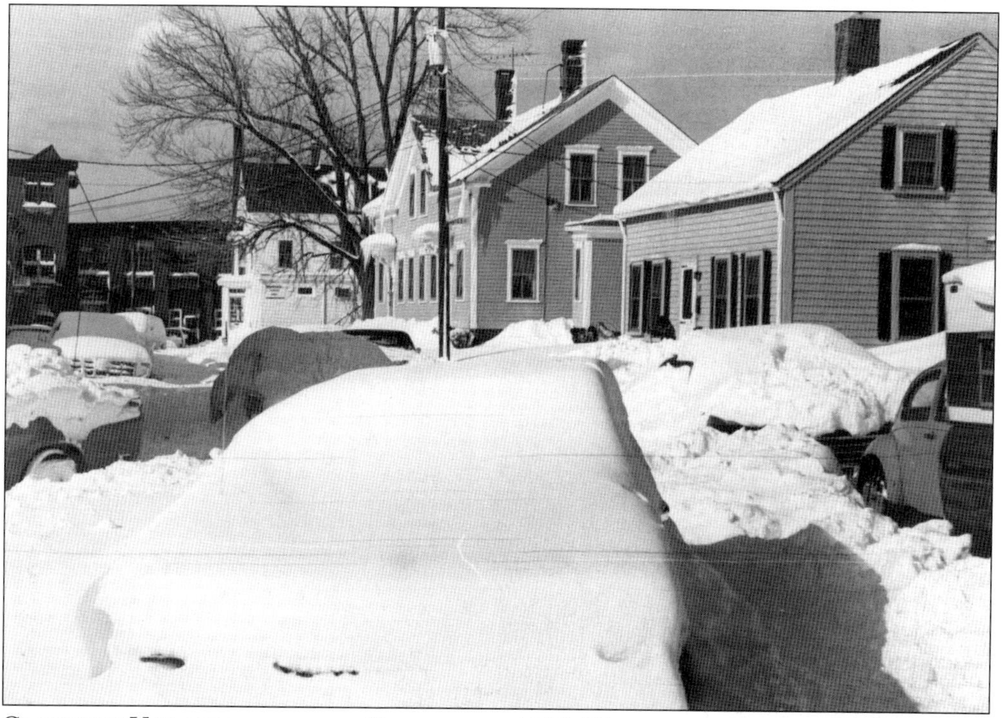

CROMPTON VILLAGE DURING THE BLIZZARD OF 1978. This surprise storm paralyzed the entire state for over a week, and this street scene was typical of even major roads and highways. Residents were forced to resort to walking or snowmobiling to get around, and many were without heat or power for the better part of a week. The governor activated the National Guard to assist in the digging out, but it was some time before things got back to normal.

The Blizzard of 1978 in Arctic.

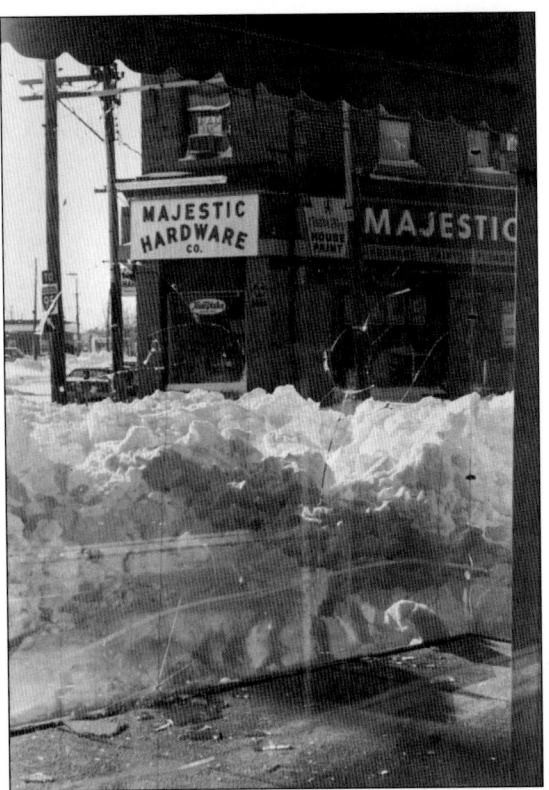

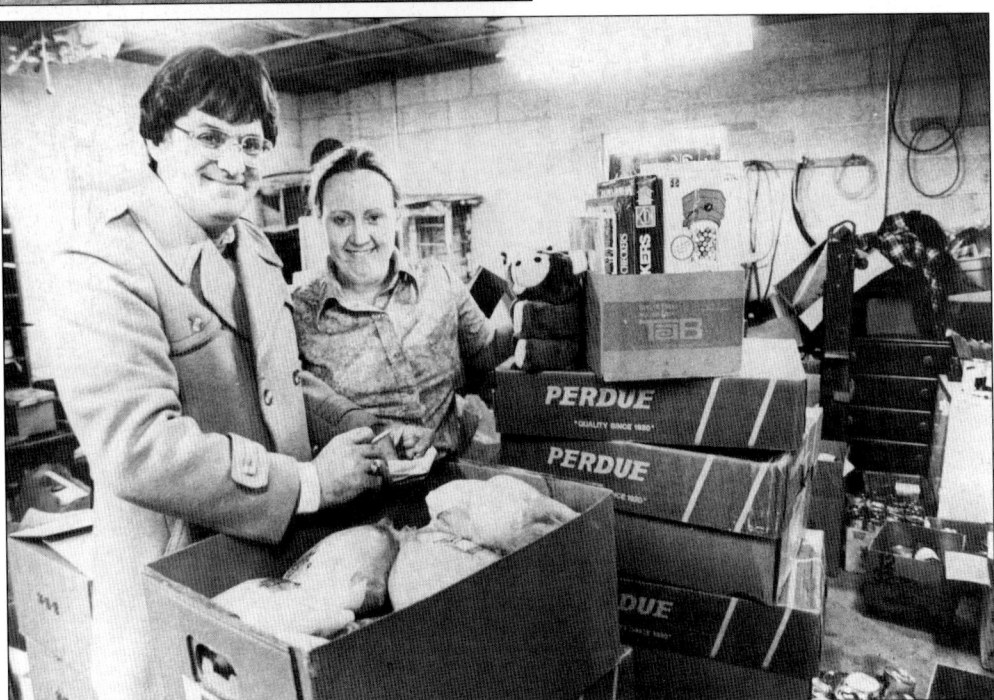

Tom Iannitti Helps Set up the Christmas Charity Drive, 1980. Each year, food and gifts are given to needy Pawtuxet Valley families through the Christmas Is charity drive.

Eight
Pawtuxet River Rebirth

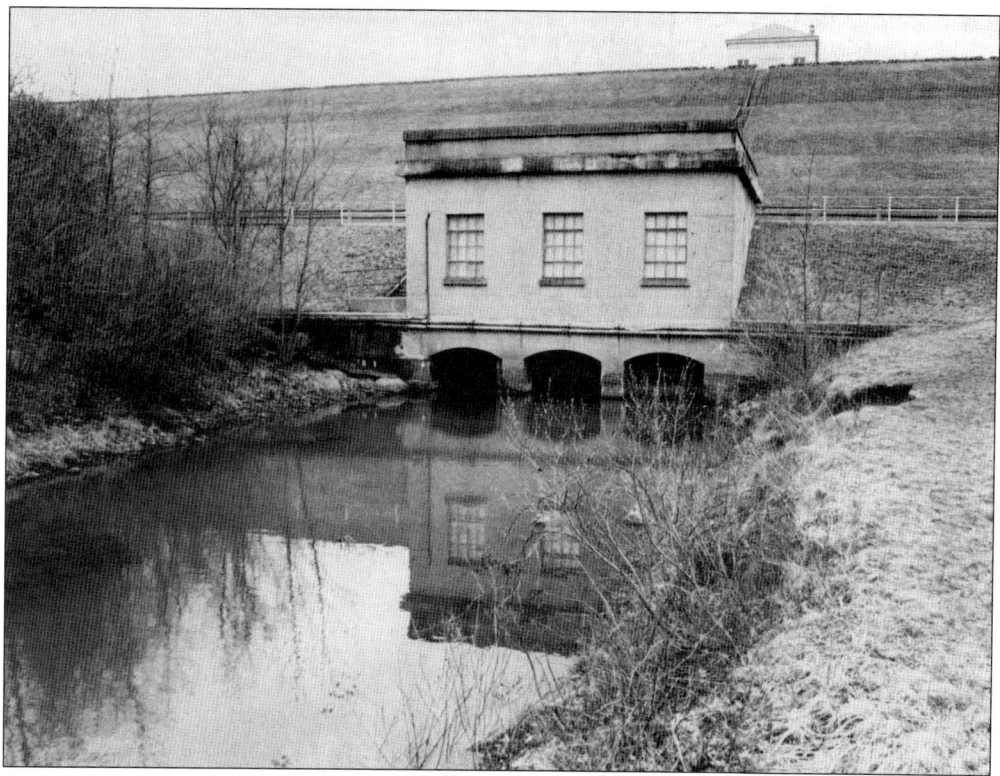

THE SCITUATE DAM, 1927. In the mid-1920s, a large reservoir was built in the town of Scituate to provide drinking water to the Providence area. This area was also the headwaters of the North Branch of the Pawtuxet River. Several small villages were inundated by the project, and the flow of the river was regulated.

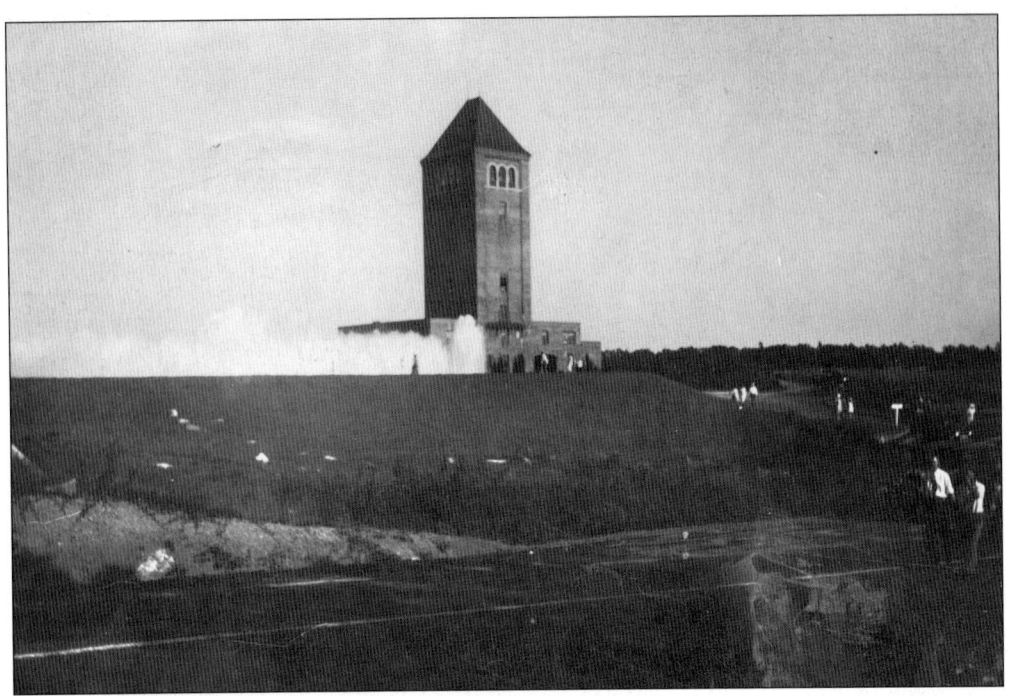

The Old Scituate Water-Purification Plant, c. 1930.

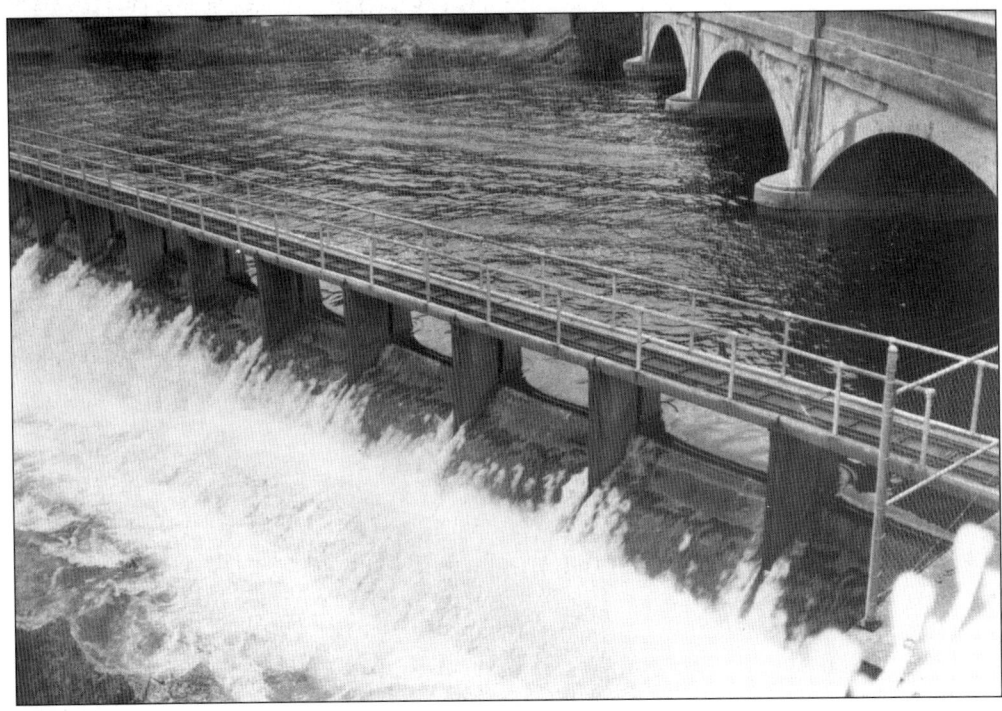

The Spillway at the Scituate Dam.

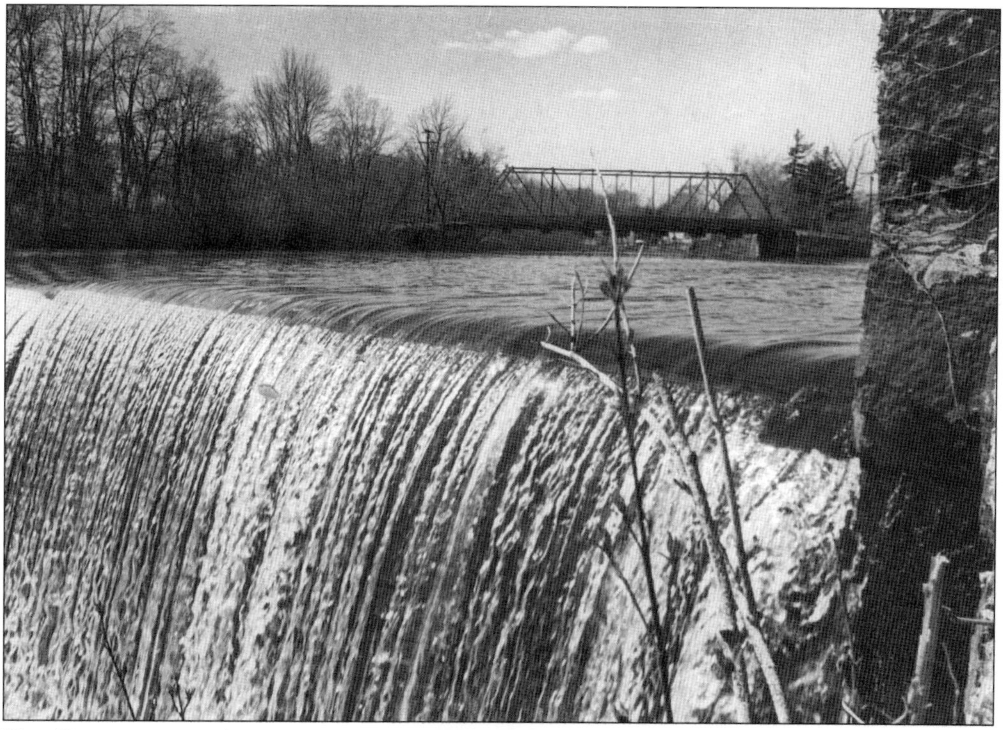

THE FALLS AT THE ARKWRIGHT BRIDGE. As industry moved from waterpower to other sources of energy, the river and its dams and banks became neglected, eventually being used as a dumping ground for litter or sewage overflow.

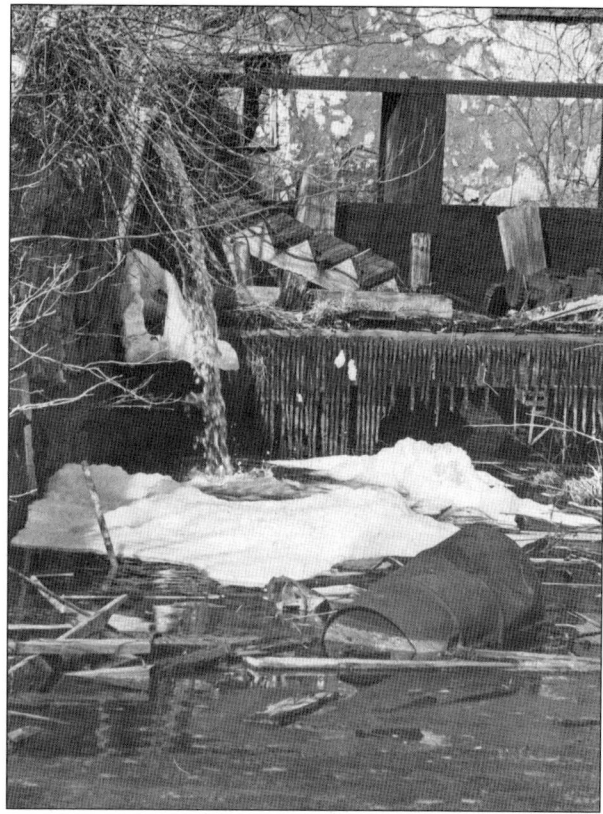

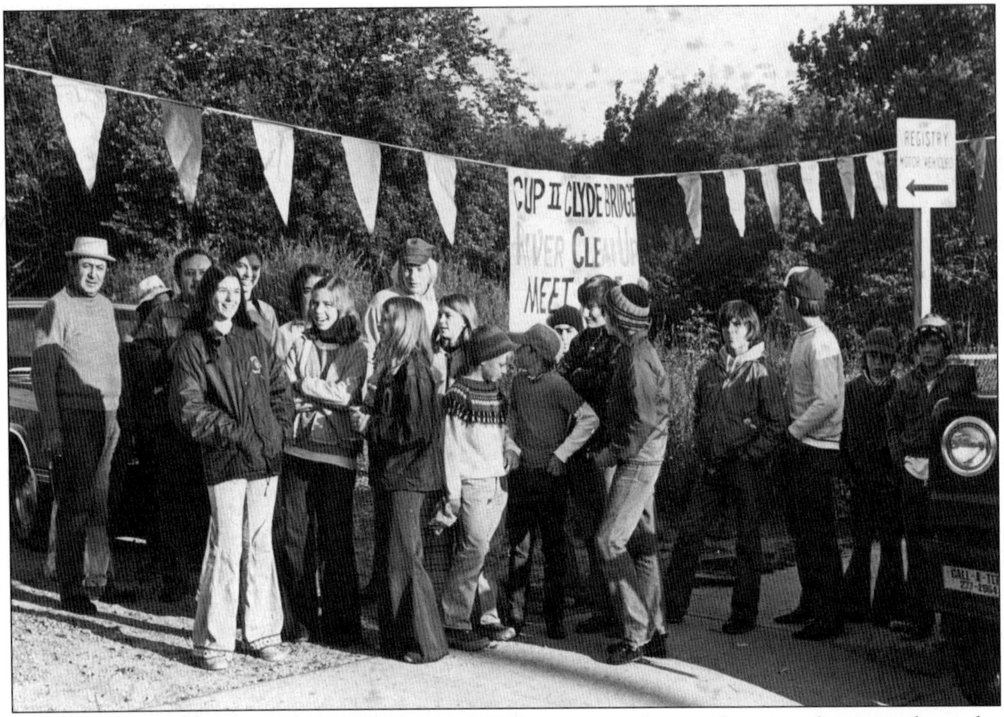

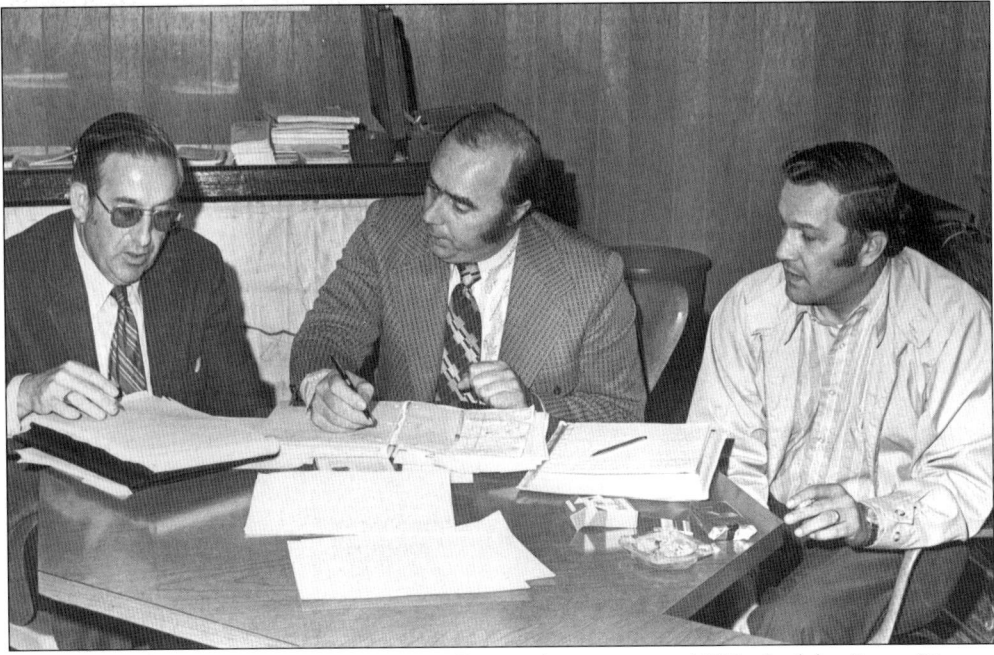

CLEAN UP THE PAWTUXET (CUP), 1972. CUP was one of several major cleanups along the Pawtuxet River in the early 1970s. This one is led by state senator Donald Roch.

THE FIRST BOARD OF THE PAWTUXET RIVER AUTHORITY, 1972. Led by Rene Dionne (center), this body grew out of the demand by the public for environmental protection and the foresight of Sen. Donald Roch. Coupled with new sewer treatment plants and strong cleanwater laws, the Pawtuxet River Authority helped to turn things around for the Pawtuxet River.

CANOEING ALONG THE PAWTUXET RIVER, 1994.

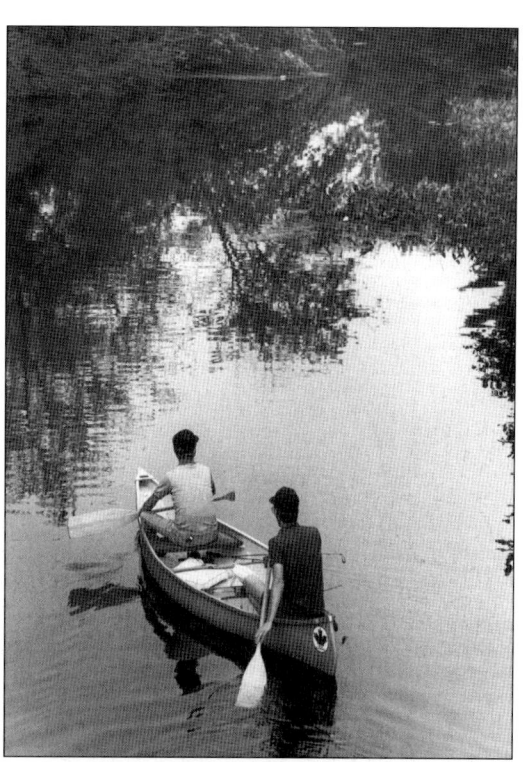

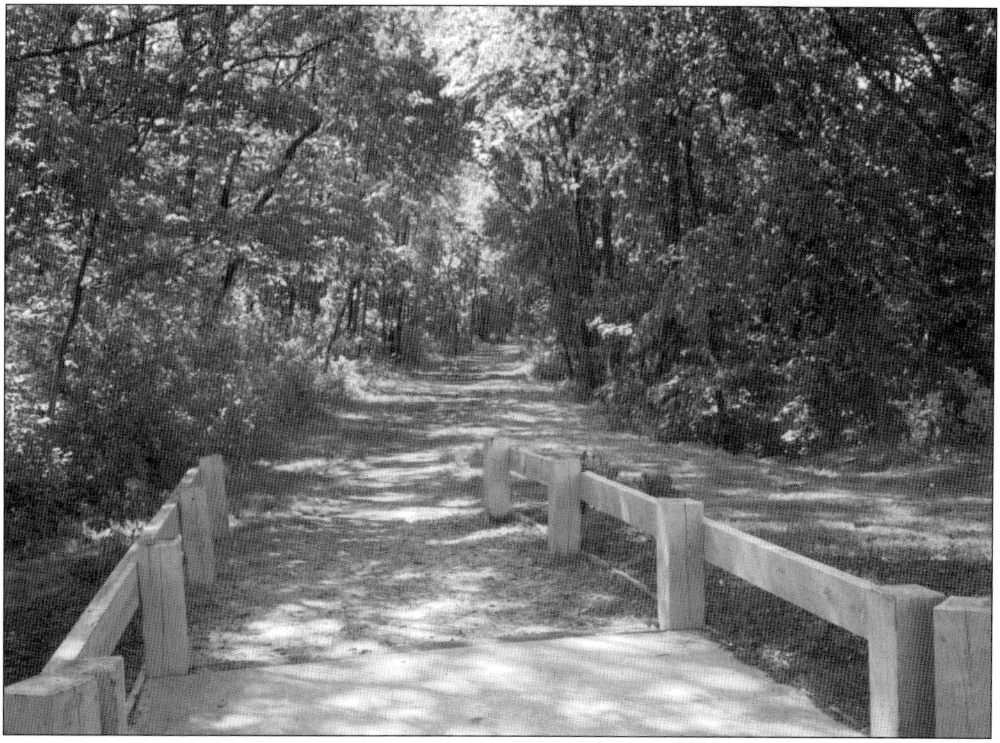

THE PHENIX-HARRIS RIVER WALK. When the railroad rights-of-way were abandoned in the 1980s, a system of river walks and bicycle paths began to be built to replace them.

A QUIET MOMENT ON THE NORTH BRANCH OF THE PAWTUXET, C. 1970. At Harris Village Dam, more people have begun to use the Pawtuxet for recreation, fishing, and hiking on the shore, as the banks and water have been made cleaner.

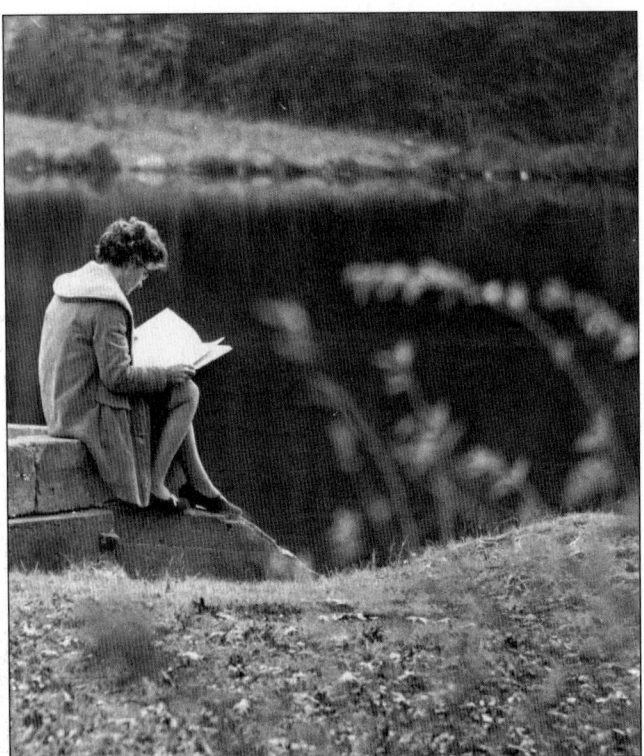

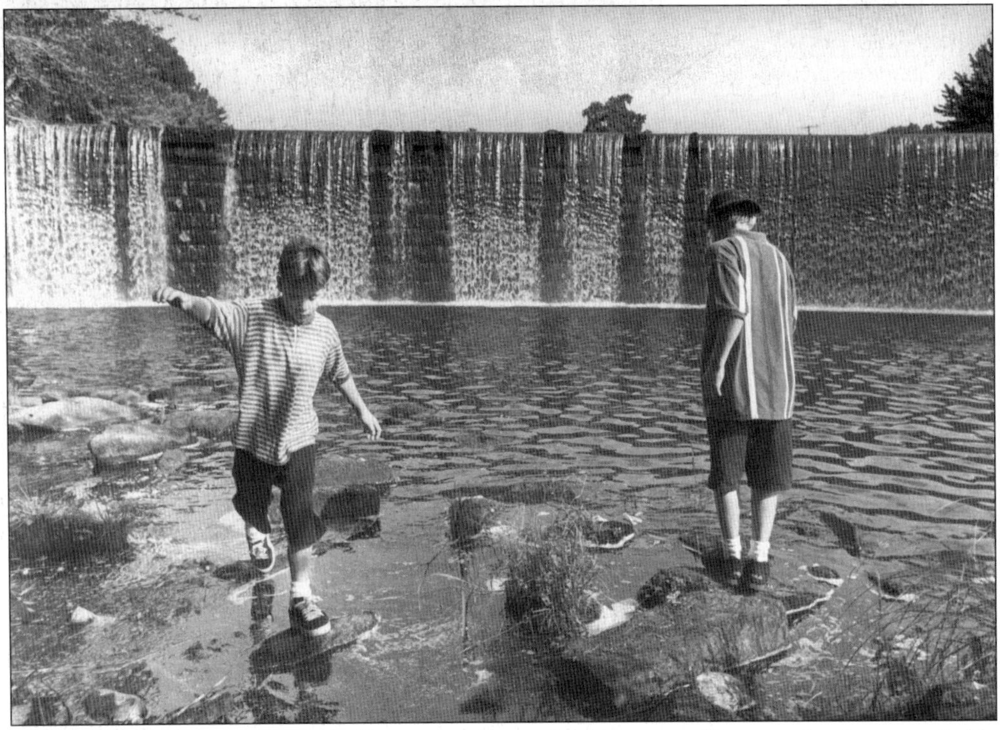

THE ARKWRIGHT DAM, 1995. Shown exploring the Pawtuxet River at the dam are Peddy Rampini (left) and Stephen Mroz.

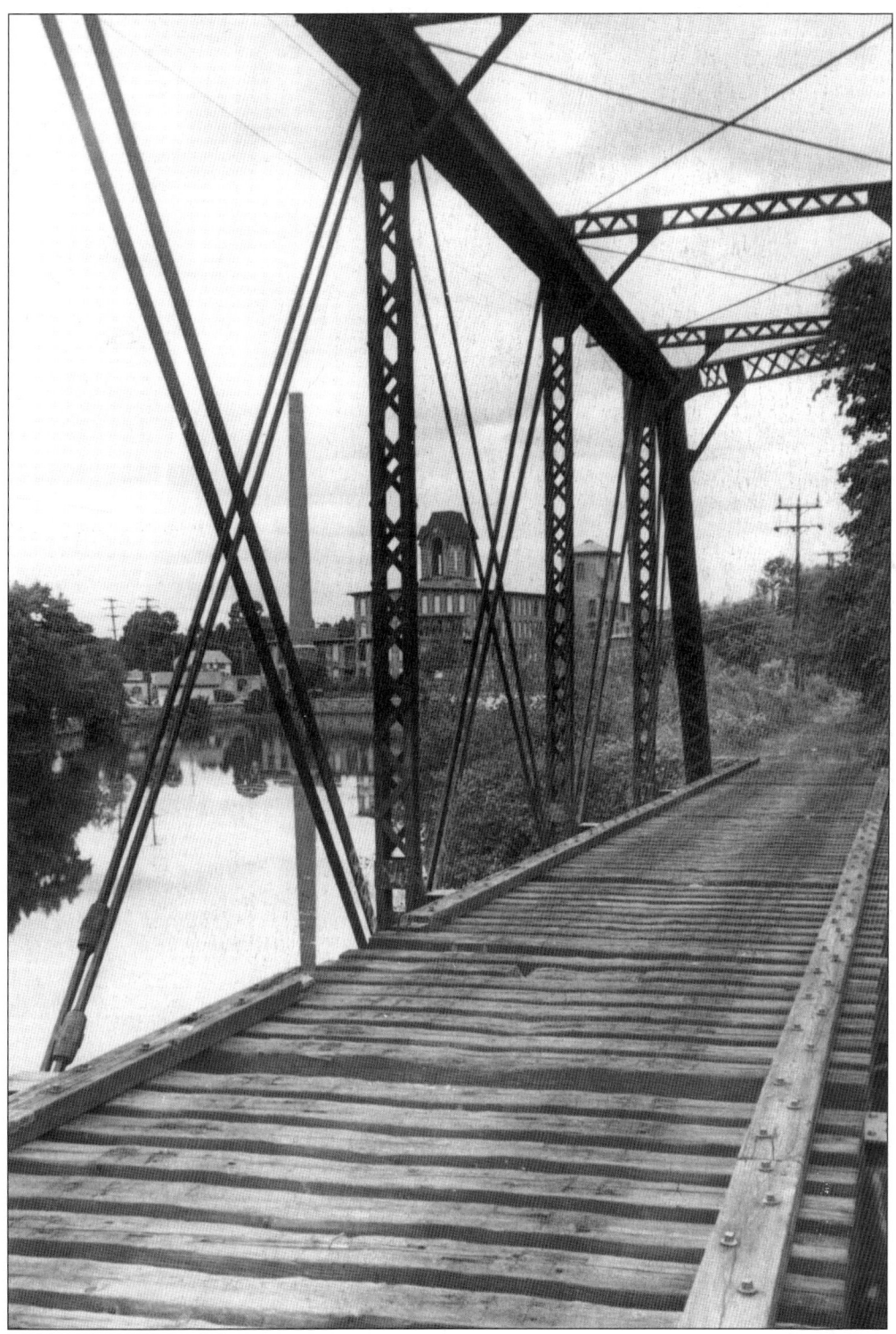

THE RAILROAD CONNECTION TO THE ANTHONY MILL. It is now being transformed into a bicycle path as part of the East Coast Greenway, which stretches from Maine to Florida.

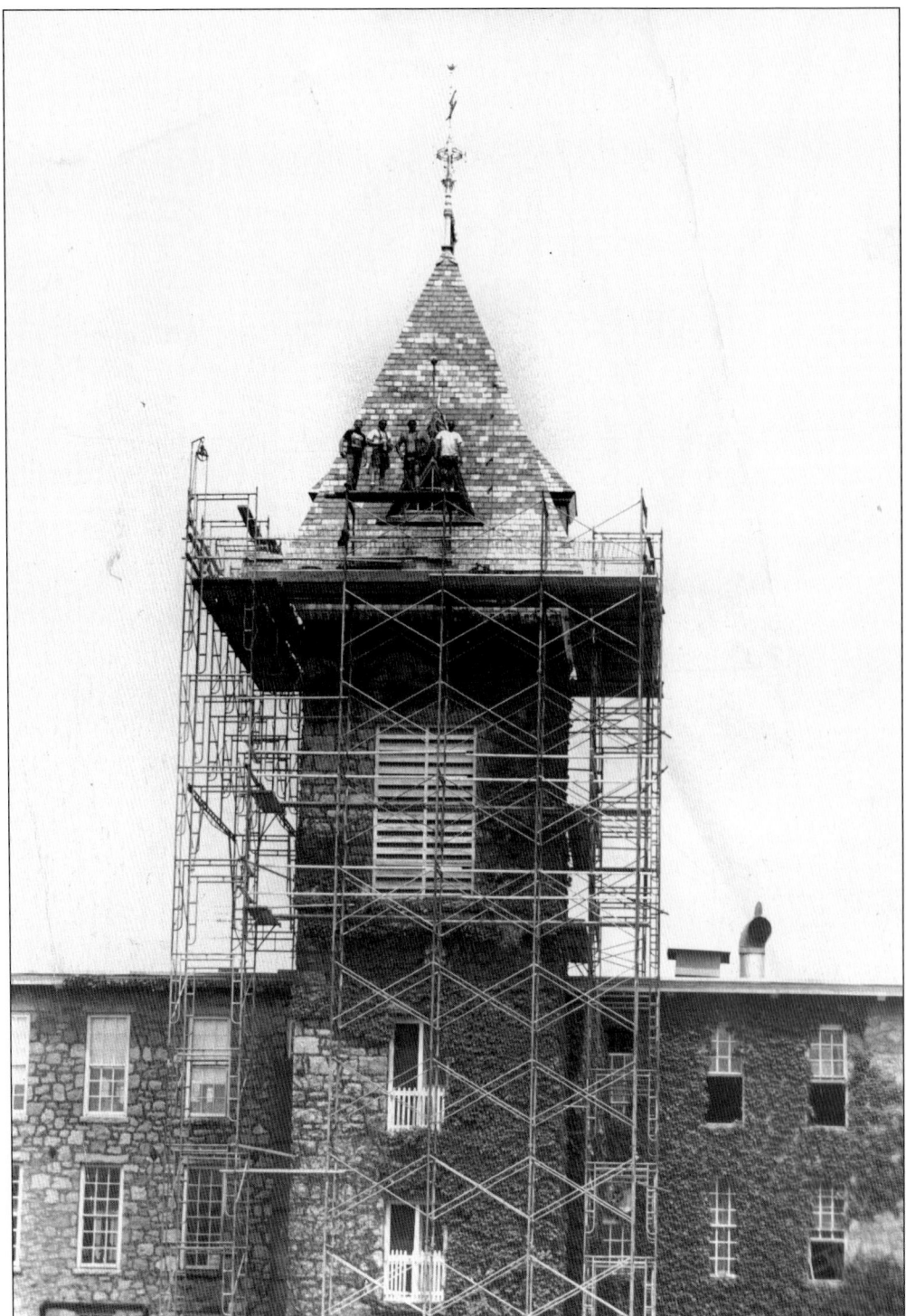

BRADFORD SOAP WORKS IN RIVERPOINT, REPAIRING THE TOWER, 1983. The former Valley Queen Textile Mill was built in 1889 and is still serving as a working symbol of the Pawtuxet Valley.